MONASTIC ARCHITECTURE IN FRANCE

MONASTIC ARCHITECTURE
IN
FRANCE

FROM THE RENAISSANCE TO
THE REVOLUTION

BY

JOAN EVANS

PRESIDENT OF THE SOCIETY OF ANTIQUARIES

CAMBRIDGE
AT THE UNIVERSITY PRESS
1964

PUBLISHED BY
THE SYNDICS OF THE CAMBRIDGE UNIVERSITY PRESS

Bentley House, 200 Euston Road, London, N.W. 1
American Branch: 32 East 57th Street, New York 22, N.Y.
West African Office: P.O. Box 33, Ibadan, Nigeria

©

CAMBRIDGE UNIVERSITY PRESS

1964

Printed in Great Britain at the University Printing House, Cambridge
(Brooke Crutchley, University Printer)

To
Kathleen and Dyneley Hussey
with love and gratitude
✻
Our lot has fallen in
pleasant places

CONTENTS

PREFACE

FRANCE is a country so rich in architecture that it is not surprising that some of her fine buildings remain unstudied and even, for the purposes of the history of art, unseen. Students of medieval architecture have endless Romanesque and Gothic churches and castles to engross their attention; students of Renaissance and later architecture have palaces, châteaux and town houses to study, of such magnificence that those who survey them tend to minimize the importance of church architecture in classical style, and, when they consider it, to concentrate upon great city churches such as the Invalides, or upon royal chapels such as that of Versailles. The domestic architecture of the monasteries, abbot's lodgings, monks' quarters and the rest, are lost among the hundreds of châteaux. As a consequence French[1] monastic architecture of later than medieval date is in the main little looked at and less considered. Monsieur Élie Lambert has made some valuable studies of single buildings and groups of buildings;[2] Monsieur Hautecœur has given a summary but useful account (scattered through many chapters) of the major existing buildings, especially of the eighteenth century, in his *Histoire de l'architecture classique en France*; Monsieur Tournier has included classical churches in his study of the ecclesiastical architecture of Franche Comté; a few biographies of architects contain references to their work for monastic patrons, but there is no handy textbook in which the student may find guidance in his studies. Only as I was finishing the chapter on the Jesuits was I able to obtain a copy of Monsieur Pierre Moisy's *Églises des Jésuites de l'ancienne Assistance de France*.[3] I already knew his studies of individual Jesuit architects and churches,[4] and it was most exciting at this late stage to be able to avail myself of his more extended and more historical researches, and to dovetail them with my own, though these are on a much smaller scale and occupied less with history than with actual buildings. I should like here to express to him my indebtedness and my gratitude.

I am well aware that it is presumptuous in a foreigner to tackle such a subject as later French monastic architecture, and am painfully conscious that any French local antiquary may be in a position to correct me on much that concerns his province; yet I feel that the need for the study of later French monastic architecture is so great that it must serve as an excuse both for my temerity and my mistakes. Any visitor to such a city as Auch must be conscious that it is likely to contain a number of former convents of which the history is known to hardly anyone but their owners; yet until a greater interest is aroused even the owners may hardly realize their significance.

[1] I have tried to confine this study to monastic houses in territory that was French at the time they were built.

[2] See Bibliography. [3] *Institutum Historicum,* 1958. [4] See Bibliography.

The Revolution turned the monastic buildings of France to a great variety of practical uses and the process has continued to our own day. I have visited administrative buildings of every sort, from splendid prefectures to modest *mairies*; schools and colleges of every kind; hospitals, lunatic asylums, old people's homes, orphanages, *colonies de vacances*, prisons, factories, warehouses, farms, manor houses, even a night club. In nearly all of them I have been kindly received, and wish to express my thanks to those who welcomed or tolerated me. It took me five months to gain authorized entry into the prison of Clairvaux, but when I gained it my welcome was most kind. My happiest memory is perhaps of my unauthorized visit to Prémontré (now a mental hospital) which occurred quite accidentally, when I joined a party of the inmates returning from a walk.

For once it may be said that England is ahead of France on a question of architectural appreciation. In this country a post-Reformation church, especially if it be Georgian, will find more admirers among the *cognoscenti* than any but the finest medieval churches. In France it is otherwise. What little money the State can there afford for preservation goes to medieval churches or Renaissance châteaux; the monastic buildings of the Renaissance centuries are altered or destroyed[1] or allowed quietly to fall into decay, without any outcry either from the *cognoscenti* or the general public. The monastery of Bon-Repos is an example of romantic dereliction, with the keystones dropping from the arches of the ruined cloister and the trees growing between the paving-stones. The fine buildings of Moutiers-Saint-Jean may stand as an example of the many that are put to the most sordid farm use. At Souvigny the windows of the monastic buildings lack glass and the roof, tiles; and peasants live in the cells and mend their *boiseries* with bits of packing cases. At Corbigny the fine and unusual church, of late seventeenth-century date, was in 1954 divided by floors and partitions to make dormitories for school children. The fine lectern and other church furniture have simply disappeared. At Fontmorigny the buildings are being destroyed as and when the proprietor can afford the necessary dynamite. In 1955 most of the

[1] A process naturally on occasion hastened by war: the house of Clarisses at Chauny, Aisne, for example, rebuilt in 1580, was destroyed in the First World War; one court at Pontlevoy, the eighteenth-century buildings of the Benedictine abbey of Bourg-Moyen, the buildings at Aulnay-sur-Odon, and the Jesuit churches of Pontoise and Dieppe and Brest in the Second. The Couvent de Bonne-Nouvelle of 1683 at Orléans (Préfecture); the Carmelite house (Hôtel de Ville) at Gisors; the seventeenth-century Augustinian buildings at Évaux; the Benedictine monastery at Vire; the chapels of the Annonciades at Boulogne-sur-Mer and at Vesoul; and the Jesuit College (later Museum) at Douai, were all destroyed in the Second World War, when the Cistercian monastic buildings at Longport and the Recollets' church at Dunkirk were severely damaged. The cloister of St Stanislas at Abbeville and the church and cloister of Saint-Jean-des-Prémontrés at Amiens were damaged and later destroyed. The sixteenth-century priory of La Chaise-Dieu at Port Dieu, Corrèze, was in 1954 submerged by the waters gathered by the barrage of Bort-les-Orgues; it does not seem to have been recorded first. The buildings of the Ursulines at Dijon, including the chapel, were in 1949 modified to the point of destruction to form a Cité Administrative; the house of the Visitandines at Gray, designed for them in 1784 by the Discalced Carmelite Père Bacquet, has lately been pulled down to make room for the new buildings of the Collège Moderne. At Tours and Saint-Flour Jesuit chapels have been remorselessly demolished.

PREFACE

house of the Benedictines at Conches was pulled down to be replaced by a modern hospital. The list can be extended *ad infinitum*. At the same time it must be recorded that the wing of the Abbaye-aux-Hommes damaged by English bombing in the last war is being nobly restored; that Lessay and Loos, gutted in the war, have been repaired; and the list of such restorations grows yearly.

Any failure to restore is the result of the inevitable impoverishment of a country that has endured two wars; any vandalism is the result of a hereditary blindness in a country where the traditions of Prosper Mérimée and Viollet le Duc die hard. Serious French archaeologists will still tell you that at Cîteaux and Clairvaux there is hardly anything to be seen, because little remains that is medieval; yet at each place there are magnificent ranges of eighteenth-century buildings. At the moment, indeed, an appreciation of such buildings in France is chiefly to be found among the members of the Orders who originally built them. Where a wise purging of later disfigurements has restored their pristine beauty, as at Cîteaux and Le Bec-Hellouin, the work has usually been done on the initiative and at the expense of the religious Orders that have once more been allowed to inhabit their own buildings.

My own attention was first drawn to the later monastic architecture of France when in the months before the invasion of 1944 I read the *Guides Bleus* from end to end, in order to draw up lists of buildings to be respected by the invading armies of the allies. I then began to realize how numerous were the monastic buildings of the sixteenth, seventeenth and eighteenth centuries, and that I had hardly *seen* them when in the years before the war I had visited French abbeys, to study their Romanesque and Gothic buildings. Forthwith I began to prepare a map of the sites to be visited: a nostalgic task that helped to sustain my belief that travel in France would once again some day be possible.[1]

It has taken much longer than I then hoped to visit the places I mapped. Difficulties of travel in the years immediately after the war, and of acquiring francs in the subsequent years,[2] brought unexpected delays, which were extended by increased responsibilities in England. Only now can I say that I have succeeded in visiting the greater number of the places where monastic buildings of the sixteenth, seventeenth and eighteenth centuries can still be seen. Furthermore, I am fully conscious that my map is necessarily incomplete. Many a priory has become a country house,[3] many a Charterhouse a farm, many a friary a group of inconspicuous dwellings, many a convent a school, without a record of the fact being available to an inquirer, and especially to an inquirer from beyond the seas. Yet though this study must of necessity be incomplete, I hope it may provide a

[1] I should like to express my gratitude to a book not then available to me—Dom L. H. Cottineau's *Répertoire Topo-Bibliographique des Abbayes et Prieurés*, published at Mâcon by the house of Protat between 1935 and 1937.

[2] I should like here to express my gratitude to the Medieval Academy of America that in making me an Honorary Research Fellow gave me an additional status when it was needed.

[3] Even ancient abbeys have become farms; for example, Les Deux-Jumeaux near Isigny.

foundation on which others may build a more complete and perfect edifice. I hope, too, that it may make these later monastic buildings more visible to the traveller, and may even cause their conservation to be more seriously considered by the authorities in whose care they rest. I hope later to complete the present volume by a briefer study of French monastic iconography in the same period.

I have limited the definition of monasticism to the members of Orders living under vows. There were important congregations of priests in France in the seventeenth and eighteenth centuries, notably the Sulpicians, the Oratorians, the Lazarists, the Pères de la Doctrine Chrétienne, and the Eudists, but though their members followed a common rule they took no vows. I have therefore excluded their surviving architecture from consideration in this book, though it is well worthy of independent study. I have not given the Department of the places mentioned in the text; it will be found in the Index and in the List of Illustrations.

My thanks are due to many friends and acquaintances who have helped me in my work: in France to two successive Surintendantes of the School of the Légion d'Honneur at Saint-Denis, Madame Meunier and Madame d'Alverny; to Madame Claude Carnot; Mademoiselle Marguérite Prinet; Mademoiselle Jeanne Vielliard; M. Jean Michoud; M. Jacques Dupont; M. Aufrère; the Governor of the prison at Clairvaux; Monsieur le Baron Thénard; the Father Abbot of Mondaye; Monsieur Mesplé of Toulouse; Monsieur René Jullian of Lyons; Monsieur Ternois of Montauban; MM. Vallery Radot, Adhémar and Weigert of the Cabinet des Estampes, Bibliothèque Nationale; Monsieur le Moël of the Archives Nationales; the Archivistes-en-Chef of the Departments of the Ardennes, Aube, Aude, Aveyron, Bas Rhin, Basses Pyrénées, Cantal, Côtes du Nord, Corrèze, Creuse, Deux-Sèvres, Haut Rhin, Ille et Vilaine, Lot, Marne, Meuse, Morbihan, Moselle, Nord, Oise, Puy-de-Dôme and Rhône; the Director of the Hôpital Villemin; Monsieur Raymond Cornou; Monsieur l'Abbé Plateau; Monsieur Quarré, the Keeper of the Museums of Dijon; the Supérieure Générale of the Sœurs de la Divine Providence of Ribeauvillé; Mademoiselle M. M. Chalufour; Miss Elizabeth Sunderland; Monsieur A. Schaaf of Wissembourg; Monsieur Charles Wetterwald of Guebwiller; Monsieur Rouquette of the Musée Réattu of Arles; Monsieur Lassalle of the Musée Archéologique de Nîmes; the Abbot of Maguzzano; the Bursar of the Hospice of Dol-de-Bretagne; Monsieur R. Couffon; and in England to Professor Dom David Knowles, O.S.B., Sir Anthony Blunt, and to Miss Vera Dallas who compiled the index. My friend Monsieur Jean Prinet of the Bibliothèque Nationale has facilitated and encouraged my researches in many ways.

I am greatly indebted to my friend Dr George Zarnecki for driving me on a tour of Northern France, for investigating and photographing buildings on the Eastern frontier and elsewhere, and for the many admirable photographs he has allowed me to reproduce in these pages. Madame Josette Fourès has kindly helped me in photographing some of the abbeys near Paris.

My debt to Mr and Mrs Dyneley Hussey, who have taken me many thousands

PREFACE

of miles to see the greater number of the abbeys I record, who have discovered others that I have overlooked and have photographed yet others for my benefit, is inadequately expressed in the dedication of the book. Without their practical help, their wise understanding, their infinite patience and their friendly encouragement, I could never have completed my work.

J.E.

WOTTON-UNDER-EDGE

INFORMATION REQUESTED

I have not seen or had first-hand information about the houses listed below, where I have reason to believe something may still remain. I should welcome information about any of them:

Benedictines

Bergues, Nord: Saint-Winoc. Entrance gate, eighteenth century.

Chanteuges, Haute-Loire. Abbot's Chapel, sixteenth century.

Lonlay, Orne. Buildings of 1664?

Montfort l'Amaury, Seine-et-Oise. Façade of church (unfinished), sixteenth century.

Nanteuil-en-Vallée, Charente. Monastic building, eighteenth century?

Saint-Evroul d'Ouche, Orne. Abbot's lodging and Gate, eighteenth century.

Saint-Gildas-des-Bois, Loire-Atlantique. Church and monastic buildings, c. 1711.

Saint-Philbert-de-Grandlieu, Loire-Atlantique. Church and buildings, sixteenth to eighteenth century.

Saint-Sulpice-sur-Risle, Orne. Sixteenth-century buildings, now a farm.

Sainte-Colombe-lès-Sens, Yonne. Refectory.

Savigny, Rhône. Gateway, seventeenth century.

Sens, Yonne (Celestins). Chapel of Lycée, 1735.

Val-Richer, Calvados. Guest-house, late seventeenth century, now priest's house.

Benedictine nuns

Chapelle-sur-Orense, Yonne: La Pommeraie. Buildings, eighteenth century.

Charenton-du-Cher. Buildings, 1698.

Cistercians

Bonneval, Aveyron. Abbey buildings rebuilt early eighteenth century. Now Trappistines. Inaccessible by car.

Champlevé, Sarthe. Church sixteenth century, with seventeenth-century retable and tabernacle.

Clairefontaine, Haute-Saône. Cloister eighteenth century; now lunatic asylum.

Noirmoutier, Vendée. Gateway and Abbot's lodging, seventeenth century; monastic building, eighteenth century.

Valcroissant, Drôme. Ruins?

Vauluisant, Yonne. Entrance gate, sixteenth century; Abbot's lodging, eighteenth century.

Cistercian nuns

Avignon, Vaucluse: Sainte-Cathérine. A few bays of cloister.
Clavas, Saint-Philibert-de-Rioutor, Haute-Loire. Some remains of monastic buildings, c. 1698?

Augustinians

Chantelle, Allier. Church (near château) with façade, c. 1700.
Écouis, Eure. Altars and stalls, Louis XIV.
Verteuil, Gironde. Monastic buildings, eighteenth century?

Premonstratensians

Bellevaux, Nièvre. Monastic buildings, seventeenth century?
Corneux, Saint-Broignt, Haute-Saône. Buildings and cloister, 1708–37.

Ursulines

Malestroit, Morbihan: Saint-Michel. Chapel, c. 1670.

Visitandines

Beaune, Côte-d'Or. Caves du Patriarche père et fils, seventeenth century.
Embrun, Hautes-Alpes. Convent, now hospital.
Saint-Amour, Jura. Convent, now Collège.

Annonciades

Saint-Amour, Jura. Rebuilt 1710, now private property.

Carmelites

Langres, Haute-Marne. Chapel, seventeenth century, now Caserne Galland.
Marnay, Haute-Saône (Carmes Déchaussés), 1675?

Carthusians

La Verne, Var. Gateway, eighteenth century, and some ruins.
Le Pin, Isère: Silve Bénite. Cloister, church, prior's house, sixteenth century. ? In Gothic style.
Revest, Var. Church, 1640.
Valbonne, Gard. 1780, by J. P. Franque?

Dominicans

Alais, Gard. Church (Présentation), 1772, and cloister.
Besançon, Doubs. Gateway and buildings now Bureaux militaires.
Le Buis, Drôme. Seventeenth century, now Justice de Paix, Mairie and Collège.

Cordeliers

Besançon, Doubs. 1719–33, now Lycée de filles.
Chariez, Haute-Saône. Now private house.

Recollets

Ciboure, Basses-Pyrénées. Cloister, seventeenth century, now Caserne des douanes.

Minimes

Draguignan, Var. Chapel, sixteenth century. ? Gothic style.

Jesuits

Auxerre, Yonne. Seminary, 1714, now Lycée Paul Bert.
Carpentras, Vaucluse. Buildings, *c.* 1607–30.
Embrun, Hautes-Alpes. Chapel, 1644; Collège, 1644–60. Now Caserne Lapeyrouse.

LIST OF ILLUSTRATIONS

Unless otherwise stated, the photographs are by the author. Those by Dr George Zarnecki are indicated by the letters G.Z.; those from the Archives Photographiques by A.P.; those by Lévy and Neurdein by L.N.

PLATES
(between pp. 152 and 153)

93 Benedictine Nunnery of Le Val-de-Grâce, Paris. Dome, 1645. [Lucien Hervé]

94 Benedictine Nunnery of Le Val-de-Grâce, Paris. Nave and choir, 1645. [A.P.]

95 Benedictine Nunnery of Le Val-de-Grâce, Paris. Vault of the nave, 1645. [A.P.]

96 Benedictine Nunnery of Saint-Pierre, Lyons, by François des Noyers de la Valfenière. Outer façade, 1659. [J. Camponogara, Lyons]

97 Benedictine Nunnery of Saint-Pierre, Lyons, by François des Royers de la Valfenière. Church, 1676–1748. [J. Camponogara, Lyons]

98 Benedictine (Cluniac) Priory of Lons-le-Saunier, Jura. By Dom Vincent Duchesne, 1680. Cloister. [G.Z.]

99 Benedictine (Cluniac) Priory of Lons-le-Saunier, Jura. By Dom Vincent Duchesne, 1680. Abbot's lodging. [G.Z.]

100 Benedictine Nunnery of La Ronceray, Angers, Maine-et-Loire. Monastic buildings, c. 1650.

101 Benedictine Nunnery of La Ronceray, Angers, Maine-et-Loire. Monastic buildings, c. 1650.

102 Benedictine Nunnery of Bonne-Nouvelle, Orléans, Loiret. Monastic buildings, 1653. (Before 1939.) [L.N.]

103 Benedictine Nunnery of Notre-Dame-de-Liesse, rue de Sèvres, Paris. Cloister, 1644.

104 Benedictine Abbey Church of Saint-Maixent, Deux-Sèvres. Nave, by François Leduc de Toscane, 1670–82.

105 Benedictine Abbey of Corbie, Somme. West front, by Nicolas Léveillé, begun 1701, finished 1719.

106 Benedictine Abbey of Corbie, Somme. West front, by Nicolas Léveillé, begun 1701, finished 1719.

107 Benedictine Abbey of Saint-Georges-de-Boscherville, Seine-Maritime. Living quarters over the chapter-house, probably by Dom Marc Rivard, c. 1670. [G.Z.]

108 Abbaye-aux-Hommes, Caen, Calvados. Cloister, by Dom Guillaume de la Tremblaye, 1704.

109 Benedictine Abbey of Saint-Maixent, Deux-Sèvres. Cloister, by Dom François Leduc de Toscane, 1670–82.

110 Abbaye-aux-Dames, Caen, Calvados. Screen, probably by Dom Guillaume de la Tremblaye, 1704.

111 Benedictine Abbey of Saint-Maixent, Deux-Sèvres, by Dom François Leduc de Toscane, 1660–c. 1670. Monastic buildings.

112 Benedictine Abbey of Saint-Maixent, Deux-Sèvres, by Dom François Leduc de Toscane, 1660–c. 1670. Cloister.

113 Benedictine Abbey of Saint-Maur, Maine-et-Loire. Monastic buildings.

114 Benedictine Abbey of Saint-Maur, Maine-et-Loire. Cloister, 1664–87.

115 Benedictine Abbey of Saint-Fuscien-aux-Bois, Amiens, Somme. Design for garden front, c. 1680. Arch. Nat. Plans N III, Somme 21 (8).

116 Benedictine (Cluniac) Priory of Morteau, Doubs. Design for garden front, c. 1680. Arch. Nat. Plans N III, Doubs 1 (3).

117 Benedictine (Cluniac) Abbey of Saint-Martin-des-Champs, Paris. Monastic buildings, by Antoine, c. 1710–22.

118 Benedictine (Cluniac) Abbey of Saint-Martin-des-Champs, Paris. Monastic buildings, by Antoine, c. 1710–22.

119 Benedictine Abbey of Le Bec-Hellouin, Eure. Guest house, c. 1680. [F. Vincent, Étretat]

120 Benedictine Priory of Framecourt, Somme. Monastic buildings, 1713. [G.Z.]

150 Benedictine Abbey of Moutiers-Saint-Jean, Côte-d'Or. Monastic buildings, c. 1680. [Cochet]

151 Benedictine Priory of Le Paraclet-des-Champs, Ailly-sur-Noye, Somme. C. 1680.

152 Benedictine Abbey of Moutiers-Saint-Jean, Côte-d'Or. Cloister, c. 1680. [Cochet]

153 Benedictine Abbey of Moutiers-Saint-Jean, Côte-d'Or. Cloister, c. 1680.

154 Benedictine Abbey of Sorèze, Tarn. Exterior.

155 Benedictine Abbey of Sorèze, Tarn. Main cloister, c. 1680.

156 Benedictine Abbey of La Réole, Gironde. Monastic buildings.

157 Benedictine Abbey of La Réole, Gironde. Cloister, c. 1690.

158 Benedictine Abbey of Montmajour, Bouches-du-Rhône. Monastic buildings, 1703–37. [Dyneley Hussey]

159 Benedictine Nunnery of Faverney, Haute-Saône. By Dom Vincent Duchesne, 1711–14. Nuns' quarters. [G.Z.]

160 Benedictine Nunnery of Faverney, Haute-Saône. By Dom Vincent Duchesne, 1711–14. Cloister. [G.Z.]

161 Benedictine Abbey of Saint-Sever-sur-Odon, Calvados. Abbot's lodging, c. 1690.

162 Benedictine Abbey of Saint-Vincent, Besançon, Doubs. By Dom Vincent Duchesne, c. 1720. [G.Z.]

163 Benedictine Abbey of Notre-Dame de Lyre, Eure. Design for cloister, 1704. Arch. Nat. Plans N III, Eure 6 (5).

164 Benedictine Abbey of Marmoutier, Indre-et-Loire. Elevation of façade, 1675, by Dom Pierre Ledo. Arch. Nat. Plans N III, Indre-et-Loire 5 (3).

165 Benedictine Abbey of Saint-Sulpice-lès-Bourges, Cher. Mill. Seventeenth century.

166 Benedictine Abbey of Méry-ès-Bois, Cher. C. 1680? [Combier, Mâcon]

167 Benedictine Abbey of Sainte Melaine, Rennes, Ille-et-Vilaine. Abbot's lodging, 1672.

168 Benedictine Abbey of Nouaillé, Vienne. Abbot's lodging, c. 1665.

169 Benedictine Abbey of Jumièges, Seine-Maritime. Abbot's lodging, 1666.

170 Benedictine Abbey of Saint-Gildas de Rhuis, Morbihan. Cloister, 1700–1705.

171 Monastery of English Benedictines, 269 rue Denfert-Rochereau, Paris. Hall and staircase, 1661–91. [A.P.]

172 Monastery of English Benedictines, 269 rue Denfert-Rochereau, Paris. Exterior, 1661–91. [A.P.]

173 Monastery of English Benedictines, Paris. The Chapel of St Edmund, 1661–91. Arch. Nat. Plans N III, Seine 18 (5).

174 Benedictine Abbey of Sainte Melaine, Rennes, Ille-et-Vilaine. Cloister, c. 1672.

175 Benedictine Abbey of Sainte Melaine, Rennes, Ille-et-Vilaine. Cloister, c. 1672.

176 Benedictine Abbey of Saint-Michel-en-Thiérache, Aisne. East front.

177 Benedictine Abbey of Saint-Michel-en-Thiérache, Aisne. Cloister, c. 1680.

178 Benedictine Abbey of Saint-Michel-en-Thiérache, Aisne. Church, c. 1680. [G.Z.]

179 Benedictine Abbey of Saint-Michel-en-Thiérache, Aisne. Church, c. 1680. [G.Z.]

180 Benedictine Abbey of Saint-Jean-de-l'Osne, Côte d'Or. C. 1696. Baldaquin. [G.Z.]

268 Benedictine Abbey of Saint-André, Villeneuve-lès-Avignon, Vaucluse. Monastic buildings, 1755.

269 Benedictine Abbey of Lure, Haute-Saône. Monastic buildings, 1770–89. [G.Z.]

270 Benedictine Priory of Fontaine-lès-Luxeuil, Haute-Saône. Monastic buildings, 1731. [G.Z.]

271 Benedictine Priory of Commercy, Meuse. Monastic buildings, 1737. [G.Z.]

272 Benedictine Priory of Commercy, Meuse. Staircase, 1737. [G.Z.]

273 Benedictine Abbey of Cluny. Staircase, 1750. [A.P.]

274 Benedictine Abbey of Saint-Germain, Auxerre, Yonne. Cloister, begun 1720.

275 Benedictine Abbey of Cluny, Saône-et-Loire. Cloister, 1750.

276 Benedictine Abbey of Cluny, Saône-et-Loire. Monastic buildings, 1750.

277 Benedictine Abbey of Saint-Pierre, Lagny, Seine-et-Marne. Monastic buildings, c. 1750. [Mme Josette Fourès]

278 Benedictine Abbey of Saint-Wandrille, Seine-Maritime. Porte de Jarente, 1754.

279 Benedictine Abbey of Saint-Wandrille, Seine-Maritime. Monastic buildings, c. 1750.

280 Benedictine Abbey of Le Monastier-Saint-Chaffre, Haute-Loire. Cloister, 1754.

281 Benedictine Abbey of Le Monastier-Saint-Chaffre, Haute-Loire. Monastic buildings, 1754.

282 Benedictine Abbey of Valmont, Seine-Maritime. Monastic buildings, 1760.

283 Benedictine Abbey of Saint-Pierre, Chartres, Eure-et-Loir. Monastic buildings, c. 1760.

284 Benedictine Abbey of Lagrasse, Aude. Central block, 1760. [A.P.]

285 Benedictine Abbey of Lagrasse, Aude. Cloister, 1760. [A.P.]

286 Benedictine Abbey of Lagrasse, Aude. Staircase, 1760. [A.P.]

287 Benedictine Nunnery of Saint-Désir, Lisieux, Calvados. Central block and one side pavilion, c. 1760. (Before 1939). [A.P.]

288 Benedictine Priory of Fontaine-lès-Luxeuil, Haute-Saône. Prior's house, 1731. [G.Z.]

289 Benedictine (Cluniac) Abbey of Lavoulte-Chilhac, Haute-Loire. Monastic buildings, c. 1760. [A.P.]

290 Benedictine Nunnery of Baume-les-Dames, Doubs. Church by Jean Pierre Galezot. Begun 1738. Interior of dome. [G.Z.]

291 Benedictine Nunnery of Baume-les-Dames, Doubs. Church by Jean Pierre Galezot. Begun 1738. Exterior of church. [G.Z.]

292 Benedictine Abbey of Saint-Martin, Séez, Orne. Abbot's lodging, 1720–39.

293 Benedictine Abbey of Saint-Seine, Côte-d'Or. Abbot's lodging, c. 1740.

294 Benedictine Abbey of Saint-Germain, Auxerre, Yonne. Abbot's lodging, c. 1750.

295 Benedictine Abbey of La Trinité, Fécamp, Seine-Maritime. Abbot's lodging, c. 1750.

296 Benedictine Abbey of Saint-Valéry-sur-Somme, Somme. Abbot's lodging, c. 1750.

297 Benedictine Abbey of Saint-Remi, Rheims, Marne. Abbot's lodging, by Durocher, 1774.

298 Benedictine (Cluniac) Priory of Paray-le-Monial, Saône-et-Loire. Prior's lodging, c. 1760.

299 Benedictine (Cluniac) Priory of Souvigny, Allier. Prior's lodging and entrance, c. 1775. [Séguy, Moulins]

587 Saint-Bruno, Bordeaux, Gironde. Decoration of north side of choir, 1672. [A.P.]

588 Chartreuse of Apponay, Nièvre. Living quarters, c. 1680.

589 Chartreuse of Vaucluse, Onoz, Jura. Courtyard, mid seventeenth century [G.Z.]

590 Chartreuse of Le Liget, Indre-et-Loire, c. 1690. Inner gateway. [Dyneley Hussey]

591 Chartreuse of Le Liget, Indre-et-Loire, c. 1690. Monastery. [Dyneley Hussey]

592 Chartreuse of Le Liget, Indre-et-Loire. Entrance gateway, c. 1690.

593 Chartreuse of Vaucluse, Onoz, Jura. Gateway, c. 1650. [G.Z.]

594 Saint-Bruno-des-Chartreux, Lyons. Dome, c. 1740. [Egéa et Gaymard, Villeurbanne]

595 Saint-Bruno-des-Chartreux, Lyons. Nave, 1733-6. (Egéa et Gaymard, Villeurbanne]

596 Saint-Bruno-des-Chartreux, Lyons. Stalls, 1744-7. [Egéa et Gaymard, Villeurbanne]

597 Saint-Bruno-des-Chartreux, Lyons. Choir, 1733-6. [Egéa et Gaymard, Villeurbanne]

598 Saint-Bruno-des-Chartreux, Lyons. High Altar, by Soufflot, 1743-9. [Egéa et Gaymard, Villeurbanne]

599 Saint-Bruno-des-Chartreux, Lyons. Details of stalls, 1744-7. [Egéa et Gaymard, Villeurbanne]

600 Chartreuse of Auray, Morbihan. Cloister, 1730.

601 Chartreuse of Auray, Morbihan. Cloister, 1730.

602 Chartreuse of Auray, Morbihan. Entrance, c. 1740. [Lauzanne, Auray]

603 Chartreuse of Auray, Morbihan. Chapel, 1730. [Lauzanne, Auray]

604 Chartreuse of Saint-Pierre, Toulouse, Haute-Garonne. Crossing, by L. Cammas, c. 1780. [B. Saltel, Toulouse]

605 Chartreuse of Saint-Pierre, Toulouse, Haute-Garonne. C. 1680. Chapter-house.

606 Chartreuse of Saint-Pierre, Toulouse, Haute-Garonne. C. 1680. Sacristy. [B. Saltel, Toulouse]

607 Chartreuse of Saint-Pierre, Toulouse, Haute-Garonne. High Altar. Angels and urn by F. Lucas, 1785. [B. Saltel, Toulouse]

608 Chartreuse of Saint-Pierre, Toulouse, Haute-Garonne. Chapter-house, c. 1680. [B. Saltel, Toulouse]

609 Chartreuse of Saint-Pierre, Toulouse, Haute-Garonne. Choir, decorated 1683 and 1749. [B. Saltel, Toulouse]

610 Chartreuse of Gaillon, Eure. 1776. After Millin, *Antiquités Nationales*.

611 Door of the Carmelite Monastery, Saint-Amand Mont-rond, Cher. Mid sixteenth century.

612 Discalced Carmelites, Paris, Saint-Joseph-des-Carmes. 1628-30. [A.P.]

613 Discalced Carmelites, Paris, Saint-Joseph-des-Carmes. 1628-30. Façade. After Marot.

614 Discalced Carmelites, Paris, Saint-Joseph-des-Carmes. Door to choir, c. 1630. [A.P.]

615 Carmelite Nunnery of Les Billettes, Paris. Façade, 1756. [René-Jacques, Paris]

616 Carmelite Nunnery of Les Billettes, Paris. Nave 1756. [René-Jacques, Paris]

617 Carmelite Nunnery of Ploërmel, Morbihan. Cloister, 1604.

618 Carmelite Nunnery of Ploërmel, Morbihan. Cloister, c. 1700.

731 Jesuit College, Dijon, Côte-d'Or. Courtyard, by Martellange, 1610.

732 Jesuit College, Roanne, Loire. Drawing by Martellange, 1611. B.N., Cabinet des Estampes. [B.N.]

733 Jesuits of Bourges, Cher. Martellange's designs, 1611. B.N., Cabinet des Estampes. [B.N.]

734 Jesuit College, Nevers, Nièvre. Chapel, 1612. [L.N.]

735 Jesuit College of Saint-Louis (now Saint-Vincent-de-Paul), Blois, Loir-et-Cher. Façade, by Martellange, 1625. [L.N.]

736 Jesuit College of Saint-Louis (now Saint-Vincent-de-Paul), Blois, Loir-et-Cher. Interior, by Martellange, 1625. [A.P.]

737 Jesuit Novitiate, Paris. By Martellange, 1631. Chapel interior. After Marot.

738 Jesuit Novitiate, Paris. By Martellange, 1631. Chapel façade. After Marot.

739 Jesuit Novitiate, Paris. Living quarters, drawing by Martellange, 1630. B.N., Cabinet des Estampes. [B.N.]

740 Plan of the chapel, Jesuit Maison Professe, Paris (Saint-Paul-Saint-Louis), by Martellange and Derand, 1627. B.N., Cabinet des Estampes. [B.N.]

741 Jesuit Maison Professe, Paris. Chapel (Saint-Paul-Saint-Louis). Interior, by Martellange and Derand, 1627–41. [Editions du Cerf, Paris]

742 Jesuit Maison Professe, Paris. Chapel (Saint-Paul-Saint-Louis). Façade, by Martellange and Derand, 1627–41. [Yvon, Paris]

743 Jesuit Maison Professe, Paris. By Martellange and Derand, 1627–41. Staircase. [A.P.]

744 Jesuit Maison Professe, Paris. By Martellange and Derand, 1627–41. Library door. [A.P.]

745 Jesuit College, Chaumont, Haute-Marne. Chapel exterior, 1629. [A.P.]

746 Jesuit College, Chaumont, Haute-Marne. Chapel interior, 1629. [A.P.]

747 Jesuit College, Vannes, Morbihan. Chapel, by Père Adrian Deran, 1660–4.

748 Jesuit College, Notre-Dame-de-la-Gloriette, Caen, Calvados. By Père André, 1684–7. [L.N.]

749 Jesuit College, Rouen, Seine-Maritime. Chapel, 1616–56. [G.Z.]

750 Jesuit College, Rouen, Seine-Maritime. Chapel, 1615–56. [G.Z.]

751 Jesuit College, Rouen, Seine-Maritime, 1614–56. Exterior. [G.Z.]

752 Jesuit College, Rouen, Seine-Maritime, 1614–56. Parlour. [G.Z.]

753 Jesuit College, Quimper, Finistère. Chapel façade, by Charles Turmel, 1640.

754 Jesuit College, Rennes, Ille-et-Vilaine. Chapel façade, by Derand and Turmel, 1624–57.

755 Jesuits of Eu, Seine-Maritime. College, founded 1582.

756 Jesuits of Eu, Seine-Maritime. Chapel, from the north, 1613–24. [G.Z.]

757 Jesuits of Eu, Seine-Maritime. Façade of chapel, 1613–24. [G.Z.]

758 Jesuits of Eu, Seine-Maritime. Doorway from the Place du Collège. [G.Z.]

759 Jesuits of Eu, Seine-Maritime. Interior of chapel, 1613–24. [G.Z.]

760 Jesuit College, Soissons, Aisne. Gateway, c. 1690. [L.N.]

761 Jesuits of Cambrai, Nord. Façade of chapel, 1692. [G.Z.]

762 Jesuit Seminary, Brest, Finistère. 1686. [L.N.]

763 Jesuit College, Angers, Maine-et-Loire. C. 1730.

TEXT-FIGURES

INTRODUCTION

The most important factors in French monastic history in the years round 1500 were not religious but economic: and their economic force lay mainly in the results of military destruction. The Hundred Years War had fallen with devastating effect upon the monastic buildings of France:[1] Notre-Dame de Saintes, Saint-Jean-d'Angely, Poitiers, Ligugé, Saint-Lucien de Beauvais, Saint-Germer-de-Fly, and hundreds more, had had their buildings wrecked. The poverty of the country in men and money caused other abbeys to fall down for want of workmen and funds to repair them; and whatever happened to abbey buildings and abbey lands, the king's taxes had still to be paid. Jean Molinet the poet described what war had done to the abbeys:[2]

> Je laisse aux abbaies grandes
> Cloistres rompus, dortoirs gastés,
> Greniers sans bled, troncqs sans offrandes,
> Celiers sans vins, fours sans pastés,
> Prelats honteux, moisnes crottés,
> Pertes de biens et de bestaille,
> Et, pour redressier leurs clochés,
> Sur leur dos, une grande taille.

The great and ancient Benedictine abbey of Fleury may stand as an example.[3] As early as 1335 the monks found it hard to live; in 1358 the Englishman Robert Knolles devastated the abbey and its lands, and his devastations in the abbey itself were completed by a fire. In 1363 a band of Bretons occupied the ruins for two years. By the end of the fourteenth century the campaigns of du Guesclin brought a measure of prosperity to the abbey estates and Fleury was on the whole fortunate in the next fifty years, until a series of commendatory abbots brought a new element to bear upon its fortunes.

The cities suffered as much as the countryside. The story of the Benedictine abbey of Saint-Martial de Limoges is typical. The buildings were damaged in the Hundred Years War, the farms and vineyards outside the city were laid waste, and every source of revenue devastated.[4] Popes and bishops, kings and lords, made claims upon the abbey property that there was none to oppose. By 1439 there were only thirty monks left, and not enough money to pay for their food. For a time the abbey was deserted; then a few monks returned to live without a Rule,

---

[1] Denifle (see Bibliography) has a list of abbeys burnt or destroyed in the war. I have already written briefly on the subject in *Art in Mediaeval France*, p. 267.

[2] Between 1478 and 1482 (Champion, II, p. 343).

[3] Chenesseau, p. 30. [4] De Lasteyrie, p. 157.

with a city family called Jovion holding all the offices and drawing what little money there was. The abbey never wholly recovered, and was secularized in 1535.

By 1500 the economic basis of society already rested as much on the money of the merchant as on the produce of the farmer. It might have been expected that urban Orders would in consequence have overwhelmed and displaced the older foundations of the countryside. In fact such was not the outcome. The characteristic new Orders of the sixteenth century are those of Clerks Regular, exercising a priestly ministry while living in a community—the Theatines, founded in 1524, the Barnabites, in 1530, and the Society of Jesus, of which the Paris house was set up in 1540. Of these, however, only the Jesuits flourished in France, and even they hardly rivalled the older Benedictine foundations.

France has two great sources of wealth which no war can destroy: her climate and her soil. Her natural riches are inexhaustible. Fifty years after the end of the Hundred Years War in 1453 the older monasteries who drew their wealth from land were already sufficiently recovered to stand firmly beside the new urban foundations. Some of them, indeed, still retained much of the material riches garnered through the Middle Ages. When the Queen of Sicily visited Clairvaux in 1517 the abbey owned so many reliquaries that each monk held one at Mass and there were many larger ones for her to look at in the sacristy afterwards.[1]

It has been estimated[2] that at the beginning of the sixteenth century France could boast at least six hundred Benedictine abbeys and about six thousand priories, about six hundred and sixty Cluniac houses and more than two hundred Cistercian; sixty Charterhouses; one hundred and thirty-nine houses of Celestines, thirty-six of Premonstratensians, four hundred of Friars of various Orders, one hundred and fifty of Regular Canons, and about five hundred Commanderies of St John, St Anthony of Vienne, St Lazare and other Hospitallers.

Between 1547 and 1550 the Chambre Ardente of the Parlement of Paris condemned more than five hundred Protestants to prison or the stake unless they retracted. None the less Calvinism flourished; at the Paris Synod of 1559 seventy-two churches were represented; by 1561 there were two thousand in the kingdom with members as illustrious as Antoine de Bourbon, King of Navarre, his brother the Prince de Condé, and Admiral de Coligny.

The Wars of Religion began in 1560 with the attempt of the Conspiracy of Amboise to seize the person of Francis II. In the next thirty years Catholics and Huguenots were eight times at war in France. Pasquier said that if a man had slept through these years he would have woken to find not France, but her dead body. Once more the abbeys and priories of the land suffered, and this time less by casual destruction than by deliberate intent. In 1576, for example, the Protestants occupied Figeac, which they did not leave until 1623. They had only been there a few months when they decided to destroy the Cluniac church of Saint-Sauveur. They removed stones from the piers, replaced them by wooden blocks,

---

[1] Assier, p. 8.   [2] Imbart de la Tour, II, 199.

2

and fired the wood. They thus brought down the choir, part of the transept and part of the nave vault.[1]

The abbey of Marcilhac was burned by the Protestants under Montgomery in 1569, and seventy years later was still in ruins. The Benedictine abbey of Saint-Michel-en-l'Herm in the Vendée[2] suffered much in a long and eventually successful siege by the Huguenots in 1568. Attempts at restoration in 1589 failed to secure the support of the commendatory abbot, Charles de Bourbon, and it was nearly a century before the abbey buildings were restored.

Some abbeys could not survive such attacks. Saint-Aignan d'Orléans, an abbey of seventh-century foundation, had been destroyed by the English in 1428. It was destroyed once again by the Calvinists in the sixteenth century and was never rebuilt.[3] The abbey of Saint-Saulve, at Montreuil-sur-Mer, was sacked by the Huguenots in 1537. The monastic buildings were never rebuilt, though the monks followed their Rule for a time in an ordinary citizen's house.

The Wars of Religion in France ended with the abjuration of Henry IV in 1593. The French monarchy and the Church of Rome were reconciled with his formal absolution by the Holy See two years later. One of the conditions imposed by the Pope was that the King was to establish a convent or monastery in every province in reparation for those that had been destroyed by the Huguenots.

Another condition imposed by the Pope was the publication in France of the edicts of the Council of Trent, which had not hitherto been officially recognized in France. Their delayed effects were in fact almost negligible in the field of art;[4] the Vatican might be in some measure dictator to the artists of Italy, but in France painters, sculptors and architects continued to go their own way. A consequence of this independence was a close approximation in style between French religious and secular architecture:[5] an approximation which continued to have repercussions long after the sixteenth century. It owed something to the fact that the spread of architectural designs by means of engravings made the same models available to all, and that these models were for the most part intended for secular use. The 'premier Renaissance' had found a more abundant and more characteristic expression in castles than in churches, though the appearance of the new style had in both been contemporaneous.[6] When Philibert de l'Orme published his *Premier tome de l'architecture* in 1567 his plates were all for secular architecture. In one of them[7]—a design for a rib vault of a flattened kind—he implies the approximation of secular and religious architecture by entitling it: 'Des voultes modernes que les maistres macons ont accoustumé de faire aux églises et logis des grands Seigneurs.'

[1] Restoration was begun in 1636.   [2] See F. Eygun in *Cong. Arch.* CXIV, 27.
[3] Migne, *Dictionnaire des Abbayes*, col. 24.   [4] Dejob, p. 259.
[5] Hautecœur, I, 368: 'Au milieu du [XVIe] siècle l'architecture religieuse subit les mêmes influences, emploie les mêmes formes, obéit au même idéal, que l'architecture civile.'
[6] The Easter Sepulchre with Renaissance detail at Solesmes (see below, p. 11) dates from 1496, five years before the Château de Gaillon was begun.
[7] P. 107.

A comparison of such a secular loggia as that of Valençay with such a monastic cloister as that of Fontevrault shows how close the approximation remained.[1]

The monastic architecture of France passed into full classicism at a pace as certain, if a little slower, than the architecture of palaces and châteaux. Yet the Benedictines, at least, did not deny their past. My study of their architecture has unexpectedly thrown into relief a 'Gothick' taste in the late seventeenth century and in the first half of the eighteenth, that found expression most frequently in architecture designed by members of the Order. Like the Oxford Gothic of the seventeenth and eighteenth centuries it had its roots in tradition and in sound historical learning; the result is no boudoir Gothick, but a serious and almost unrecognized element in the history of French classical architecture.

A study of the architecture of any Order, except possibly the individualist Augustinians, will gradually reveal characteristic forms and tastes. It has long been usual to speak—usually without much documentation—of a Jesuit style in architecture; it is, I think, no less true to speak of a Benedictine style in the classical period. Even the Ursulines have a style of their own, that in its decent economy recalls the women's colleges of Oxford and Cambridge.

The student will find the history of each Order in great measure self-contained. He will have to complete the picture by the study of the men and women whose influence extended over more than one Order and indeed over the whole Church of France: men and women like St Vincent de Paul, Cardinal Bérulle, Madame Acarie, André du Val, St François de Sales and Père Joseph (François Joseph Leclerc du Tremblay). He will understand the history, the pictures, and even the architecture of monastic France the better for this knowledge; but it cannot be given in a book such as this.

At the time of the Revolution all monastic property in France was confiscated by the State, most of it into the immediate hands of the newly constituted local authorities. Many churches were destroyed, some on principle, more—as at the English Dissolution—for the sake of their building materials. Others were stripped of their roofs and left to decay. The monastic buildings, especially when they were of comparatively recent construction, were usually turned to some administratively useful purpose. The names of several Paris convents are familiar because they were prisons; the house of the Jacobins is remembered not as a Dominican convent, but as the meeting place of a club. The house of the Petits Augustins of Paris acquired a lasting fame as the building where all that Alexandre Lenoir could save of the medieval splendour of France was housed. After 1820 it became no less famous as the École des Beaux Arts; little of interest of its monastic architecture is left.

The Revolution, and the reorganisation of the State that followed it, produced a great need for buildings to house the new bureaucracy and the new social

---

[1] Sir Anthony Blunt (*Philibert de l'Orme*, p. 8) has shown how even Rabelais's imaginary Abbey of Thélème (1534) was influenced by current château architecture.

services. The monastic buildings of France offered ready-made quarters for Préfectures, Sous-Préfectures, Hôtels de Ville and Mairies. They could house the police and their prisoners, and the Courts of Justice; they could meet the needs, more acute since the nursing and teaching Orders had been disbanded, of hospitals and homes for the demented and the aged, and of schools and colleges of every degree.[1] They provided barracks and depots for the armies of the Revolution and the Empire. Military occupants are peculiarly difficult to dislodge. As early as 1826 local archaeologists and historians began to try to get the army out of the Abbaye-aux-Dames at Saintes. The manœuvre was only accomplished a hundred and ten years later.

Some monastic buildings were turned—churches and all—into factories for the new industrialism. The remoter houses, that could not be turned to any administrative or commercial use, were sold to become, with little change, farms or manor-houses.

The Jesuit churches, though most of them were attached to buildings which continued in scholastic use, none the less underwent varied avatars, not only in the Revolutionary period but also in our own day. M. Pierre Moisy[2] records the destruction of many, and the transformation of others into classrooms, concert halls, gymnasia, sports clubs, museums, libraries, courts of justice, cinemas and prisons.

The poverty of France at the Restoration prevented any wholesale expropriation in favour of the Orders that were now able to return. It was, on the whole, cheaper and easier for the government to encourage them to build new and more modest quarters, than to drive out the administration from what had once been monastic houses. Throughout the nineteenth century there was some destruction but little change of use, and the process has continued to our own time.

The traveller who finds the time and the patience to see the later monastic churches of France for himself will be rewarded. He will not enjoy the majestic certainty of such Romanesque abbeys as Cluny, nor the Gothic glories of the late medieval abbeys. He will instead find himself admitted to the buildings, and often even to the atmosphere, of a life that vanished at the Revolution. When he is lucky enough to find a building that has not been turned to base uses—some farm or country-house, some monastery once again dedicated to the religious life—he will breathe an air sometimes heavy with dead learning, sometimes a little insipid, smelling of the pot-pourri of forgotten sentimental pieties, and sometimes still vital with impulses of truth and kindness. Sunlight on old stone, the decay that forms a bloom on faded leather bindings, the scent of old paper and stale incense, dust sweet in the sun, will recreate a little busy world of piety and learning and charity that by force of order and tradition achieved a sepia-tinted beauty of its own: a beauty that endured for the centuries before the Revolution and can still sometimes be felt today.

---

[1] In recent years the abbess's house of the noble nunnery of Beaurepaire near Marchiennes has been turned into a miners' welfare centre.   [2] Les églises Jesuites, p. 25.

CHAPTER I

THE BENEDICTINES

I. 1498–1610

At the end of the Middle Ages the Benedictines were not only the most ancient but also the most widespread Order in France. The two great Benedictine reforms, those of Cluny in the tenth century and of Cîteaux in the twelfth, had not changed the essentials of the Rule: poverty, chastity, obedience and enclosure. The daily observance of liturgical prayer might vary a little from abbey to abbey, but essentially all were under the same Rule.

Cluniacs, Cistercians and autonomous Benedictines had been the architectural innovators of the early Middle Ages, but by the fourteenth and fifteenth centuries their churches had accepted a late Gothic style not essentially different, except in the details of its iconography, from that of the cathedrals and the parish churches.

The Hundred Years War not only damaged the buildings and property of the Benedictines but also the fabric of discipline within the Order. Plague had been joined to the ravages of war and had killed many in the monastic dorters. It was inevitable that in houses where too few monks were left to fulfil the complicated and inexorable duties of work and prayer and chant, the Rule should be modified and relaxed; and that in those of which the lands no longer brought in enough to live on, men should leave the cloister rather than starve.

Five years after the final defeat of the English in 1453 the work of reform had begun. Jean de Bourbon, abbot of Cluny,[1] issued statutes designed to restore the ancient discipline of his abbey and its many dependent houses. Circumstances were too much for his efforts. His successor, Jacques d'Amboise, continued to attempt reform, though still with little result. In 1494 further statutes had to be enacted, aimed principally against the monks who went to Saint-Martin-des-Champs and the Collège de Cluny at Paris to pursue their alleged studies, and stayed in the capital with students' privileges for an unconscionable time.

Meanwhile others of the great Benedictine abbeys had also attempted reform: Marmoutier in 1466, and Chezal-Benoît, in alliance with Cluny, in 1480. The revised Rule arrived at by the Chapter of Chezal-Benoît was accepted by four or five other Benedictine houses; together they formed 'la Congrégation Casalienne'.

It is fair to say that by the end of the fifteenth century Benedictine reform was

---

[1] I have included the Order of Cluny with the Benedictines, since it followed the same Rule, had the same architectural needs, and in the main pursued the same development: but since the Cistercians developed rather outside the main stream of Benedictinism I have considered them separately in chapter II.

far ahead of that of the friars.[1] It consisted in the main in a return to the original Rule with minor modifications that were simplifying and superficial. The abbey churches and monastic buildings continued to be perfectly adapted to the needs of the Order, and no great campaigns of building were needed except to restore the damages of war. One or two Benedictine nunneries moved from the country into the towns in the second half of the sixteenth century for greater security, and a few houses near the frontier built 'refuges' to which the monks could withdraw in case of need. Two survive at Laon: typical town houses, their façades framed within a pair of stair-turrets [1].[2]

The great difficulty of the Benedictines, once the damage of war had been repaired, lay in the fact that their abbots were appointed *in commendam* by the King. The abuse had first arisen in the stormy years of the eleventh century, but had been abolished in 1122. It had arisen again at the time of the Papal Schism of 1378–1417. It was particularly rife in France, where the statutory Benedictine right of the free election of the abbot by the Chapter had almost lapsed by the end of the fifteenth century. By the Treaty of Bologna the Pope had ceded to Francis I the right of nomination to all the benefices of the kingdom: a strange result of the victory of Marignano that was to weigh upon France for two centuries and more.

The King's nominations were by no means always bad. The first abbot *in commendam* of Fleury, Jean de la Trémoille, appointed in 1486, was always ready to fight for its rights, and built a fine new chapter-house.[3] Yet the abbeys still remembered their ancient privileges, and in 1484 there were protests against the admission of the abbots introduced by Louis XI to Bourgdéols, Massay and Saint-Maixent. Further protests were made under Louis XII against his nominations at Fécamp, Ferrières, Saint-Germain-des-Prés and the Cistercian abbey of La Bénisson-Dieu.[4] When the Cardinal de Boissy came to enter his abbey of Le Bec-Hellouin in 1516, he came accompanied by a troop of men-at-arms and occupied his abbey like a conquering invader. Such abbots did not provide even for the most necessary repairs; at Bec the nave of the church fell down for want of care in 1591, and the then abbot did nothing to restore it.

When in 1493 Louis XI held a commission of bishops and doctors at Tours to consider the reform of the French clergy, the abbots of Cluny, Chezal-Benoît, Marmoutier, Cîteaux and Bonport (all busy with the reform of their abbeys) were unanimous in condemning the nomination of commendatory abbots and the influence over elections exercised by Princes and even Popes. Their advice, however, was not followed: to give a man an abbey *in commendam* was too easy a way for the King to reward a servant or to bribe a waverer for him to renounce

---

[1] Exceptionally a Benedictine house preferred secularization to reform; Saint-Maur-les-Fossés at Paris was secularized and attached to the See in 1536 (Clouzot, p. 259), and Saint-Martial de Limoges in 1535 (see above, p. 1).

[2] The references are to the plates following p. 154.

[3] Marchand, p. 47. [4] Imbart de la Tour, II, 119.

it. Francis I rewarded Primaticcio with the abbey of Saint-Martin-ès-Aires near Troyes[1] and Philibert de l'Orme was nominated to Saint-Eloi-lès-Noyon and other abbeys. He was titular abbot of Ivry-la-Bataille; a door in the church is said to be of his design. Ronsard (who was at least in minor orders) was Prior of Saint-Cosme-lès-Tours, and of Croixval a dozen miles away, and had a part share in other monastic endowments.

Even Huguenots were nominated. Odet de Coligny (who had been elected a cardinal at the age of seventeen) was made titular abbot of Fleury in 1562.[2] It was a moment when members of the Reformed Church were tolerated, and he declared himself a Huguenot, but did not quit the purple or renounce his abbey. When Calvinist troops invaded the abbey in 1562 and 1568 his name did something to protect it, though the gold and silver of the sacristy were looted, the reliquaries and sacred vessels destroyed, the organ and many documents burned, and the statues of the north porch mutilated.[3] His eventual excommunication was followed by his marriage, but he continued to hold his benefices until removed from them by the Parlement in 1569, and even then was able to put in a nominee and to keep the revenues of Fleury. When he died in 1571 his brother Gaspard de Coligny, the famous admiral, still received the revenues, while Claude Soublet, his *homme de paille*, officially held the abbatiate. In 1572 Soublet attempted a very mild reform; it had little effect. By the time the abbey had paid its titular abbot it was so poor that land had to be sold every year to provide food for the monks. At Ferrières-en-Gâtinais the attacks of the Huguenots were led by the titular abbot himself, the same Odet de Coligny. At Le Bec-Hellouin Henri IV appointed a married man as abbot.

An exceptional commendatory abbot who entered the Benedictine Order and became a regular abbot was Jacques de Billy, a scholar who in his day held the abbacies of Ferrières, Taussigny, Notre-Dame-des-Châtelliers and Saint-Michel-en-l'Herm. He proved a good disciplinarian, and turned his scholarship into patristic channels. More often a commendatory abbot might do something for the beautification of his titular church; in 1530, for example, Chancelier Duprat brought rich marbles from Italy to pave the sanctuary of his abbey of Fleury, and built an arcade like a triumphal arch before the high altar.[4] At Maillezais, again, a house which, though it became the seat of a bishopric, still sheltered its Benedictine community,[5] Geoffroy d'Estissac in 1536 redecorated the sanctuary in considerable splendour. He erected a very rich screen in Renaissance style, with Ionic pilasters, coffered soffits with rosettes, garlands of flowers and fruit, angels and putti.[6] More frequently the institution of a commendatory abbot brought a

---

[1] An Augustinian house: see below, p. 74. [2] Chenesseau, p. 35.
[3] Chenesseau, p. 36. They had begun to burn the library when Pierre Daniel, an amateur of Orléans, arrived and bought the remaining MSS., which later passed in part to the Queen of Sweden (and so to the Vatican) and in part to Berne. A few MSS. remained at the abbey and are now in the Public Library at Orléans and other collections. (Chenesseau, p. 88.) [4] This was destroyed in 1642.
[5] See Crozet in *Cong. Arch.* CXIV, 80. [6] The remains of it are now in the Museum of Niort.

campaign of restoration to an end. The Madeleine of Châteaudun, for example, had been burned in 1463; the apse had fallen in 1522. The restoration, begun in 1529, stopped when the abbey passed *in commendam* in 1536.

The institution of a commendatory abbot had one immediate and inevitable effect on any abbey: separate quarters had to be built for him, since he did not follow the common Rule. At Cluny Jacques de Bourbon, titular abbot from 1456 to 1485, erected a lodging near the outer wall of the abbey precinct. It is a modest building, Gothic in feeling, with heavy mullioned windows and fine hooded fire-places decorated with the achievement of the builder's arms. It has even the monastic feature of a cloister, formed of a single gallery between two polygonal staircase-turrets.

It was not splendid enough for his successor Jacques d'Amboise, abbot from 1485 to 1510, who built himself a new lodging alongside the first [2]. The square bays of its southern façade are fantastically mixed in style; the lower part is carved with sham windows with elaborate flamboyant tracery, whereas the upper part is covered with a veneer of alabaster delicately sculptured in the Italian manner with rosettes, fleurs-de-lis, masks, arabesques and hunting scenes, so disparate and so ill-fitted to their position that they look as if they might have been mass-produced in Italy and imported ready-made.

At Rouen the abbot of Saint-Ouen built himself a splendid palace at the turn of the century. It was entirely secular in style, with great pinnacled *lucarnes* and a vast expanse of sculptured tracery. John Sell Cotman painted it twice[1] in 1817, the year in which it was demolished [3]. At Fleury Etienne Poncher, the second abbot *in commendam*, built himself a lodging (now destroyed) between 1508 and 1524.[2] At the Cluniac priory of Notre-Dame d'Airaines a small block of buildings of about 1530 precariously survives.[3] It is matched by a longer three-storeyed building of equal plainness at Sorde.

At Brantôme Pierre de Mareuil, abbot under François I, built himself a charm-ing Renaissance gazebo and a series of classical summer-houses [4, 5]. At Souvigny a new lodging for the prior [6, 7] was built in the time of Henri II; on one side it incorporates a cloister that is still Gothic in design.[4]

Another abbot's lodging of the middle of the century survives at the Trinité at Vendôme[5] [9], and another chequy in brick and stone at Bernay [8]. At Beaulieu-lès-Loches a charming little Vignolesque house has most of the metopes of its frieze filled with religious symbols, while the two over the door are carved with Masonic signs [11].

[1] One picture is in the Cotman Collection in the Norwich Museum, the other in the collection of Lord Mackintosh of Halifax.
[2] Marchand, p. 47.
[3] Another may be cited at Luxeuil, Haute-Saône, but it was built before Luxeuil became part of France.
[4] The buildings of the Benedictine house at Thouars—now a mill—are of much the same date but have been in the main reconstructed.
[5] Parts of the abbot's quarters at Saint-Savin seem also to be of this date, but have been modified.

All these buildings are handsome rather than sumptuous, and apart from a few chimney-pieces have little interior decoration. Clearly it was recognized that a commendatory abbot would not spend much time in his abbey, and would travel with his own tapestries. Residence in Paris was another matter.[1] At Saint-Germain-des-Prés an abbot's lodging[2] was built in 1586 for the Cardinal de Bourbon by Guillaume Marchant.[3] Its style is more mature [12] and its interior was more splendid; originally it was famed for a splendid gallery decorated with stags' heads.

Few houses embarked on rebuilding their monastic quarters, though many had to repair medieval buildings damaged in war. The abbey of Sainte-Austreberthe at Montreuil-sur-Mer had its living quarters rebuilt in an austere style suited to its windswept site [15]. The Benedictine nuns of Pont-l'Evêque built themselves a high square pavilion, depending for its effect on the alternation of brick, stone and pebble [14]. Monstierneuf built a dovecote of unexampled splendour, with a lantern at the top and sculptured *lucarnes* [10]; it looks as if its designer had drawn inspiration from an engraving of the tomb of Cecilia Metella.

In one or two monasteries new cloisters were erected, usually to project from existing buildings.[4] The most beautiful surviving cloister of the Renaissance in France is the lesser quadrangle of Saint-Martin de Tours, built between 1508 and 1519 by Bastien François, a nephew of Michel Colombe[5] [16]. It is inspired less by the cloisters of the Middle Ages than by the great Italianate galleries of such castles as Gaillon. The low-pitched stone vaults rest on delicately sculptured ribs with shields in rosettes for bosses. The exterior, in spite of its structural buttresses, is entirely of the Renaissance in its modillion cornice, its elaborate frieze of scrolling foliage, and the death's heads that adorn the spandrels [17]. The cloister at Decize, on the other hand, is of clumsy simplicity. It is not vaulted, but is covered by a ceiled penthouse roof. The arcade of round-headed arches rests on squat quadrangular pillars on a rather high plain base. It appears to date from the middle of the century. At Marmande the roughly contemporary cloister [18] is also not vaulted, but its delicately sculptured arcade is of the utmost elegance, with capitals of Florentine delicacy and richly panelled rectangular columns.

In 1555 the mature classic style of Henri II was used at Saint-Germain-des-Prés for a cloister in two storeys,[6] the ground floor [13] which in part survives being Doric and the upper storey (backing on to the Library) Ionic, with elaborate capitals each differently ornamented. It is not, I think, fantastic to see in it the

[1] A new abbess's lodging was built 'en forme de pavillon' at Montmartre in 1555 by Philibert de l'Orme.

[2] Parts of it survive at 3 rue de l'Abbaye and in the rue de la Petite Boucherie.

[3] Marchand, p. 47.

[4] Those built at Cadouin and Ambronay early in the sixteenth century are still essentially Gothic. That erected at Jumièges in 1530 has disappeared except for a few capitals at Highcliffe. (See E. Remnant, p. 107.)

[5] The cathedral cloister of La Psalette, finished by his brother Martin in 1513, affords an interesting comparison.

[6] Sauval, I, 339.

direct influence of the Bramantesque cloister of Monte Cassino, which must have been known to the abbots of many of the greater Benedictine houses. It is the application of a classical pilastered order to a cloister there adopted which appears in a plainer form at Saint-Germain-des-Prés, Pontlevoy [40, 41] and many later French monastic cloisters.

The style of the Italian Renaissance early found its way into the churches of the Order of St Benedict. The earliest instance that can be precisely dated is the Entombment group in the abbey church of Solesmes, carved by an artist of the school of Michel Colombe in 1496.[1] The group itself is Gothic in style, though some Italianate influences are evident in its modelling. The architectural setting is in the main Flamboyant, but the two side pilasters are decorated with Italianate candelabra of the type used on the façade of the Certosa of Pavia. It is possible that the group was in part due to the generosity of Charles VIII, who brought sculptors from Italy to work at Amboise. The cloister of Saint-Wandrille, another great Norman abbey, has a washing fountain dated 1502, with equally elegant arabesque decoration.

Some five years later the abbey church of Fécamp was enriched with a series of Italianate sculptures. Its abbot, Antoine Bohier, visited Italy in 1507; he brought back some sculptures for his church, and seems to have invited Italian craftsmen to Normandy to decorate it. He acquired from Pace Gaggini of Genoa the tabernacle[2] [19] which enshrines the relic of the Precious Blood and from Girolamo Viscardi of the same city the tabernacle, sarcophagus and reliefs still to be seen above the high altar. These show that the abbot had a true feeling for the history of his abbey, for they represent Richard I and II, Dukes of Normandy, protectors of the abbey, who were buried in its choir. Then, before his death in 1519, he had the Gothic chapels of his choir divided from the sanctuary by screens in Renaissance style [21]. Their extravagantly varied designs rather suggest that they were made by French sculptors working from engraved designs. The sacristy door [20] is French in the shape of its arch but Italianate in ornament.

The elaboration of such screens to form as it were an interior building in a church is well shown in the abbey church of Moissac. The over-rich cresting, the multiplication of varied columns, the elaboration of reliefs, the whole Mannerist complication of the design, suggest a style that has not yet been fully assimilated.

Meanwhile, the new style was being extended to greater schemes of church building in the Benedictine abbeys. The church of Saint-Victor at Paris was sumptuously rebuilt between 1517 and 1540; nothing of it remains. A splendid Renaissance façade [22] completed the rebuilding of the abbey of Saint-Michel at Dijon. The church was begun in 1499 and consecrated in 1529 and the façade

[1] See Hautecœur, I, 95; Blunt, *Art and Architecture*, p. 5; Vitry, p. 276. Antoine Bohier was the brother of the man who began to build Chenonceau in 1515.

[2] Gaggini later worked in France: see Blunt, *Art and Architecture*, p. 7. His family, originally Florentine, also worked in Sicily.

seems to have been begun soon afterwards.[1] The base keeps the Gothic tradition of three deep portals, but they are united to form a kind of triumphal arch.[2] The piers that frame them and the frieze above are all classical, in the style derived from engravings. The arcades of the portals are treated as coffered ceilings, the coffers enclosing reliefs of extraordinarily varied subjects which all appear to be based on engravings: Minerva, Apollo and Venus consort with Solomon and Judith. Above this two towers of later date, having the series of classical orders on each storey, end in lanterns. They mask the Gothic side view of the church; only the gable peers above the screen that joins them.[3]

Another early campaign of Renaissance building took place in the choir of the priory church of Saint-Florentin. The entire choir was rebuilt about 1530; the side-screens are dated 1539. The main lines of the exterior and interior are wholly Gothic, with a rib-vaulted apse, a pointed arcade, gables and rose windows; the doorways (dated 1611–13) are classical, in the Roman manner, with flat pilasters, anthemion brackets and a coffered voussoir.[4] They afford an interesting filiation with the doorway at Decize[5] [24], with that at Mozac, dated 1542, which bears the arms of the commendatory abbot Duprat [23], and with the simpler doorway with the name of the monastery in noble Trajanic capitals at the Cluniac priory of Monstierneuf. The Easter Sepulchre at Saint-Florentin shows how fatally strong the influence of engravings upon sculpture was at this time; its friezes and reliefs, crowded with tiny figures, are mere translations from graphic art into stone.[6] The retable of the high altar is more medieval in its equestrian figures of St Martin and St Florentin.

Near Fécamp the church of the abbey of Valmont was rebuilt by the Estoute-ville family, certainly before 1540 and probably about 1525. The Benedictine tradition of a long nave and a rounded apse is there frankly accepted [25]. Its classical pillars and high rounded arches, its coupled arcade in bays over the ambulatory, seem a strangely belated development from the Romanesque of about 1130, though its window tracery is of Gothic derivation. An odd hybrid quality is evident in the piers of the crossing: the arch is Gothic; the inner side is decorated

[1] See Hautecœur, I, 154. In 1527 Jean Boudrillet of Tours carved new backs for the stalls of Saint-Bénigne-de-Dijon 'à l'antique', that is, with arabesques in Renaissance style. (Hautecœur, I, 179.)

[2] The south door, finished in 1537, still has Gothic niches and canopies; the north door, finished in 1540, differs only in detail; the central door, also of 1540, still has a figure of St Michael against the mullion in the medieval style, but the bracket on which he stands is covered with Renaissance detail. The tympanum still has the Last Judgment, but the frieze has Satyrs and Labours of Hercules.

[3] An interesting description of the façade will be found in John Ruskin's *Diary* for 23 September 1846 (ed. Evans and Whitehouse, I, 347).

[4] Two men named Boullon from Tonnerre, perhaps father and son, are recorded to have worked at Saint-Florentin between 1600 and 1607. (*Cong. Arch.*, Auxerre, 1958, p. 24.)

[5] It is interesting to see the scheme reappearing with a rounded arch in the seventeenth century in the remote Breton abbey of Saint-Maurice de Carnoët.

[6] Blunt, however (*Art and Architecture*, p. 6), considers its detail to be too accurate not to be of Italian workmanship. The fine stained-glass windows are under the same influence, as is usual at this time.

The superb choir screen of about 1540 at La Trinité de Vendôme affords an interesting analogy.

with Gothic tracery in relief up to capital height; but instead of a capital there is a classical moulding, and the soffit of the arch is adorned with classical medallions.[1] Beyond the choir lies a Lady Chapel, dating from between 1517 and 1552, the date of its fine stained glass. Its splendid vaulting [26] is of late Gothic form, though its ornament is classical. Its sculptures are no less disparate: a medieval God the Father rises from a classical garland; a group of the Education of the Virgin fills the spandrel of a classical arcade. Only the latest of the sculptures, Germain Pilon's Annunciation on the high altar, succeeds in being entirely of the Renaissance.

The Benedictines were far from denying their medieval past. The commemoration of the eleventh-century Dukes of Normandy by Antoine Bohier, abbot of La Trinité at Fécamp, has already been mentioned.[2] Elsewhere, too, history was not forgotten. The great door of Saint-Martin-des-Champs, set up in 1575, was adorned with statues of the founders Henri I and Philippe I.[3] The shrine of Saint-Remi set up at Rheims[4] was adorned with statues of the six ecclesiastical and six lay peers of France who used to take part in the Coronation, together with statues of St Remi and of Clovis.

In the second half of the century few monasteries were rich enough to build churches. The Benedictine nunnery of Montmartre, reformed in 1549, was burned in 1559,[5] and Henri II promised the nuns to help rebuild it. His architect Philibert de l'Orme planned a new building for it[6] of a sensational new form. It was to be spherical, some sixty or seventy-five yards in diameter, with a peristyle-cloister of two Ionic storeys and several storeys of cells linked by galleries above, the whole surmounted by a heavy cornice and a high wooden dome and lantern [27]. He said of it: 'Elle eust représenté à ceux de Paris, un globe terrestre ou céleste qui eust été très beau, et encore plus admirable si, par curiosité, on y eust marqué les heures du jour par l'ombre du soleil ou quelque géographie que l'on eust peu discerner sur la couverture.' Unfortunately, Henri II, the destined benefactor, died, and the gigantic monastic sundial was never erected, even in a modified form. Indeed, most monasteries had to content themselves with an episodic version of the highly classical style of the time. At the priory of Notre-Dame de Vitré in 1578 an elegantly classical door, with pediment, triglyph frieze and coupled Doric columns, was inserted into a much-pinnacled Gothic façade with astonishing effect.

The Benedictine nuns at Jouarre rebuilt a good deal of their nunnery[7] in 1588; tall and high-roofed, it is more like a town house than a monastic building.

The eccentric Pope St Celestine V established a branch of the Benedictines

[1] It may be compared with the priory of Saint-Eusèbe at Auxerre, of which the choir was built in 1530. Here, however, every detail is late Gothic.
[2] See above, p. 11. [3] Piganiol de la Force, IV, 10.
[4] The statues survive but were reset in 1847. [5] Roy, I, 368.
[6] *Inventions pour bien bastir*, reprint, p. 304; Blunt, *Philibert de l'Orme*, p. 81.
[7] It is still a nunnery.

which bore his name. The Celestins never had many houses in France, but the cloister of their Paris monastery [28], built between 1539 and 1550, was considered one of the most splendid in the city.[1] It retained the medieval tradition of double bays and twin columns; but the capitals were Corinthian, the bays were divided by classical pilasters, a triglyph frieze ran above the arches, and the barrel vault was panelled in classical fashion. The church was Gothic, but four splendid bronze statues of the Evangelists were set up in the time of Henri IV at the corners of the altar. No church in France but Saint-Denis held the tombs of more great people; nothing remains. The stalls from their abbey at Marcoussis [29], now in the parish church, remain their sole memorial.

2. LOUIS XIII, 1610–43; LOUIS XIV (REGENCY), 1643–61

The reign of Louis XIII was a time when the realm of France prepared itself for future greatness. The history of the country as a whole was paralleled in that of its Benedictine houses. The political architects of French monarchism in his reign were not only churchmen but also had direct contact with the abbeys of France. Richelieu was commendatory abbot of some twenty abbeys, headed by Fleury and Cluny; he was nominated abbot of Cîteaux by the community and had power and influence over an inordinate number of Benedictine houses. Mazarin held twenty-seven abbacies.

At the beginning of the century the flame of devotion burned low in the Benedictine abbeys. Chenesseau[2] has described the condition of things at Fleury.

The documents show us the Abbey at the beginning of the seventeenth century as a sort of boarding-house where every man made his little way of life as personal as possible, by reducing the ancient obligations of the Rule to the indispensable minimum. If the endowed masses—in any event not numerous—were said, if the regular liturgical service was performed, it was enough. The offices of the monastery served as a pretext for individualism, and almost every monk managed to secure a titular post. They drew for their own use the revenues attached to their charges of treasurer, almoner, cénier[3] and so on. They used to busy themselves visiting their lawyers and their farms, and making sure that their tenants paid all their dues.... They spoke of their wine and their corn as possessions as personal as their books and their furniture and their savings.... In effect the monastery had become a haven for some fifteen little bachelor capitalists, friendly and gregarious; decent folk leading a decent life, so far as one may judge, but men who considered the ancient practices of austerity, of seclusion from the world, of silence, of life in the cloister, to be altogether obsolete and out of date.

The time had come for reform; and reform was imposed from above. The Council of Trent had ordained that all monasteries that were not under direct

[1] Piganiol de la Force, IV, 186 and 252.

[2] P. 39. I translate.

[3] The cénier was an officer found at Fleury, Saint-Germain-des-Prés and Saint-Denis (and probably at other abbeys), who was originally in charge of the monks' supper during the summer; see Godefroy, Dictionnaire de l'ancien français, s.v., and Ducange, s.v. cœnarius. The post later became a valuable sinecure.

episcopal jurisdiction should be united into congregations, or lose their exemption from diocesan control. The edict was directed mainly against the Benedictine houses, which were autonomous (except for those included in the Orders of Cluny and Cîteaux) and, by their deeds of foundation, in most cases exempted from the jurisdiction of the bishop.

The Congrégation Casalienne[1] made little progress, and there was as yet no general movement towards the organization of congregations. Cardinal Charles de Lorraine, on his return from Trent, tried to reform his titular abbey of Cluny, but without result.[2] A partial reform based on a return to the original Rule was instituted in 1621, but without any attempt to form a congregation.

The Parlement, however, had registered the decree of the Council in 1576, and the French Benedictines had to accept reorganization in congregations in some form or another. The first congregation, formed in 1583[3]—the Congrégation Gallicane des Exempts—only consisted of five abbeys: Marmoutier, Fleury, Saint-Sauveur, Notre-Dame de Dôle[4] and the Trinité de Vendôme.

In 1598 Dom Didier de la Cour, Prior of Saint-Vannes in Lorraine, instituted a strict reform in his abbey. Other monasteries accepted it, and it gradually extended to some forty houses.[5] By the beginning of the seventeenth century the Benedictine houses of Lorraine, Champagne and Franche Comté were organized into a reformed Congregation of Saint-Vannes and Saint-Hyadulphe. The reform spread from Lorraine into France through the influence of Dom Laurent Bénard, Prior of the Collège de Cluny,[6] and soon extended to Limoges, Nouaillé, Meaux, Jumièges and to the Guillemites (Blancs-Manteaux) of Paris.[7] A General Chapter of the Congregation of Saint-Vannes was held at Toul in 1618, at which an independent congregation of reformed French houses was instituted under the name of the Congregation of Saint-Maur, to be for France what Saint-Vannes was for Lorraine. By 1621 the new Congregation, to which royal letters patent had been granted, included about a dozen of the great abbeys of France. In 1636 it was united to the Congrégation Casalienne and by 1648 its numbers had risen to about eighty.

The true creator of Maurist greatness was the first Superior General of the Congregation, Dom Grégoire Tarrisse,[8] who died in 1648. He not only did

---

[1] See above, p. 6. In 1516 Leo X forced the nuns of Saint-Pierre-de-Lyon to join the congregation, in which they remained until 1637.

[2] Hélyot, *Dictionnaire*, I, 1015.   [3] Chenesseau, p. 38.   [4] Not yet in France.

[5] The history of the Maurist reform is fully recounted in Dom Martène.

[6] He refused office in the Cluniac Order, and went for a second novitiate to Saint-Vannes, where he renewed his profession in 1615.

[7] Plans for their house, dated 1640, will be found in Arch. Nat., Plans N III, Seine 432 (1–5) and 435 (1–10). The church was rebuilt in 1685 and remains; it has a narrow nave, with Corinthian pilasters and an arcade leading to narrow aisles. Piganiol de la Force (IV, 321) says of it: 'Il règne dans l'ordonnance de son architecture une monotonie de pilastres corinthiens, dont le trop grand nombre fatigue l'œil....Les bas côtés sont trop étroits, et dans le genre d'une cour à remises, plutôt que dans celui d'une église.' Parts of their buildings are embedded in the Crédit Municipal in the rue des Francs-Bourgeois.

[8] See his biography by Rousseau.

much by his powers of conciliation to introduce the Maurist reform into rich and proud abbeys such as Saint-Germain-des-Prés and Saint-Denis, but also by his own work and his encouragement of the researches of others did much to found the tradition of Maurist learning. The spread of the Maurist Congregation was largely due to Richelieu, who desired the union of all the Benedictine houses of France into a single congregation. The Cardinal became titular abbot of Fleury in 1621, and incorporated the abbey in the Congregation in 1627.[1] There was some opposition from the older monks, but he met it by pensioning them off out of the abbot's revenues. He became titular abbot of Cluny in 1629, and at once summoned monks from Saint-Vannes. By 1634 the whole Order of Cluny was united with the Congregation of Saint-Maur, but the union only lasted for ten years. Chezal-Benoît, that had had its own reform, stood out against Richelieu, but he forced a commendatory abbot and the Maurist reform on them in 1635. By the end of the eighteenth century the Congregation, with Saint-Germain-des-Prés at its head, included a hundred and ninety-two houses divided into six provinces: a hundred and fifty-five abbeys *in commendam*, thirty-four priories and three other houses,[2] as well as nine colleges.

The aim of the Maurist reform was a return to the Benedictine principles of residence, silence, abstinence, obedience and the full liturgical *opus Dei*.[3] The practice of private meditation and prayer was encouraged, travel was permitted for study and research, and there was a new stress on intellectual work. On the other hand, no manual labour was imposed; the regulations about fish, eggs, cream and honey were eased; and, greatest change of all, separate cells were permitted instead of a common dormitory.

The Maurists dealt competently and systematically with the problem. They had their own architects who went round the abbeys and priories that entered the Order, and made plans of them as they were with suggestions for their repair and modification, and exceptionally for their rebuilding. A great series of these plans, mostly of the second half of the seventeenth century, but extending into the eighteenth, survives in the Archives Nationales at Paris,[4] to which it passed at the Revolution from the library of Saint-Germain-des-Prés. They show, in most instances, medieval buildings in a bad state of repair, and give some idea of the practical problems that faced the Maurists.

The acceptance of membership in the Congregation of Saint-Maur saved many abbeys from annihilation, since by membership they shared not only in a common inspiration but also in common funds. The abbey of Saint-Riquier, for example, had been burned in 1487 and rebuilt in a campaign that finished in 1536. The

---

[1] Chenesseau, p. 41. Richelieu gave the handsome *boiseries* of the sacristy at Fleury.

[2] Prat, p. 12.

[3] Dom Laurent Bénard's *Instructions monastiques sur la règle de Sainct Benoist* was published in 1618, the year of the foundation of the congregation. It is traditional and pietistic, with nothing about *consuetudines*.

[4] Arch. Nat., Plans N III. The plans are basic for the detailed study of individual buildings, but can hardly find a place in a general view such as this.

abbacy was then put *in commendam* and the discipline relaxed. It was again burned in war in 1554, and after the commendatory abbot's revenues had been paid there was not enough money left for rebuilding. The monks continued to live miserably in the ruins until the Marquis d'Aligre, a commendatory abbot who ruled from 1645 to 1695, introduced the reform of Saint-Maur. The abbey church was restored, still in late medieval style, and provided with splendid furnishings, of which much survives[1][30]. Finally, in 1690 he held a competition for pictures for his church. The Marquis d'Aligre and the Maurists also built two blocks of monastic buildings at Saint-Riquier[2] in a simple institutional style [31] that re-appears in parts of the living quarters at Fécamp [33] which became Maurist in 1649.[3]

The abbey of Sainte-Croix de Bordeaux was in such a state when the Con-gregation took it over[4] that the infirmary, guest-house, monks' living quarters, library and cloister had to be rebuilt. At Saint-Wandrille the central tower of the church fell in 1631 and caused much ruin. The commendatory abbot Ferdinand de Neufville invited the Maurists to take over the abbey in 1636. They set about restoring the church and buildings [35] and further erected a great hall for the meetings of the General Chapter of the Congregation.

On the other hand, several ancient abbeys that refused to join the Congregation came to an end. Moissac was secularized in 1625, and Tournus in 1627. At Arcisses by 1630 there were only two monks left, and the buildings were ceded to nuns.[5]

The formation of the Congregation of Saint-Maur, and the influence it exer-cised even over monasteries that remained outside it, had two direct consequences on monastic architecture. The Maurist emphasis on historical erudition, and their need for sensible economies, encouraged a tendency to repair old buildings rather than to build new ones, and the Maurist permission for each monk to have his own cell led to a campaign of rebuilding the domestic quarters of the Benedictine houses.

The generation of Dom Jean Mabillon, Dom Luc d'Achery and Dom Jean Martène, who made the Maurist house of Saint-Germain-des-Prés at Paris a true centre of historical and literary learning, was represented in many provincial houses by other Benedictines hardly less learned, even if less famous. It is signifi-cant that their literary work finds a parallel in architectural reconstruction in

---

[1] His gifts include not only two missals and two Canons of the Mass bound in copper gilt, but also three gilt bronze choir-staves, and silvered bronze altar candlesticks, cross and sanctuary lamp. All are still in the sacristy of the church. See Catalogue of Royal Academy Exhibition, 'Age of Louis XIV' (1958), nos. 327-31.

[2] On the Maurist buildings at Saint-Riquier see E. Rostand, 'Les Constructions mauristes'.

[3] It seems also to have been followed at Vierzon in 1628, but the monastic buildings (now the Hôtel de Ville) have been greatly modified. A very plain version of it is used for the long wing of monastic buildings at Ambierle, apparently of about 1630.

[4] Chauliat, p. 327.

[5] Migne, *Dictionnaire des Abbayes*, col. 51.

Gothic style.[1] At Saint-Etienne de Caen the vaults of the church were rebuilt in their original form after their destruction in the Wars of Religion. At La Réole the church has sexpartite vaults rebuilt in the seventeenth century. At Bernay the refectory,[2] built about 1630, has Gothic vaults with sculptured pendants and brackets. At Chancelade, in the Dordogne, the Romanesque nave was revaulted and fenestrated in 1629 by the abbot of Solignac, in flamboyant ogival style. At Nieul-sur-l'Autise the chapter-house had its vault rebuilt in Romanesque style in 1646. Elsewhere long campaigns of rebuilding were continued without change of style although their completion fell in a strongly classical age. Even in Paris the wooden ogival vaults of Saint-Germain-des-Prés were rebuilt in stone between 1644 and 1646, although the detail of the portal is in contemporary style.

The second great change propagated by the Maurists was the institution of separate cells in lieu of a common dorter. The French adaptation of the Monte Cassino Rule published by Jean du Breul in 1603 had authorized it on grounds of decency and privacy for devotions. The provision recurs in the Constitutions of 1637 and 1646; the latter fix nine feet square as a minimum, with no side longer than eleven feet. As a consequence a great number of abbeys found themselves under the necessity of rebuilding their living quarters.

In Normandy a generation of Benedictine architects arose to meet the need. Dom Denis Plouvier worked as an architect at Préaux in 1650, at Saint-Vigor de Bayeux in 1655, at Saint-Wandrille (his own monastery) from about 1655 until his death in 1669.[3] In 1658 he was at Corbie, and in 1661 at Samer. Everywhere he showed himself a competent, economical and conservative architect. Dom Anselme Boisseau, the Cellarer of Saint-Vigor, acted as architect to his own cloister and infirmary about 1644.[4] Frère Victor Tixier designed good monastic buildings in brick with stone quoins for the Maurist house at Compiègne in 1647; his cloister still has pointed arches. Many of these new monastic quarters built in the first half of the seventeenth century were strongly influenced by secular architecture. Part of Bernay was rebuilt in 1628[5][38] in an economical provincial version of such a Mansart town house as the Hôtel de la Vrillière, with three storeys of similar windows divided by panelled spaces of wall, the length marked by a single moulding above the first and a double above the second floor. The attic has double windows under pediments in the centre and on each side of the projecting wing. At Saint-Georges-sur-Loire, again, the two wings[6] [39] recall

---

[1] Their surveyor-architects (who may well have been Benedictines) shared in the same interests; for example, the surveyor of Saint-Wandrille between 1656 and 1671 made careful drawings of the late medieval details of the tower. Arch. Nat., Plans N III, Seine-Maritime 15.

[2] Now the Tribunal Civil.

[3] Rostand, *L'œuvre architecturale*, pp. 18 ff.; Hautecœur, II, 717.

[4] Emmanuel Boinet, a converted Huguenot, also worked here for some thirty years after 1654. (Rostand, *L'œuvre architecturale*, p. 28.)

[5] Now the Hôtel de Ville, etc. The fine refectory is now the Salle du Tribunal. The Romanesque church was retained but its capitals were covered with classical stucco work. It is now a garage.

[6] One now the Mairie and the other a dilapidated tenement.

a château in their sober elegance. The likeness to secular architecture is no less marked when the building is in brick as at Fécamp [33], the abbey of Toussaint at Angers[1] [34], and the priory of the Val-aux-Grès outside Bolbec [32].

Richelieu, who became titular abbot of Pontlevoy in 1629, restored and enlarged it before handing it over to the Congregation of Saint-Maur, who added a school to its monastic activities. It eventually had no less than four cloisters,[2] with two storeys and an attic with dormer windows headed alternately with angular and rounded pediments. It was some time before they were finished, but they are consistent in style [40–43]. The remaining fragment of the abbey of Josaphat, near Chartres, is of comparable architecture[3] [44].

At Saint-Wandrille the buildings erected after the abbey's acceptance of the Maurist reform in 1636[4] show the same approximation to secular architecture [35]. They might easily pass as a modest château by an architect of the school of Le Mercier. The interior, however [36, 37], is more austere than that of a private house would be, with some deliberate archaizing in the vault of the staircase. The monastic buildings of Saint-Savin-sur-Gartrempe[5] [45], begun in 1640, have a certain resemblance to those of Saint-Wandrille, but achieve a deliberate austerity by a flat and unbroken façade seventeen windows long on one side, and by a bare wall broken only by classical doorways on the other. A similar building, on the scale of a small town house, was erected for the Benedictines of Selles-sur-Cher;[6] others are at Corme-Royal[7] [47], Solignac[8] [46], Ébreuil [48, 49] and Massay.[9]

The buildings at Saint-Jean d'Angely [50, 51] are less austere; the varied windows and central pavilion make them indistinguishable from a château. At Brantôme, which joined the Congregation of Saint-Maur in 1636, the monastic buildings were rebuilt with a long flat façade broken by a central feature with pedimented windows, under a rounded pediment framed in volutes[10] [52]; the block has at each end a square pavilion with a curved roof and bell-cote [53]. The design is rather ambitious, but notably provincial. The buildings at Livry[11] seem originally to have followed a similar plan; they are secular in style. At La Chaise-Dieu the

[1] Now the Manutention Militaire.
[2] One was deliberately destroyed by the Germans in the last war.
[3] Now part of the hospital.
[4] The plans (Arch. Nat., N III, Seine-Maritime 15) date from 1656–7; they are not exactly followed in the buildings erected.
[5] Now tenements. [6] Now Hôtel de Ville and post office.
[7] The church was done up in 1624 and the monastic buildings look little later.
[8] Now the seminary of the Missions des Pères Oblats de Marie Immaculée. A simpler version of the same style will be found at Saint-Seine-l'Abbaye.
[9] Saint-Jacut, Ploubalay, became Maurist in 1648. Plans for its rebuilding in the style of a Louis XIII manor survive in Arch. Nat., Plans N III, Côtes du Nord 1.
[10] Parts of the central block were modified about 1900.
[11] Now a factory and in bad repair. Their local name of 'Château de Sevigné' seems to recall the fact that in the middle of the seventeenth century Christophe de Coulanges, uncle of Madame de Sevigné, was titular abbot. I owe this information to the kindness of Mme Josette Fourès.

buildings have a monumental quality that is meridional [54], achieved by a masterly use of proportion. The architect is unknown. The same note is struck in the monastic buildings at Ferrières-en-Gâtinais [55].

The abbey of Flavigny, again, rebuilt its monastic quarters.[1] It seems possible to detect two campaigns; one (represented by a plan of 1655)[2] [56] with very simple architecture depending for its effect entirely on proportion and fine stone, and one [57] with more pretensions: a ramped base, moulded windows, and an entresol lit by hooded *œils-de-bœuf* between the first and second storeys.[3] These are repeated, without hood-moulds, on the cloister side of the building. The cloister is extremely simple both in arcade and vault. A second vaulted passage runs behind it.

Many of these monastic buildings necessarily included cloisters. Some of these, like that at Pontlevoy, followed a simplified version of the formula employed at Monte Cassino,[4] but on the whole the influence in France of the style of Bramante seems to have been less strong than that of secular architecture.[5] The Place-Royale (now Place des Vosges) [58], which Henri IV began to build in 1605, probably on plans by Androuet du Cerceau, became not only a centre of Parisian society but also a model for monastic cloisters. Its Italianate arcades and vaults classicized the idea of the roofed arcade that had been common both to the *villes neuves* of medieval France[6] and to her monasteries.

There is a striking parallel between Henri IV's secular arcade, built between 1605 and 1610, the cloister at Redon dating from Richelieu's titular abbatiate [59] and those at Souillac[7] [61] and La Réole [60]. At Paris and Souillac the square piers are alike on every side; at Redon the arches are closed by a low wall which serves as a base to a simple pilaster which receives the arch. On the external side the piers end in double scrolls, suggesting vestigial buttresses. At Paray-le-Monial [62] the groin-vaulted cloisters are supported by buttresses with square Doric capitals, that swell out in an elegant curve below. At Redon the doors to the church and the sacristy are enriched with sculpture entirely in the secular classical style [64].

A variation on the theme occurs in the abbey of Sainte-Croix de Quimperlé[8] [63], probably built after the abbey joined the Congregation of Saint-Maur in 1665. At Le Bec-Hellouin [65, 66] the cloister built between 1644 and 1646 has a scheme that closely resembles Redon without the wall. Each side has six bays with Corinthian pilasters on the inner side and a kind of buttress on the outer. The vault, however, keeps the medieval tradition. This cloister follows the tradition of Redon in having sculptured niches and doors [67].

---

[1] Now a factory for aniseed liqueur. [2] Arch. Nat., Plans N III, Côte-d'Or 7.
[3] A comparable feature occurs at Le Val-de-Grâce. [4] See above, p. 11.
[5] The much-battered cloister at Vendôme, however, is in late medieval style.
[6] See Evans, *Art in Mediaeval France*, p. 224.
[7] Now a storeroom of the Régie de Tabac. The cloister at La Charité, now a vintner's store, is in the same style.
[8] Now Mairie, Tribunal and Gendarmerie.

Several monasteries of which the monks' quarters were rebuilt at this time have impressive gateways.[1] Saint-Wandrille has a delightful garden gateway with fanciful watch-towers at the side, and an upper arch crowned by a round-headed tympanum [68] and Souvigny has a massive and rather squat entrance pavilion [69].

The Maurists definitely declared themselves against luxury in abbots' lodgings, and the surviving buildings seem to show that their protestations were sincere. According to Dom Martène,[2] Dom Grégoire Tarrisse, the superior of their Congregation from 1630 to 1648, did not wish 'que dans les nouveaux édifices, dans les jardins et autres lieux, il n'y eût rien que ressentît la pompe et l'éclat des personnes de qualité, voulant seulement qu'on y vît reluire la modestie, la pauvreté et la simplicité religieuse'. These austere standards seem chiefly to have been followed in such poor and remote houses as Landévennec in Brittany. In richer independent houses another note was struck. Léonor d'Etampes, bishop of Chartres and titular abbot of Bourgueil, about 1630 had his salon there painted by Mosnier with 'l'histoire d'Apollon et de Daphné d'une manière fort galante'.[3]

There was no change in Benedictine liturgy that demanded a change in their churches, as the institution of cells did in their monastic buildings, yet a number of abbey and priory churches were rebuilt or embellished under Louis XIII. All show a veneer of classicism on an essentially Gothic base. Saint-Germain-des-Prés acquired a door with a broken pediment [70]. The church of Saint-Nicolas de Rethel, a priory of Saint-Remi de Reims, had a great square tower added to it in 1614, with three superposed orders and a pedimented doorway: an unusual translation of a medieval form into classic guise.[4] Saint-Gildas d'Auray, a priory of Saint-Gildas de Rhuis, had its church completely rebuilt between 1623 and 1641. The windows are still ogival, but the porch, dated 1636, is classical [71]. The church of the abbey of Saint-André at Le Cateau [72, 73] was begun in 1625.[5] Its façade, dated 1635, is definitely Flemish in style, and owes much to books of engraved architectural ornament. The interior shows an interesting compromise between classical and Gothic style; the aisle, for example, is definitely classical, but the ambulatory and the vault are still medieval. It has a deep transept with apsidal ends. The interior offers a close analogy with the church of the abbey of Saint-Sépulchre at Cambrai[6] [74], which suggests a later work by the same architect. The ambulatory is more classical; the nave is more Ionic; the façade is very much less Flemish and altogether better designed; but the two are clearly related.

More often a medieval church was modernized by the addition of contemporary woodwork. Good examples of the middle of the seventeenth century are the

[1] For example, Saint-Pierre-le-Moutier. As late as 1648 the monks of Fleury constructed a gate with the exceptional survival of a drawbridge. (Chenesseau, p. 183.)
[2] Cited Hautecœur, II, 858.   [3] Pointel, I, 171.
[4] It was considerably damaged in 1940.
[5] It was severely damaged in the First World War but has been conscientiously restored.
[6] Now the cathedral; it too has been badly damaged and well restored. It looks as if the post office buildings next to it were based on the monastic quarters.

choir screens at Nouaillé, the retable of St Benedict at Marmande and the stalls at Saint-Jouin-de-Marnes [75]. Charles d'Aligre, commendatory abbot of Saint-Riquier between 1645 and 1695, gave new stalls carved with bas reliefs, of which two show Charlemagne and Angilbert restoring the abbey, perhaps in allusion to his own restorations. They maintain a medieval tradition in their splendid animals [76]. Many abbeys acquired a new pulpit[1] or a new organ loft;[2] a few remade a shrine. At Fécamp Guillaume de Dijon, the first abbot, was given an elegant classical tomb; at Fleury, in 1637, St Benedict was given a great 'mausolée'. A number[3] acquired a new sacristy with fashionable panelling; a delightful example from Saint-Wandrille survives in the church of Caudebec-en-Caux.

Such *boiseries* were complemented by no less elaborate work in stone. At Pontlevoy, for example, the high altar and side chapels were in 1651 all adorned with elaborate baroque retables [77] and at Saint-Remi de Reims a splendid screen was erected seven years later, in a rather old-fashioned style [78]. Many choir-screens in wrought iron were set up; they were occasionally supplemented by such a splendid iron lectern as that which survives in the church of Saint-Julien-le-Pauvre at Paris.

Everywhere it was felt that the simple stone altars of the Middle Ages were no longer splendid enough for modern needs. Dom Martin Marrier of Saint-Martin-des-Champs was the historian of the Order of Cluny, and in 1636 he wrote[4] with evident regret

There was in our church an ancient altar dating from so old a time that few appreciated it. It was therefore desirable that, as had been done in other places, an altar of this kind should be demolished to make way for one more splendid, higher, shining with gold, marbles, columns and paintings, for the greater glory of God. In fact, by force of such reasoning, we soon agreed to replace the old altar by one more accomplished and more sumptuous.

The new altar—now in its turn destroyed—at Saint-Martin-des-Champs[5] was by François Mansart with paintings by Vignon. It may stand as the type of many such renewals.

No nuns were included in the Maurist congregation but those of the royal abbey of Chelles, and since few women's houses were exempt from episcopal supervision, it was not possible for them to be united in a congregation. None the less a wave of reform spread through the Benedictine nunneries, which after the difficult centuries of war were in need of reorganization. The Benedictine nuns of Le Val-de-Grâce of Paris were reformed by their abbess in 1618. 'L'Ordre mitigé de Saint Benoît' was instituted in 1648 in the convent of Notre-Dame de Bon-

---

[1] For example, that from Saint-Jean-des-Vignes, Soissons, now at Oulchy-le-Château.

[2] For example, the very fine one at La Chaise-Dieu, with splendid sculptured caryatids, given in 1683 by Cardinal Serroni; and that of 1704 from Fleury now in Orléans Cathedral.

[3] For example, Souvigny.   [4] P. 540. I translate.

[5] See Derel, *Le Maître Autel*, p. 161.

Secours, founded in the rue de Charonne in Paris in 1648. A good deal of its buildings remains incorporated in more recent secular houses[1] [79]. A house of Benedictine nuns called the Filles du Saint Sacrement was founded in Paris in 1652 by Mère Mechtilde (Catherine de Bar) to follow an elaborate scheme of devotion.[2] Reformed Benedictines, the Religieuses de la Madeleine de Trainel, set up at 100 rue de Charonne in 1654;[3] and the reformed Benedictine nuns of Le Val-d'Osne, an old foundation in Champagne, were brought to Paris about 1661 to occupy the site of the Protestant Temple at Charenton and to sanctify it by the perpetual Adoration of the Sacrament.[4]

Even in the seventeenth century the Benedictine Rule had not lost its attraction. One of the contemplative Orders that were inspired by the mystical devotions of the time chose to follow it: the Order of Calvarian nuns, that arose out of that of Fontevrault, and was recognized in 1617, when Madame Antoinette d'Orléans became its head. It was dedicated to the mystical adoration of Calvary; the chief devotion of its members was to imagine themselves in the position of Mary at the foot of the Cross. Marie de Médicis established them in the rue de Vaugirard in 1625, and they had another house in Paris, nine houses in the Loire valley and seven or eight in Brittany. Their church was dedicated to Our Lady of the Sorrows, and her image was carved over its door.[5] Parts of their building survive in the rue de Vaugirard,[6] very handsome but curiously secular in style [80].

The tendency for country nunneries to seek safety in and near the towns continued until the end of the Wars of Religion; in 1622 the Benedictine house of La Pommeraye, two leagues from Sens, was brought into the faubourg by its abbess, and in 1629 the nunnery of Notre-Dame de Bricol, an ancient house two leagues from Sézanne, was likewise brought inside the walls.[7] The Benedictine nuns of Valognes moved their house inside the town in 1631, and the buildings survive[8] [81, 82]. Their fine and simple church, with four side chapels on either side, has a façade that oddly reconciles a Gothic arch with a classical 'frontispiece'. The cloister finds its only ornament in the rustication of its arches; the buildings above it are of an utter simplicity only relieved by steep-roofed pavilions at the angles.

The Benedictine nuns of Châtillon-sur-Seine rebuilt their house in 1629 as plainly as might be [83];[9] the ladies of the Abbaye-aux-Dames at Saintes[10] were a

---

[1] 97, 99 and 101, rue de Charonne.

[2] Hélyot, *Dictionnaire*, I, 162. Plans for their house survive in Arch. Nat., Plans N III, Seine 459 (1–8).

[3] Plans for their house will be found in Arch. Nat., Plans N III, Seine 461 (1–5).

[4] Hélyot, *Dictionnaire*, III, 827. They followed a mitigated Benedictine Rule and became tinged with Jansenism. [5] Piganiol de la Force, VII, 269.

[6] No. 19. Of their house at Chinon, a little rather featureless building survives.

[7] Migne, *Dictionnaire des Abbayes*, col. 133.

[8] Now the hospital. [9] Now the Hôtel de Ville.

[10] Now turned to many uses, from administration to tenements; it was for a long time a military prison. The later parts of the buildings are said to have been due to the abbess Françoise de Foix, 1666–8. (Crozet in *Cong. Arch.* CXIV, 118.)

little more ambitious [*84, 85, 86*]. The way their cloister is integrated into the building clearly owes something to secular architecture. Some of the interior sculpture is ambitious and highly provincial [*88*]. It compares unfavourably with a door from the Benedictine nunnery of Puyberland[1] [*87*] which, if with a considerable time-lag, recalls the *jubé* of Saint-Etienne-du-Mont. It probably dates from the foundation of the convent in 1644.

The chief patron of Benedictine nunneries at this time was the Queen, Anne of Austria. In 1638 she decided to rebuild the Benedictine nunnery of Le Val-de-Grâce outside Paris,[2] in gratitude for the birth of the Dauphin (to be famous as Louis XIV) after twenty years of married life. The first stone was laid by the child, then seven years old, in 1645; the work was delayed for a time by war, but was finished by 1665. The Queen intended to have fine apartments in the nunnery, but gave up the plan to leave more money to be spent on the church and the nuns' quarters. In the end she had only two or three simple rooms in the north-east corner of the cloister, with an elaborate entrance porch on very French Ionic columns. The cloister, built in 1655, still exists [*91, 92*]; it has two storeys of galleries (now glazed) one above the other, with buttresses between, running up for the whole height. The low-pitched vault of the lower floor is rather old-fashioned, like the balusters of the staircase. The storey above is perfectly plain, with unadorned windows, and dormers above. The chief façades are centred by rounded pediments with the royal arms[3] [*90*]. The buildings might be splendid, but the life led in them was austere.[4] Beds were of boards with a mattress of straw, sheets of serge and pillow-cases of wool. Earthenware vessels and wooden spoons served for meals in the refectory. Each cell, even that of the abbess, contained besides the bed only a prie-dieu, a crucifix, a chair and three pious engravings.

The general plan of Le Val-de-Grâce[5] included a lesser cloister fitted in between the nave and the transept (and beyond it) in the traditional way, with a staircase in the corner (Fig. 1). Behind it lay a greater cloister with projecting pavilions at the angles.[6] The chapter-house and the refectory [*89*] have ogival windows and projecting buttresses that recall the earlier style. It is noteworthy that the monastery is separated from the church with unusual completeness, doubtless because it was anticipated that many royal ceremonies would be held in the church, which was, indeed, planned on a royal scale.[7] Its façade, of the familiar two-storeyed plan

[1] Now in the Hospice at Melle.

[2] The nuns had originally been established at Bièvre-le-Châtel. They moved to the Faubourg Saint-Jacques, after they had been reformed, in 1624. They had branch houses at La Celle, Charenton, La Charité, Montreuil-sur-Mer, Calais, and elsewhere. The nunnery is now a military hospital.

[3] The engraving in Marot's *Recueil* shows small oval windows over the second storey, but there is no sign of alteration in the façade.   [4] Ruppricht-Robert, p. 27.

[5] Perelle's engraving is reproduced in Blomfield, II, plate c.   [6] Ruppricht-Robert, plate 3.

[7] It proceeded slowly after the death of Anne of Austria in 1666 and was barely completed in 1710. (See Hautecœur, II, 51.) So ambitious an ensemble must, however, have been planned as a whole from the start.

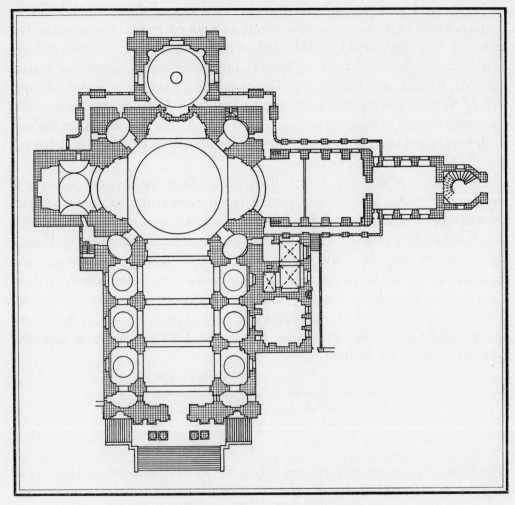

Fig. 1. Benedictine Nunnery of Le Val-de-Grâce, Paris.
Plan of church, 1645. (After Ruppricht-Robert.)

framed in scrolling buttresses,[1] was the central feature of a great three-sided courtyard formed of monastic buildings and shut off by a grille that in its design recalls the forecourt of Mansart's château at Maisons.

For the first time the medieval tradition of Benedictine church planning was broken (Fig. 1). The church was designed not only to serve the community but also to be the place of sepulture for the hearts of the royal house. François Mansart therefore planned it[2] with the nuns' choir not in the main axis of the church but occupying the south transept. The nave has barrel vaults on a heavy cornice above fluted pilasters with splendid Corinthian capitals. The soffits of the

[1] It invites comparison with the façade of the church of the Sorbonne by Jacques Le Mercier.

[2] See Ruppricht-Robert. An excellent brochure on the church has recently been published by Pierre du Colombier in the series *Nefs et Clochers*. The work, begun by Mansart, was carried on by Le Mercier and completed by Le Muet. The main altar of the church has a wooden retable with twisted columns of much the same date; and the wooden screen of a side chapel seems to date from the same campaign.

arches are richly coffered, as is the great terminal arch of the choir[1] [94]. The six domed chapels of the nave are more completely cut off from it than usual; it was intended[2] that they should be dedicated to three sainted kings: Canute of Denmark, Eric of Sweden, Louis of France, and three sainted Queens of France, Clotilde, Bathilde and Radegonde. The great dome over the crossing[3] followed that of St Peter's in its external treatment [93] with single engaged columns as buttresses instead of coupled columns as at Rome. The whole edifice, indeed, both in plan and style, is notably of Roman inspiration; it could not be what it is but for St Peter's and the Gesù.

The influence of the Gesù is particularly noticeable in the elaborate planning of the domed crossing. The dome on pendentives rests on four massive and complex piers in each of which an oval chapel on two floors has been set. Unlike the Gesù, the church of Le Val-de-Grâce has a trefoil plan at the crossing: the central apse is less important than one would expect; the Chapel of the Holy Sacrament, under its own cupola, lies behind it. On the right is the nuns' choir, on the left the Chapel of St Anne, destined to be the burial place of the hearts of the royal house.[4] The exterior of the nuns' choir is admirable in its proportions and in the delicate diminution of the scrolled buttresses. It was with reason, if not with taste, that Molière wrote of the church:

Tout s'y voit
Assaisonné du sel de nos grâces antiques,
Et non du fade goust des ornements gothiques,
Ces monstres odieux des siècles ignorants
Qui de la barbarie ont produit les torrents.

The dedication was remembered not only in the pictorial decoration of the church but also in the sculptured decoration with which it was enriched.[5] Here again Italian influence is manifest; many of the figures and much of the scheme come directly from the *Iconologia* of Cesare Ripa.[6] The barrel roof of the nave [95] is adorned with an elaborate network of guilloche mouldings, framing circular medallions of the kings and queens to whom the chapels were dedicated, and oblong panels of angels holding scrolls. The arcades of the nave and choir have statues lying on them in the manner of those in St Peter's at Rome. The subjects, straight out of Ripa, are the Virtues of the Virgin.[7]

The arcades of St Anne's chapel and of the nuns' choir are adorned with 'emblems' from the chisel of Michel Anguier. They were designed especially for

[1] By 1714 it was felt that this splendid arcade was less classical than a plain architrave would have been. See Decordemoy, p. 108.

[2] Piganiol de la Force, VI, 198.   [3] It was rebuilt on an iron frame in 1865.

[4] Thirty-six of them were buried in it. After 1694 it became also the place of burial for the bodies of the house of Orléans, who could no longer claim burial in Saint-Denis.

[5] The sculpture was begun in 1662 and seems to have been finished in 1667.

[6] The first edition of 1593 was not illustrated, but that of 1603 had engravings. The French translation by Baudouin published in 1644 was still more fully illustrated.

[7] See Mâle, p. 422.

their position, possibly by a nun of the abbey; at all events a manuscript that records them came from the possession of such a nun.[1]

The great painting of the dome, commissioned from Mignard in 1663 and finished in 1666,[2] was designed by the learned Du Fresnoy. It comprises nearly two hundred figures some sixteen feet high, and elaborate inscriptions.[3] It portrays Anne of Austria, led by St Louis and St Anne, holding out to God a model of the monastery she has built.[4] Round her, in concentric circles, are the Prophets, the Evangelists, the Apostles, the Martyrs, the Fathers of the Church and the founders of religious orders. Above her are the Trinity and a kneeling Virgin and angels with a cross. A seven-branched candlestick, a Paschal Lamb, and the inscription *Sic exultant in Gloria Dei* show that even in the seventeenth century the Benedictines had not forgotten the Apocalyptic theme which had adorned their most splendid Romanesque churches.[5]

This was the most ambitious iconographic scheme of the church, yet each subsidiary part was no less appropriate. The half-cupola of the Chapel of the Sacrament, for example, was painted by Jean-Baptiste de Champaigne with the figure of Christ in clouds, holding the Host.[6] One of the Queen's salons was adorned with paintings of all the empresses and queens who had been held to be saints.[7]

A second great nunnery that was rebuilt in the middle years of the century was that of the Dames de Saint Pierre at Lyons,[8] a sixth-century foundation for noble ladies with its own rights and privileges.[9] As a consequence the ladies in course of time had built themselves a lot of little houses within the enclosure; each belonged to the builder during her lifetime, and then passed to the abbess who nominated a nun to occupy it, as a bishop might nominate a canon to a house in the close. The nunnery was occupied by the Huguenots in 1562 and despoiled, and patched up again. A measure of reform was introduced in the middle decades of the seventeenth century, and it was rebuilt in the years after 1659, after endless disputes with the city authorities, who were building their town hall on a new site, which the nuns considered encroached upon their property. Anne of Austria helped to

---

[1] *Bib. Nat. nouv. acq. franc.* 10171; see Vauthier, p. 146.

[2] See Lemonnier, p. 314.   [3] See Piganiol de la Force, VI, 185.

[4] It finds a parallel in a great picture in the sanctuary of the Benedictine nunnery of Le Val-d'Osne, which showed Madame d'Orieux, the foundress, holding the church and putting it under the protection of the Virgin, with Louis XIV and Cardinal de Noailles beside her. (Hélyot, *Dictionnaire*, III, 827.)

[5] The angels with a cross recall the iconography of the Gothic tympana. The Apocalyptic vision was later painted on the cupola of the transept of Sainte-Glossinde de Metz by J. Girodet of Lunéville, artist to Stanislas Leczynski.

[6] Guillet de Saint Georges, I, 347.

[7] *Ibid.* I, 242. About the same time Sacquespée painted for the choir of Saint-Wandrille the saints of the abbey and the Order. (Pointel, I, 245.) The Queen also ordered a set of pictures of the Life of St Benedict from Philippe de Champaigne for her private apartments. (See Guillet de Saint Georges, I, 242 and J. Descamps, *La Vie des peintres.* 1754, II, 68.)

[8] Now the Palais des Arts. (See Hervier, and Charvet, 'Thomas Blanchet', p. 158.)

[9] *Ibid.* Charvet, 'Thomas Blanchet', p. 7.

settle the dispute on her way through Lyons in 1658, and the design adopted was to be on a scale to balance that of the town hall. The abbess, Anne de Chaulnes, spent five years in prayer, and had more than five thousand Masses said, before she was confirmed in her decision. She then engaged an elderly Avignonese architect, François des Noyers de la Valfenière, to design the work.[1] The foundation stone was laid early in 1659, at a solemn ceremony, by a poor child symbolizing the Infant Christ. The architect accepted the necessities of a town site, set the cloister a little askew, and from the first the abbey had shops built in on the ground floor of its façade to the Place des Terreaux [96], set between Doric pilasters with little windows above the main shop. The *piano nobile* was framed in Corinthian pilasters; its pedimented windows were surmounted by a row of plainer windows, with attics above. The new buildings were a hundred metres long and some seventy-six deep; the interior court was sixty-four metres by forty: all this to house forty nuns and twelve lay sisters. It was originally planned that there should be domes over the end pavilions, but these were never built because of financial difficulties. There are staircases at each angle, with an extra one near the entrance, to serve the abbess's lodging, so planned that it has double stairways for the use of the cloistered sisters and those coming from the world outside. The abbess's own quarters were in the projecting central block; they included a richly panelled suite of rooms (with a billiard room), an oratory, and a covered terrace for exercise two hundred feet long and forty wide. The whole might well pass as a noble palace in Turin.

Abbess Anne de Chaulnes died in 1672, and was succeeded by her sister, who finished the remaining two sides[2] and undertook the decoration. She employed the artist Thomas Blanchet; his work remains in the refectory, designed as a double cube, begun in 1681; it was completed by Simon Guillaume. The cloister of forty-eight arcades has its exterior designed with simple pilasters and a plain cornice;[3] the centre of each arch has an acanthus console. The arches were originally closed by grilles.

The church itself [97] is a noble building with its arcade formed as part of an order of fluted Ionic pilasters. It follows the traditional aisled Benedictine plan. The rib-vaulted roof has round-headed clerestory windows.

In 1644 the Benedictine nuns of Notre-Dame de Liesse, who had come from Rethel, were established in the rue de Sèvres at Paris. About half of the lower storey of their cloister survives in the Hôpital Necker [103]; it is well proportioned but extremely plain. A similar austerity is evident in the buildings of La Ronceray at Angers[4] [100, 101]; the canted filling of the angles is a slight concession to elegance. The cloister follows the masculine Benedictine tradition. The nunnery

---

[1] It was completed by his son Paul.
[2] The main block was finished in 1669, the wings in 1687.
[3] The heavy masonry above is a nineteenth-century addition.
[4] Now the École des Beaux Arts.

of Saint-Bonnet de Bourges is framed in pavilions with curved roofs like the gateway at Souvigny.[1] The Benedictine house of Bonne-Nouvelle at Orléans was another that had its monastic quarters rebuilt[2] half-way through the century [*102*]. The ground floor was rusticated; the first floor was treated as a *piano nobile* with pedimented windows; and the second had Corinthian pilasters between every window. The central feature was framed on each floor with a pair of columns, Doric, Ionic and Corinthian, and was surmounted by a rounded pediment. The whole was less elegant than the work of François Mansart, but bears the stamp of his posthumous influence.

3. LOUIS XIV, 1661–1715

When Colbert became Minister to Louis XIV in 1664 he thought out the economic basis of the realm of France from its foundations. In the functional society he envisaged the monastic life appeared to be an anachronism.[3] About 1666 he presented a note to the King:[4] 'Les moines et les religieuses non seulement se soulagent du travail qui irait au bien commun, mais mesme privent le public de tous les enfants qu'ils pourraient produire. Pour cet effet il serait peut-être bon de rendre les voeux des religieux un peu plus difficiles, mesme retrancher l'usage des dots et pensions des religieuses.' The King replied: 'L'on devrait réduire le nombre de cette profession à ceux qui servent à l'instruction des peuples et à l'administration des sacrements ou qui par un austère exemplaire, sont un grand exemple.'

Orders were given that no fresh community was to be established without the King's leave,[5] and that the capital of religious houses was to be spent in rebuilding cloisters, abbot's lodgings and monastic quarters. In fact such building was usually financed by borrowing, or by the sale of timber from the abbey woods. The abbeys were not rich in property that could be realized. At Saint-Etienne de Caen there was no building between 1706 and 1710, because of the general poverty; and at Jumièges the cloister was left unfinished between 1704 and 1712 in order that the available revenues might be spent on the repair of the abbey church.[6]

The chief intellectual event of the time was the massive emphasis of the Congregation of Saint-Maur on learning, which gave the Benedictine Order an

---

[1] The church survives, across the road, as a light engineering factory. There is a good seventeenth-century staircase door.

[2] Now the Préfecture. Wings were added in the nineteenth century, and the building was severely damaged in the Second World War.

[3] Colbert not only had two brothers who were bishops and a third who was Archbishop of Rouen, but also had sisters who controlled the great abbeys of Chaillot, Sainte-Claire de Reims, and Le Lys, and a fourth brother who was Superior of the Premonstratensians.

[4] Quoted Hautecœur, II, 851.

[5] Exceptionally two abbeys of ancient foundation were secularized: Baume-les-Messieurs in 1680 and Saint-Martin d'Ainay at Lyons in 1685.

[6] Rostand, *Frère Guillaume*, p. 14.

intellectual prestige in the *grand siècle* that it had hardly enjoyed since the twelfth century.

The studies of the learned Maurists were rarely architectural. The great scholar Dom Mabillon seems to have been curiously little interested in visible history, and does not suggest any architectural or iconographical studies in his *Traité des études monastiques* of 1691. He even advises monks not to spend time in studying ancient medals, 'cette étude qui est trop engageante, et qui peut détourner de meilleurs choses, lesquelles ont plus de rapport à notre état'. His colleagues, Dom Thierry Ruinart of Saint-Remi de Reims, Dom Edmond Martène and Dom Martin Bouquet of Saint-Germain-des-Prés, were no more visually minded. Moreover, they tended to stress the early period of ecclesiastical history, which had left fewest architectural remains, in all that they wrote. Only Dom Bernard de Montfaucon, a Southerner who had passed from La Daurade at Toulouse to Saint-Germain-des-Prés, was not only a brilliant editor of ancient texts but also a man who could study the medieval art of his own country as well as the classical architecture of Greece and Rome. His *Antiquité expliquée et representée en figures* of 1719 was followed by his *Monumens de la monarchie française*, between 1729 and 1733. Such learning was paralleled in the field of architecture.

Sometimes, even in the age of Louis XIV, Maurist builders endeavoured to respect a pre-classical style. When the church of the mother-house of Saint-Germain-des-Prés, the chief centre of historical study, was largely rebuilt in 1645, it followed the old design.[1] The church of Saint-Etienne at Caen was restored in a manner that still puzzles archaeologists.[2] The abbey church of Saint-Maixent had been ruined in the Wars of Religion. It was restored between 1670 and 1682, after it had become Maurist, by Dom François Leduc de Toscane, a Benedictine, who had worked at the cathedral of Luçon where he built a classical façade with a Gothic spire above it.[3] At Saint-Maixent he retained the Romanesque outer walls and the Gothic transept, but within them built an extraordinary Gothic church [104] of which the inspiration is clearly derived from Luçon. He completed it, however, with retables and stalls in the style of his own day.

At Corbie the rebuilding of the ancient church had been begun in 1498, under abbot Pierre II d'Ostel, on the designs of Nicolas Léveillé, the architect of Saint-Riquier. Wars prevented the church from rising much above the foundations until in 1701[4] its building recommenced, still in bastard Gothic. It proceeded slowly, and the façade [105, 106] dates from 1719;[5] its scheme is entirely medieval, but the detail is classical. No less remarkably, the late seventeenth-century build-

---

[1] Bouillart, p. 237. The plans from Saint-Germain-des-Prés have been published by M. Élie Lambert.
[2] See Gouhier.
[3] *Bulletin de la Société Nationale des Antiquaires de France* (1945–7) (20 March 1946), p. 141. The plans are now in the Archives Nationales.
[4] Dom Thierry Ruinart the historian was at this time a monk of the abbey.
[5] A very rich reliquary chapel, begun after 1750, was, however, entirely classical. It was destroyed at the Revolution.

ings at Saint-Georges-de-Boscherville [107] were designed, probably by the Benedictine Dom Marc Rivard, to enshrine the twelfth-century chapter-house, of which the arcades appear on its ground floor.

It is, indeed, easy to believe that in some instances it was realized that the medieval church could harmonize with the later classical buildings of a monastery. At the Abbaye-aux-Hommes, for example [108] Dom Guillaume de la Tremblaye added a new classical cloister with the happiest effect to the Romanesque church, of which the style had been respected when it was restored at the beginning of the seventeenth century. At the Abbaye-aux-Dames a severer entrance screen, also probably of his design, is no less happy in its alliance with the medieval towers that appear above it [110].[1] At Saint-Maixent a similarly happy marriage of styles was achieved [109] by Dom François Leduc de Toscane between his mainly Gothic church and the monastic buildings. It seems as if those who had lived as monks in medieval buildings learned even in an age of classicism to have an affectionate understanding of their beauty.

The Congregation of Saint-Maur continued to be the chief factor in Benedictine progress. In 1700 it was divided into six provinces: France, Normandy, Brittany, Burgundy, Chezal-Benoît and Gascony. It continued to do much to restore ancient abbeys that had fallen into decay. Molesme, of which the buildings had been destroyed in 1472 and again in the Wars of Religion, was almost derelict when it joined the Congregation in 1648. Saint-Bénigne de Dijon was equally derelict until the Maurists assumed responsibility for it in 1651 and restored it.

The practice of giving abbeys *in commendam* continued; Louis XIV, for example, gave to the Comte du Vexin, his son by Madame de Montespan, the two great abbacies of Saint-Denis and Saint-Germain-des-Prés. Some commendatory abbots liked to use their abbeys as supplementary country houses; Philippe de Lorraine, for example, titular abbot of Fleury from 1680 to 1702, restored the abbot's lodging and chose to live there from time to time. His example was followed by his successor, Jerôme Dufaur de Pibrac. The commendatory abbot of Saint-Père de Melun built himself a lodging[2] that is indistinguishable from a château.

Yet, even so, the practice was recognized as an infraction of monastic autonomy.[3] Gabriel Gerberon, a Maurist Benedictine who had risen to be sub-prior of Corbie, in 1674 published anonymously *L'Abbé Commendataire*, condemning the abuse. Louis XIV ordered his arrest, but he escaped to the Low Countries.

The rebuilding of monastic quarters continued to be one of the main activities of the Benedictine houses. The work was given a fresh impetus by Colbert's edict

---

[1] It was less easy to harmonize the Gothic with the classical; at Pontlevoy, for example, the chapel seems curiously episodic beside the classical cloister.

[2] Now the Préfecture; it has been considerably modified, notably by the addition of pavilions at either end.

[3] In certain abbeys, too, its influence was disastrous at this time. Noirlac, once a large abbey, passed *in commendam* in 1510; in 1666 only four monks were left and they quartered the old dorter into cells.

of 1666,[1] commanding them to rebuild their cloisters, abbot's lodgings and conventual buildings. An enormous amount of rebuilding took place, and a new scale of splendour was achieved.

The Maurists' mother-house at Saint-Maur on the Loire[2] was among those rebuilt at the time of Colbert's edict. Its façade to the river [113] appears to be by the same hand as the design for the garden front of Saint-Fuscien-aux-Bois at Amiens [115], which became Maurist in 1650. The buildings at Saint-Maur have suffered considerably, but it seems possible that the cloister [114] never had more than three sides. It follows the type established at Redon thirty years before, with rather more elaborate vaulting. At Blanche-Couronne[3] in 1675 a very plain building was given form by two almost detached end pavilions.

At Saint-Maixent Dom François Leduc de Toscane continued his work[4] by building in 1670 a block of monastic quarters[5] with a cloister [109, 111, 112] and a fine staircase with four floors of wrought-iron balustrading, which probably dates from the continuance of the work under Dom Guillaume de la Tremblaye after the edict. In 1668 the abbey of Saint-Aubin at Angers began to rebuild its monastic quarters in a simple yet massive style;[6] they survive as the Préfecture, but have been considerably modified.

Even the Paris houses, which were often held *in commendam* by great men who had their own *hôtels* in the capital, embarked on rebuilding schemes. At Saint-Martin-des-Champs the old cloister was pulled down in 1702, and a new one begun which was only finished in 1720, together with new monastic buildings thirty-one windows long, with eleven in the wings [117, 118]. The inner cloister, towards the garden, had Doric columns inserted into it. A superb parallel staircase, magnificently proportioned and decorated, led only to the cells. Further, in direct obedience to Colbert's decree, part of the land round the abbey was, in 1712, exploited by the erection of buildings to be let to lay tenants.[7] The Maurist documents include a number of plans of the date; a typical set is that for the Cluniac priory of Morteau[8] [116].

A great campaign of building, comprising everything but the church,[9] was authorized at Saint-Lomer de Blois[10] at a meeting of the Congregation of Saint-Maur held at Fleury in 1663. The building, designed by Paul and Jacques Hubert, was begun in that year[11] [121]. The façade, with its windows framed in stone

[1] See above, p. 29.   [2] Now a school.
[3] See Arch. Nat., Plans N III, Loire Atlantique 5 (16). The house had become Maurist in 1646.
[4] See above, p. 30.   [5] Now the Caserne Canclaux.
[6] They were finished in 1692; the better side contains the Préfect's private apartments and is not visible. The grille now in front of them comes from Fontevrault.
[7] See Derel, *Constructions civiles*, p. 151.   [8] Part survives as the Hôtel de Ville.
[9] The Abbé Fouquet de la Varenne had already repaired the great rose of the church in 1606, but work on it had still to be done in 1642, 1661 and 1687. (Hautecœur, I, 545.)
[10] Now the Hôtel Dieu. It has a good traditional cross-vaulted cloister with two storeys of pilasters to divide off each bay.
[11] Hautecœur, II, 881.

quoins and its dormers, closely resembles that at Saint-Maur, but it has an important central feature marked by four giant pilasters, surmounted by a scrolled *couronnement* which leads up to an elaborate bell-cote. The whole may be compared with such secular buildings as the Château de Clagny.[1] A simplification of this dignified style of architecture continued in use in smaller monasteries and in the dependencies of greater houses until the beginning of the eighteenth century. It occurs in the monastic buildings at Airvault, now a farm, in the guest-house at Le Bec [119], and in the little priory of Framecourt, which bears the date 1713 [120].[2]

In the greater monasteries of France the Benedictine architects, stimulated by Colbert's edict, began to adapt the secular style of the time into a recognizably monastic architecture. The tradition of Benedictines acting as architects that had begun in the reign of Louis XIII[3] was continued; in Normandy Dom Marc Rivard worked at Saint-Evroul, Saint-Georges-de-Boscherville, Saint-Étienne de Caen (Abbaye-aux-Hommes), and Lonlay in the years round 1664; Dom Pierre Ledo designed a façade for Marmoutier in 1675[4] [164], acted as architect at Saint-Pierre-sur-Dives in 1677 and finished the dorter at Saint-Wandrille in 1685;[5] Dom Alexis Bréard, also known as a writer, planned buildings at Saint-Vigor de Bayeux about 1679.[6] The most important of them all, Dom Guillaume de la Tremblaye, began his work at Le Bec-Hellouin about 1678[7] [123]; finished the cloister and built the main conventual building at Saint-Lomer de Blois in 1703 [121]; designed the conventual buildings of the Abbaye-aux-Hommes at Caen in 1704[8] [130, 131], and planned new buildings at Fleury, now destroyed, in 1712.[9] The new quarters of the Abbaye-aux-Dames at Caen [125–9], designed in 1704 seem also to be his work.

Dom Guillaume de la Tremblaye's early work at Le Bec[10] is chiefly remarkable for its severity. Its only interior ornament is the structural vaulting; the exterior arcade, however, is decorated with rich cartouches. By the time he reached Blois his style is far more accomplished. There are analogies of style between it and the monastic buildings of Saint-Remi de Reims[11] [122], though here an attempt was made to magnify the modest columns of the first storey into a sort of giant order.

[1] Hautecœur, II, 419. Parts remain in the École des Arts et Métiers.

[2] Cf. the plans and drawings for Saint Martin d'Auchy-lès-Aumale 1704–5. Arch. Nat., Plans N III, Seine-Maritime 14.

[3] See above, p. 18.

[4] Arch. Nat., Plans N III, Indre-et-Loire 3. Marmoutier had become Maurist in 1637.

[5] It had been begun by Emmanuel Boynet in 1658–72. (Hautecœur, II, 830.)

[6] The latest Benedictine architect seems to have been Dom J. B. Miserey, who designed monastic buildings for the Abbey of Lyre. Rostand, *L'œuvre architecturale*, p. 27.

[7] The altar he designed is now in Sainte-Croix de Bernay and the pulpit in the cathedral of Évreux.

[8] An altar with baldaquin that he designed for Notre-Dame de Caen in 1707 is now in the Trinité at Caen.   [9] Chenesseau, p. 134.

[10] It seems to descend from such secular work as that of J. H. Mansart at Le Val, planned in 1675 (Hautecœur, II, 530), and his Orangery at Versailles, built in 1681–6. (*Ibid.* II, plate 436.)

[11] Now the hospital.

His finest work is at Caen. In 1703 or 1704 the nuns of the Trinité de Caen invited a monk of the Abbaye-aux-Hommes—and it is hard to see who it can have been but Dom Guillaume de la Tremblaye—to design new buildings for them.[1] They are on a noble scale. A simple screen of round-headed arches is set inside the grille to form a further barrier to the world. Its outward face [126] has the arches broken by consoles and the frieze enriched with cartouches; the inner side is perfectly plain [124]. It serves as a link between the main building and a further wing. The richly vaulted roof links it with the first cloister [125]. The second cloister [127] is glazed; it has a projecting pavilion [128] to hold the stair-case from the cells above. The beautifully curving stairs[2] open on to a columned hall [129] which leads to the church; a niche on the half-landing holds a statue of the Virgin. This second cloister is three-sided; the fourth side is occupied by a grille with a gate. The whole is of an astonishing elegance, in plan, in architecture and in detail.

The brother house of the Abbaye-aux-Hommes began to build at almost the same time, in 1704, certainly under the direction of Dom Guillaume de la Trem-blaye. The buildings[3] are planned as two parallel blocks linked by a cross-piece which contains the entrance [131]. The cloister vaults are on the same octagonal plan as those of the Abbaye-aux-Dames; the buttresses are stepped; the arcade is Ionic. The façade [130] has high arcaded windows on the ground floor. The pediment of the main block contains fine figures of Faith and Scholarship, fit emblems of the ideals of the Congregation of Saint-Maur. The work seems to have proceeded rather slowly; the interior is all of the next reign.[4] The great arched windows turn to monastic use the arcades of the Grand Trianon, built seventeen years before.

Dom Guillaume de la Tremblaye went on to Fleury in 1712, to design monastic quarters on much the same plan as those at the Abbaye-aux-Hommes, with a ground floor of refectory, library and so on and two floors of cells above.[5] An eighteenth-century drawing[6] shows them with the arcades of the cloister as a base, and two floors of equal windows above, framed in simple pilasters. The dormers are centred by a rather small rounded pediment and bell-cote; an effect of end pavilions is given to the long façade by two terminal pediments.

Dom Guillaume de la Tremblaye's characteristic style is evident in the buildings of many monasteries in and near Normandy; we do not yet know whether they were designed by him or planned under his influence. In 1670 the monks of Bernay began to build a great range of monastic quarters. In their latest part [132]

---

[1] Now the Hôtel Dieu.

[2] A similar branching staircase was built about the same time at Saint-Remi de Reims.

[3] Formerly the Lycée Malherbe; they are now being repaired for use as the Hôtel de Ville.

[4] See below, p. 48. The buildings at Saint-Pierre-sur-Dives, probably designed by Dom Pierre Ledo, date from 1693 to 1751; they have been badly defaced by being split up into private houses and tenements.

[5] They were finished about 1730, and destroyed for building materials after the Revolution. (Chenes-seau, p. 134.)   [6] Ibid. p. 139.

we see the tall round-headed ground-floor windows that Tremblaye uses at the Abbaye-aux-Hommes. They reappear, sometimes on the ground floor and sometimes on the *piano nobile*, in the buildings at Saint-Georges de Boscherville that are probably due to the Benedictine architect Dom Marc Rivard [*134, 135*]. They appear again at Beaulieu-lès-Loches [*133*] towards the end of the century and on the great façade of the nuns' quarters of the Abbaye de Saint-Georges at Rennes,[1] begun by the abbess Magdelaine de la Fayette in 1670 [*136*]. It is nineteen windows long, with two floors and a dormered attic above the lofty cloister. The end pavilions seem rather slight to balance such length. The small central tympanum is filled with a great achievement of arms; over the arcade the abbess's name is spelled out in letters of iron. Round-headed windows appear on one of the lesser blocks of living quarters at Saint-Riquier [*137*] and on the buildings said to be of 1735 at Bourgeuil[2] [*146, 147*]; and square-headed at Saint-Serge d'Angers[3] [*138, 139, 140*].

Beyond the perimeter of his direct influence Tremblaye's typical arcades appear in less lofty form. At the abbey of Sainte-Croix de Bordeaux the infirmary, guest-house, dorters, library and cloister were rebuilt and finished in 1672[4] [*141, 142*]. The building was on three floors with a mansard attic above, with a great pavilion at either end and a fine central door. The monumental staircase has stone balustrades. The building was planned with considerable originality for the special needs of the abbey. On the ground floor were the kitchen, refectory, procurator's office, archives and a classroom; on the first floor forty cells and rooms for the sick; on the second the great library; with servants' rooms and storerooms in the attics. A second building included two large halls, six rooms for guests, a parlour, a porter's room and a small chapel. (There was no attempt to rebuild the Romanesque church.) Everywhere PAX, the Benedictine motto that seems at this time to have become the special mark of the Maurist Congregation, appeared as a device, for the rebuilding was undertaken after they had taken over the decayed monastery.[5] A rather stunted version of Tremblaye's windows is a feature of the façade. The abbey of Saint-Sulpice at Bourges—called *Navense* because it stood near the pool for ships on the river—became Maurist in 1636. Some forty years later, to judge by the style, a great garden front was planned for it, with round-headed windows everywhere[6] [*143*]. At the abbey of Toussaint at Angers they

---

[1] It is now used as public buildings. The exterior was damaged by a fire in 1921.

[2] These were never finished. Martellange's drawings of 1624 (Cabinet des Estampes, Ub 9, fol. 14224) show very plain buildings that appear to be of the mid-sixteenth century. Bourgeuil is now a school. There is a fine staircase with a wrought-iron balustrade.

[3] Now the Lycée Joachim du Bellay. It has two wings at right angles to the main block, and a central feature framed in three pairs of pilasters.

[4] Part of the building survives, considerably disfigured, as the École des Beaux Arts.

[5] Chauliat, p. 327.

[6] Arch. Nat., Plans N III, Cher 23. The remaining buildings, of many dates, suggest that the plan was never fully carried out, but one Louis XIV block survives in the hospice of the Little Sisters of the Poor, and the splendid gate of the abbey bears the Maurist motto PAX.

adorn a single storey [144]; at Montivillers [145] and Châteaudun [148, 149] they are on the *piano nobile* and at Ailly-sur-Noye they dignify the little priory[1] of the Paraclet-des-Champs[2] [151].

The abbey of Moutiers-Saint-Jean in Burgundy, that had been destroyed three times in war, in 1567, 1592 and 1629, was in its turn rebuilt at the end of the seventeenth century. It still exists as a farm,[3] in a state of melancholy decay. A classical gateway leads to a courtyard between two blocks of buildings, one perhaps for guests and servants, the other, containing the cloister, for monastic use [150]. The familiar Norman arcade, a little dwarfed, frames the ground floor. The surviving cloister walk [152, 153] is particularly elegant in style and proportion, with heavy quadrangular piers, divided by a low wall, with a simple pilaster on each of their four sides.

Sorèze was an ancient abbey which was developed on the scholastic side early in the seventeenth century, to counteract the influence of the Protestant Academy of Puylaurens [154]. Its main cloister [155] shows a development of the style of Moutiers-Saint-Jean. The interior is very simple but is not lacking in dignity. An unusual rusticated pier was adopted for the cloister of Notre-Dame de Lyre[4] when it was rebuilt in 1704 [163].

The rectangular-windowed style established by Dom François Leduc de Toscane had an influence no less distinguishable. At Saint-Michel-en-l'Herm[5] (Maurist after 1661), of which the rebuilding was begun in 1676,[6] he himself employed it in a rather conservative form, enriched only by high attic windows and heavy baroque doorways. His style finds a nobler reflection at La Réole[7] [156, 157], where both the great façade and the fine cloister framed by good ironwork bear his stamp. It is no less evident at La Sauve-Majeure,[8] at the abbey of Sordes[9] and in parts of the Madelaine de Châteaudun. Farther south, at Montmajour, the great buildings begun by Pierre Mignard in 1703 [158] are Italianate in their austerity. On one face the usual storeyed scheme is broken to include pilasters linking two of the floors.

In eastern France another Benedictine, Dom Vincent Duchesne, was the architect of the church of Saint-Pierre at Chalon-sur-Saône,[10] of Benedictine monas-

---

[1] Now a School of Agriculture.

[2] An unexpected echo of Tremblaye's style will be found in the Grand Théâtre of Bordeaux, built by Louis between 1773 and 1780. The side aisles of the entrance hall are a multiplication of the enriched bays Tremblaye uses at the angles of his cloisters.

[3] The church was destroyed at the Revolution.

[4] Now destroyed. The designs for it survive in Arch. Nat., Plans N III, Eure 6.

[5] It had been destroyed by the Huguenots in 1568 and became Maurist in 1661. It is now a private house which I was allowed to visit but where I was not allowed to take photographs.

[6] See Eygun, p. 27. The church, dating from 1724-5 and destroyed at the Revolution, was in classical style.

[7] Now Mairie, gendarmerie, etc. There is a staircase with a wrought-iron balustrade in the usual Benedictine style.

[8] Burnt in 1910. A pillared entrance hall survives in a derelict state.

[9] Burnt at the Revolution.   [10] See p. 39.

teries at Besançon, Corneux, Lons-le-Saunier, Faverney and Vaux-sur-Poligny;
of convents for Benedictine and Cistercian nuns at Besançon and Orgelet, and of
a number of parish churches. His surviving work at Lons-le-Saunier is in sound
provincial style. At the nunnery of Faverney his buildings,[1] erected between 1711
and 1714, provide one of the finest monastic ensembles of the age of Louis XIV
in eastern France. The church, but for the door of the west porch and the towers
of the south transept, was not rebuilt, but all the residential quarters were remade,
within an enclosure with handsome gateways. The minor constructions have been
considerably modified, but the great main block [159] survives. On the northern
side it is linked to the church by a long wing, which holds one walk of the three-
sided cloister [160]. His buildings for Saint-Vincent at Besançon[2] [162] have been
modified for academic use, but followed the same conventional formula.

The attempt to give a more classical form to the characteristic many-windowed
Benedictine façade by the introduction of pilasters is characteristic of the time,
but was doomed to failure. At Marmoutier Dom Pierre Ledo wished to attempt
a giant order [164], but when the monastic quarters were rebuilt after the province's cession to France in 1704, it was found that the Rule decreed that the
windows of monastic dorters should not be more than four and a half feet wide
and four feet high and these could not be combined satisfactorily with great
pilasters or columns.[3]

At the other end of the scale monastic buildings were erected in a farmhouse
style: an example is the Cluniac priory of Saint-Révérien. In a few instances such
buildings are notably backward in style; at Montiéramey, for example, the
monastic buildings erected by the abbot Rémond Renouard in 1669 are some
thirty years out of fashion.[4] At Méry-ès-Bois the buildings of the abbey—an
abbey with no recorded history—remain a dignified example of a small but
perfect monastery on the scale of a manor house[5] [166]. The smaller abbeys and
priories, indeed, lived mainly by the supervision of agriculture and milling. The
fine mill of the Benedictine house of Saint-Sulpice just outside Bourges [165]
remains as testimony; its severe and utilitarian style contrasts with the splendid
gate of the abbey.[6]

Comparatively few abbots' lodgings[7] were built in the years following Colbert's decree. At Pommiers-en-Forez the lodging survives as a château,[8] which

---

[1] Now the seminary.

[2] 1650–1724; see Tournier, p. 316. Arch. Nat., Plans N III, Indre-et-Loire 5 (3).

[3] Perrault, *Voyage à Bordeaux*, p. 146, cited Hautecœur, II, 853. The monastic buildings do not survive.
The choir and five-sided apse were rebuilt at the same time in rather old-fashioned style.

[4] There are a few slight remains of the chapel, which appears to date from the time of Louis XV.

[5] It has become a private house and figures in Alain Fournier's *Le Grand Meaulnes*.

[6] The farm buildings are now a garage.

[7] Professor Knowles reminds me that the Maurists had not abbots but priors; I use the term 'abbot's
lodging' generically.

[8] The owners were away and I was not able to see it; a good deal of it appears to be of the sixteenth
century.

in effect it always was. At Nouaillé [168] and at Sainte-Melaine de Rennes[1] [167] the lodgings are rather old-fashioned in style; that at Jumièges[2] [169] comes closer to the style of contemporary châteaux. It followed immediately on Colbert's edict; it was built between 1666 and 1671. The commendatory abbot for whom it was built was a bishop; none the less it is a quite unclerical manor-house, with a slightly projecting central pavilion crowned by a modest pediment, and a high mansard roof. At Saint-Sever-sur-Odon the lodging approximates to a small town villa [161].

In only a few Benedictine houses were both church and monastery built or rebuilt. The prolonged if intermittent persecution of English Catholics caused the foundation of a house of English Benedictines in the rue Denfert-Rochereau at Paris.[3] It was enlarged between 1661 and 1691. In the monastic quarters the convention of the town house has been accepted [172], but the familiar arcade none the less appears. The beautiful hall and staircase [171] and the elegant parlour are rather secular in spirit. Their quality may be compared with that of some modest monastic buildings in small towns, such as that of the Benedictines at Selles-sur-Cher. The church was designed on a system of flattened arches, with medallions above, and a gallery over a heavy frieze [173].

At Rennes the monks of Sainte-Melaine had the façade of their church rebuilt in 1672 with a Doric and a Corinthian storey surmounted by an elegant octagonal lantern that completely overwhelms the Romanesque nave. The detail of the doors is particularly fine. The cloister [174, 175] would appear to be of the same date. Its sculptured decoration is unusually rich: not only does each bay have a sculptured *clef de voûte*, with a large relief of St Benedict in glory and the Ascension in the surviving angles, but externally the spandrels are richly and delicately carved with foliage, each arch is centred by a bracket formed of a cherub's head, and each of the scrolled buttresses merges into a Daphne-like figure of an angel. The rich effect is enhanced by the sculptured cornice's being broken above every buttress. The whole is both splendid and feminine and in amusing contrast to the massive austerity of the cloister of the women's abbey of Saint-Georges in the same city.

At Saint-Michel en Thiérache, near Hirson, the whole monastery[4] was rebuilt, and all the church but the fine late Romanesque choir. The *ensemble* is comfortable, dignified and a little squat and provincial [176–9]; there are Norman round-headed windows on the ground floor. At Saint-Gildas de Rhuis in Brittany the nave of the church was rebuilt in a simple classical style between 1700 and 1705 and the monastic buildings[5] and the little cloister were reconstructed even more simply a little earlier [170].

---

[1] Now the Faculté de Droit of the University. [2] Now the Museum.

[3] James II of England was buried in the church. Plans made in 1788 are at the Arch. Nat., Plans N III, Seine 517, 1–9.

[4] Now a school.

[5] Now a children's home. The plans and elevations, dated 1655, are in Arch. Nat., Plans N III, Loire-Atlantique 8.

The Benedictine priory of Saint-Jean-de-l'Osne was destroyed in the Thirty Years War, after a gallant defence against the Emperor's troops. The church was rebuilt about 1696; it incorporated earlier elements with rather unhappy results. The baldaquin and the sacristy door [180, 181] are, however, worthy of the time.

The monks of Saint-Clément de Metz in 1680 engaged the Italian architect Spinga, who designed them a splendid church in which Gothic windows and vaulting are combined with great files of classical columns [182].

In a few houses only the church now survives. The church of the Benedictine abbey of Saint-Pierre at Chalon-sur-Saône was rebuilt in 1697 on the designs of Dom Vincent Duchesne of Besançon[1] and consecrated in 1713. The original abbey, outside the walls, had been destroyed in 1562, and the community had moved into the town. They joined the Maurists in 1662, and it must have been under the Maurist influence that the church was rebuilt. It remains both overcharged in ornament and tentative in style. The plan is medieval, with a three-bay vaulted nave, a cupola at the crossing, a transept (one arm is longer than the other), and a choir of three bays with a semicircular apse, with a heavy vault[2] [185]. The elaborate cornice and truncated piers of the crossing give a certain richness to the interior, but the complicated ornament of the façade [184], with a heavy classical frontispiece framed between the two towers of the medieval Benedictine tradition, is a good deal less successful. The side entrance, with a façade of two storeys divided by a triglyph frieze, is almost equally elaborate and but little better designed.

The Maurist documents in the Archives Nationales include a plan and section of a church by the architect Chauvin of Saint-Jean d'Angely that seem to date from soon after 1712, for the priory of Mortagne-sur-Sèvre, which joined the Congregation of Saint-Maur in that year. The site was difficult, in a beautiful narrow valley of granitic rocks; the difficulty was met by the interesting design of an oval nave, with a circular choir and a large organ gallery with an entrance to the monastery beneath [186]. A second altar was set in a small chapel in the nave opposite the entrance giving on the street. The section shows this [187] and indicates the simple style of the interior.[3]

Aniane in the Hérault is famous in history as the cradle of the reform of the Benedictine Order in the time of Charlemagne. Here the rebuilding of the church was undertaken early in the eighteenth century; the façade, framed in great volutes [188], is dated 1714. It is rather provincial and old-fashioned in style, with reminiscences of the Paris architecture of nearly a century before. The nave is hardly less arriéré, with narrow groined vaults, an acanthus frieze and putti over the Ionic capitals of the pilasters [189]. The choir is richly ornamented with putti holding the instruments of the Passion in the spandrels. The nave is similarly

---

[1] Tournier, p. 316.   [2] Hautecœur, II, 721.

[3] The monastery was burnt at the Revolution. There are said to be some remains but I have not been able to see them.

adorned with figures holding musical instruments and has side chapels; a false transept is formed by omitting two of these. The five-sided apse is decorated with five great pictures of the life of Christ. The church, indeed, represents the last wave of the influence of Le Val-de-Grâce.

The French acquisition of territory on the eastern frontier under Louis XIV encouraged the erection of new buildings by monasteries that found themselves able to count upon a measure of royal patronage. At Saint-Mihiel, for example, building began soon after it passed to France, and continued into the early years of the eighteenth century. The Romanesque porch and west tower of the church were retained but the rest was rebuilt in a style that recalls the monastic churches of Flanders, with a more French delicacy of detail [183]. The nave has fluted columns with capitals that owe little to the Orders; the rib vaults are Gothic. The choir has flattened cupola vaults, rising from pilasters that are more or less Corinthian. The exterior [190] is more Gothic than one would expect, with a high pitched roof and buttresses that have been incompletely classicized. The window tracery is cusped; their frames are Gothic. The woodwork of the stalls, however, and the frieze above them, are completely *style Louis XIV*. The monastic build-ings[1] [191] are more elegant and more consistent in style. They present a fortress-like exterior to the world on the west, but within the courtyard and to the east they are pilastered and gracious.

If few churches were rebuilt, many were made fashionable with new and splendid furnishings. At Almanèches, when the choir was rebuilt in 1674, it was finished by a tremendous retable with a broken pediment, framing a painting of the Adoration of the Shepherds between statues of St Benedict and St Scholastica, while the chapels of the transept received lesser retables with figures of the Virgin and the patroness Sainte-Opportune.

The stalls of the great abbey of Saint-Sernin de Toulouse [193] date from 1670; a more architectural quality is evident in the balustrade and in the fluted columns that frame each stall. No lesser house could afford to emulate such magnificence; but the stalls of Le Moûtier-d'Ahun, carved by Simon Bauer of Menat in 1673, show what the provinces could do[2] [194]. The ends are formed of turbaned caryatids, animals and great leafy scrolls. The medallions on the Epistle side are carved with scenes of the life of the Virgin; on the Gospel side, of the life of Christ.[3] Stalls of a similar richness survive in the ancient monastic church of Moirax, with elaborate historiated panels framed in rich mouldings. At Bassac in the Charente the woodwork of 1700 is more severely classical, with Ionic pilasters, an acanthus frieze and Atlantid consoles. The delightful *boiseries* of the

---

[1] Now the Collège.

[2] See *Cong. Arch.* (1921), p. 137. The carved dates show that it was finished in 1681.

[3] Thirty stalls of the time of Louis XIV from Val Richer are in the church of Saint Jacques at Lisieux; four more are at Surville near Pont l'Évêque. Stalls from La Charité are in Saint-Bénigne de Dijon. Good rather plain stalls are to be found in the abbey of Sainte-Valérie at Chambon-sur-Voueize, and remains of others in many churches, for example, Souillac.

sacristy of Saint-Germain-des-Prés date from 1715. Even remote country monasteries did their best. The pulpit at Locronan erected in 1707 is adorned with medallions of the life of St Benedict. He lived in the sixth century, but the story is told in contemporary guise; the saint wears a soutane and the officers of the king the uniform of the army of Louis XIV.

The high altar, in its turn, was often modernized. That from Bernay, of red marble, now in the church of Sainte-Croix, is said to have been made in 1685 from the designs of a monk of the abbey. That at Saint-Germain-des-Prés[1] was designed by Oppenord in 1704. It was designed with a great curved and foliated baldaquin on an elliptical plan, resting upon six composite columns of cipollino and a broken architrave. Above the altar two angels upheld the Gothic shrine of Saint Germain, dating from 1408; the altar cross, of 1706, was designed by a monk of the abbey. The silver altar frontal might date from 1409, but it contributed magnificence, not style. Classical architecture and classical ornament had been completely adopted by the Benedictines, and they had learned to turn it to the uses of their Order.

4. LOUIS XV, 1715–74; LOUIS XVI, 1774–93

No marked turning-point in Benedictine history can be perceived when the Regent succeeds Louis XIV, and yet one is conscious of the beginning of decline. The age of sentiment, of the 'philosophes', of the Encyclopedia, of the Grand Tour, of the boudoir and the alcove, did not provide an atmosphere in which it was easy for monastic austerity to flourish. No monastic house of men was founded in Paris in the eighteenth century.[2] Comparatively little Benedictine building was attempted; on the whole such minor work as the fountain of Saint-Germain-des-Prés[3] sufficed. Even in the provinces foundations for either sex were rare and unimportant. One of the few Benedictine houses established was Notre-Dame-de-l'Hermitage, at La Bastide-de-Jourdans,[4] founded in 1740 by a lawyer of Aix on the ruins of a Commandery of Templars. On the other hand, certain ancient foundations fell into decay. Saint-André-le-Bas at Vienne had only twelve monks left in 1698.[5] By 1716 it was menaced with closure, and in 1743 was united to the chapter of Saint-Chef by a royal edict. Saint-Amant-de-Boixe, an abbey of tenth-century foundation, had never joined the Maurist Congregation; it was suppressed in 1774 for want of monks.

[1] Piganiol de la Force, VIII, 15. The baldaquin at the Priory of Saint-Jean de Château-Gontier seems a version of the theme in less precious material. Another typical form with twisted columns is well represented in a side chapel at Tournus.

[2] The Capucins of the Chaussée d'Antin were transferred, not founded, and that because of town-planning.   [3] Now in the Square Monge.

[4] Near Pertuis, Vaucluse. The tendency of nunneries to move into towns continued. In 1736 the ancient house of Almanèches, between Séez and Argentan, took over an existing church and moved to the latter town. (Migne, *Dictionnaire des Abbayes*, col. 33.)

[5] *Cong. Arch.* (1923), p. 39.

Many surviving houses could not maintain their buildings. At Massay, which had been ravaged by the English and the Protestants in turn, a plan for rebuilding could not in 1716 be carried out for want of money. Twenty years later the abbot handed over the church in lieu of one which had fallen into ruin.

The Maurist interest in history continued, with its stress on early and medieval times,[1] and with it a respect for the architecture of the Middle Ages[2] that began to be shared by professional architects. J. F. Blondel, writing in the middle of the eighteenth century, had to exclaim: 'Combien de monuments de la première beauté quoique Gothiques!'[3] He even wished to apply certain Gothic principles to the current style of classical church architecture, by heightening the nave and making its columns support an impost-like entablature to take the vaults, as in certain seventeenth-century churches in Flanders.[4]

Such interests and such tastes had no effect on great buildings at this time (though such work as the church at Corbie[5] was being completed), but find an occasional reflection in detail.

Monastic buildings—and of these those of the Benedictines were the most numerous—came under severe censure from the classicists. Piganiol de la Force wrote[6] of conventual buildings:

It is very rare, and indeed almost impossible, that they should be in a good style and free from even the most obvious faults, since most of those who live in them are habitually occupied only with works of piety, or the study of holy books, and so are necessarily ignorant of the rules of architecture and good proportion. Pleased with a well-drawn plan, they confidently adopt it, and especially if it be the work of one of their Fathers who has the gift of making architectural scribbles. Without a police regulation that would make our public buildings subject to the examination of the Academy or of architects of renown, Paris will be eternally spoiled by an infinity of ridiculous monastic productions.

Desgodets in 1722 lectured on church architecture to the students of the Academy,[7] and included in the illustrations of his discourse[8] designs for monastic and conventual churches. These, however, though apparently intended for Benedictine use, are influenced by the style of the Jesuit churches of Paris and by those of its fashionable nunneries. J. F. Blondel, in his lectures on architecture given in 1750 and the succeeding years,[9] likewise gives special consideration to monastic churches[10] and includes designs for conventual churches [208, 209]. Besides the

---

[1] The great history of Saint-Germain-des-Prés published by Dom Jacques Bouillart in 1724 has only one book out of five (though admittedly the longest) to cover the time from the reform of Chezal-Benoît in 1513 to 1700.

[2] The two bays of the nave added to Saint-Vincent-de-Metz in 1754–6 exactly copy those of the existing thirteenth-century nave, and the eighteenth-century church of Marmoutier is in late Gothic style.

[3] Cited Prost, *Blondel*, p. 26.   [4] *Ibid.* p. 27.   [5] See above, p. 30.

[6] 1765 ed., IV, 316. I translate.   [7] See Herrmann, p. 49.

[8] *Traité des Ordres de l'Architecture*, ch. v, sec. 1: Cabinet des Estampes.

[9] Published as the *Cours d'architecture* in 1771.   [10] II, 323.

general recommendation of simplicity and fine materials in place of much gilding and painting, he advises that monastic churches should be even simpler than those for parochial use. They should have space enough for a lay congregation;[1] they should have side chapels in place of aisles; and only those of rotunda form should attempt splendour, and that without ostentation.

The considerable number of Benedictine churches built between 1715 and 1770 do not in the main go contrary to his recommendations. The majority of them are in eastern France, in the recently reconquered districts that had a special claim to royal munificence. The Louis XIV church of Saint-Clément at Metz was completed between 1715 and 1737 by a façade [195] that is a little heavy and emphatic, but not a bad piece of provincial architecture. It is notably richer than most contemporary abbey churches (for example, that of the nuns of Sainte-Austreberthe at Montreuil)[2] [196] and stimulated the rival abbey of Saint-Vincent in the same city to erect a still more splendid façade, begun in 1768 and only finished in 1786 [197]. The architects Barlet, Louis and Lhuillier, seem to have drawn the inspiration for their deeply recessed façade of three Orders from that of Saint Gervais at Paris.

In 1727, when Alsace was already French, the church of Ebermünster was rebuilt with three towers with bulbous tops in the German style; its elaborate stalls, pulpit, confessionals and organ loft are enriched with gilding in a way that Blondel would not have approved. In 1743 Jean Querret designed a new aisled church for the abbey of Lure;[3] it does not survive.

Between 1760 and 1762 it was decided that two ancient Benedictine abbeys of women at Metz, Saint-Pierre and Sainte-Marie, should be united to form a new noble Chapter of Saint-Louis. J. F. Blondel designed new buildings for them between 1760 and 1767[4] [Fig. 2, 198]. The church was to be entirely dominated by a great dome on Corinthian pilasters masking heavy piers, which was to form the sanctuary. It was to be preceded by a narthex-like aisled nave of one bay, and to lead to a nuns' choir behind the altar. The plan is so splendid that it is hardly surprising that it was never executed.[5]

The plans for Saint-Louis de Metz are, however, but little more splendid than the actual church of Notre-Dame at Guebwiller [199]. In 1766 the last Prince-Abbot of Murbach decided that his ancient abbey was to be transferred within the walls of the neighbouring city and transformed into a noble chapter. The exterior was designed by the Besançon architect Beuque with the two towers of the Benedictine tradition: only one was completed. Between them is a classical version of the traditional Rhenish 'Westwork', with a two-storeyed pedimented

---

[1] He cites the churches of the Jacobins and the Petits Pères of Paris as examples.

[2] Now the Ecole Primaire Supérieure. [3] Tournier, p. 323.

[4] M. Jean Rigault, Archivist of the Moselle, kindly informs me that the original plans exist in the *liasse* N. 4036 of the archives of the Moselle. See also Bouteiller, Lesprand, Hautecœur, III, 599, and Prost, *Blondel*, p. 37.

[5] There were, too, civic claims to the site. See Prost, *Blondel*, p. 37.

façade and a heavy frieze to link it with the towers [199]. The aisled interior [200] is in Corinthian style, with barrel vaults. The transept has apsidal ends. Its richness is concentrated in the choir; the apse has a tremendous relief by Sporrer, all clouds and *putti*, of the Assumption of the Virgin, between two sober classical medallions.

A whole group of abbey churches was rebuilt in Normandy: Saint-Vigier de Rouen, by J. J. Martinet, between 1719 and 1721; Saint-Martin d'Aumale,

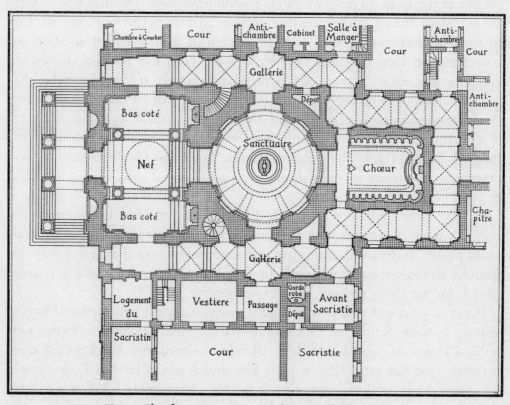

Fig. 2. Plan for Saint-Louis, Metz, by J. F. Blondel, 1760–8.

1729–44; Saint-Évroul d'Ouche, about 1746, and Fontenay, Calvados, between 1753 and 1770. All have been destroyed; and little remains at Cérisy, built between 1750 and 1757.[1]

The church of Saint-Léonard de Corbigny was rebuilt, with the rest of the abbey, just after 1754; it forms one of the wings projecting from the central block.[2] It is an aisleless building with a rounded apse, and tall windows with heavy mouldings which harmonize with those of the monastic quarters planned at the same time. Its only decoration is the Ionic half-columns between the windows on the inside, which help to mask the fact that its design has been subordinated to that of the rest of the building.

[1] At Langonnet, in the Morbihan, the abbey chapel, built about 1724, has been much restored.
[2] It was in 1954 divided up into classrooms and dormitories; its ancient fittings then vanished. Hautecœur (II, 419) illustrates a fine lectern in carved wood, of which I can now obtain no news.

The splendid church of the abbey of Saint-Vaast d'Arras[1] has a relatively simple façade [201] designed to bring it into relation with the immense range of monastic buildings, also begun in 1754. Its exterior shows the traditional flying buttresses given a classical air. Its real beauty lies in the superb interior, all in fine pale stone [202], and all severely classical. There is a deep transept, a dome on pendentives at the crossing, and an almost circular Lady Chapel reached by a flight of steps behind the high altar.

The abbey of Saint-Jean d'Angely began to be rebuilt after the Wars of Religion, but its rebuilding proceeded very slowly. The façade of the church, designed in 1740 [203], was begun in 1755[2] [204, 205]; it remained unfinished at the Revolution. It is one of the few French monastic churches of the eighteenth century, away from the eastern frontier, to maintain the medieval tradition of two towers at the west end. The classical façade in two storeys, with a splendid central window, is surmounted by two square turrets with rounded corners and coved roofs. The exterior was to have been heavy and Doric.

In 1764 the abbey church of La Daurade at Toulouse [206, 207] was designed by Hardy as a miniature version of St Peter's at Rome, in the form of a Latin cross, with a huge choir, a rounded transept, and a dome. This too was never finished.

That such ambitious projects were not completed is hardly surprising. The year 1764 was the last in which the monasteries could undertake great campaigns of church building with confidence. In that year the first warning of hostility to the monastic Orders was given by the expulsion of the Society of Jesus from France. In the following year a general assembly of the clergy of France was summoned to consider the reform of the regular clergy, and in the next year a commission to inquire into the monasteries was set up. In 1768 an edict raised the age at which vows might be taken and tried to extinguish a number of houses at which only a few monks were left.

The Benedictines were quick to see the signs of the times. In 1769 the Council of the Benedictines of Saint-Maur decreed[3] that no expenditure on buildings of more than 500 *livres* should be made without the consent of the monks in Chapter, or of over 3000 *livres* without the consent of the Visitor, on plans which he had seen. No building costing over 10,000 *livres* could be begun without the consent of the 'Définiteurs' of the Chapter General.

It can have been with little hope of their realization that in 1769, the year of the restrictive edict, Contant d'Ivry included a number of conventional projects for nameless monasteries and their churches in his *Œuvres d'Architecture*. In fact none of them seems to have been more than a studio design.

---

[1] Now the cathedral. It was severely damaged in the First World War but has been well restored.

[2] An engraved design for it dated 1740 is in the Cabinet des Estampes (Topographie, Charente-Maritime).

[3] Rostand, *L'Œuvre architecturale*, p. 14.

Yet in spite of the unfavourable climate of opinion represented by the commission of 1766, some Benedictines continued to build churches, though at a slower pace. At Saint-Georges-sur-Loire [210] a plain church, with rich furnishings, was completed by a severely classical façade. In 1772 Franque designed a new church for the Cluniac priory of Saint-Pierre d'Abbeville;[1] exceptionally it was intended to rebuild the church and to leave the buildings as they were, though there were still seven monks in the house.[2] The façade [212] is severely classical; its formality is a little broken by a single bell tower to one side. The interior [213] is elegant, if no less plain, with unadorned pilasters and clerestory windows set in lunettes.

The Benedictine nuns' church of Saint-Désir de Lisieux was rebuilt about 1770 in an astonishingly free style [214]. A cold classic gateway is set in a vast arch with curved wings to frame it and mask the aisles. The sides are very plain with two storeys of similar aisle and clerestory windows, round-headed and marked by plain stone mouldings. The interior [215] has a classical nave, with a heavy cornice resting on Ionic pilasters, that curves in at the apse to frame an arch like the proscenium of a theatre, within which a very richly decorated choir appears like a scene on a stage. Above the arch a gilded glory surrounds an angel accompanied by a crowd of cherubim. The ancient abbey of Saint-Etienne d'Uzès rebuilt its church in 1775 [216] with an outwardly curving front of great elegance. The interior of the church is more classical [217] with a rounded end, a short nave and transept, and triforium-like galleries with ironwork balustrades. These, and the very heavy cornice, are in the local Provençal style, but the plain twin pilasters with elegant French-Ionic capitals show the influence of Gabriel.[3]

Yet another late Benedictine church at the other end of France is Saint-Martin-des-Champs, Morlaix, a priory of Marmoutier, which was rebuilt in Doric style [218] between 1773 and 1788[4] with double aisles in the transepts, which have apsidal ends. Its interior [219] shows, however, the influence of insecurity, for the columns are of stucco and the vaults of painted wood.

In other Benedictine houses a modern air was given to an ancient church by the erection of a new and classical façade. Instances are Saint-Pons de Thomières, 1716; Saint-Taurin d'Évreux, 1719; Fécamp, 1750 [220, 221], and Saint-Pierre de Montmartre—an exercise of economy in classicism [211].

More often modernity was achieved only in accessories. At Fécamp, new stalls and throne [226] were erected in 1748, and a splendid baldaquin [222] was erected over the high altar in 1751,[5] with a great angel in gilded wood to hold the pyx. The chapel of the Virgin was given new panelling and the choir new stalls in the

[1] Arch. Nat., Plans N III, Somme 18.
[2] These buildings were rebuilt later in a plain style; they were not complete at the Revolution. At the Restoration they were completed by the Ursulines, who still occupy them.
[3] The church appears to be by the same architect as that of Saint-Jacques at Tarascon, not far away.
[4] The façade has been defaced by a nineteenth-century tower.
[5] It and the stalls were both designed by France.

same year. The Abbaye-aux-Dames at Saintes acquired a splendid baldaquin of Languedoc marble about the same time.[1] Mozac, again, received a whole set of new *boiseries* about 1760 in choir and sacristy, and Saint-Pons de Thomières a very rich choir decoration in metal and marble [*223, 224*]. Saint-Bénigne de Dijon was given a grand abbatial throne [*225*], Saint-Georges-de-Boscherville was equipped with confessionals with the arms of Tancarville and medallions of St Benedict and St George; and at Sainte-Croix de Bordeaux and Saint-Pierre-sur-Dives splendid altars and retables were erected. At Saint-Pierre-sur-Dives the crossing was ornamented with pyramidal reliefs, richly ornamented with symbols of the arts; at Cambrai the transepts were adorned with elaborate plaster reliefs of the lives of Christ and the Virgin. The superb stalls at Marmoutier, with trophies and tree-columns worthy of a palace, were set up in 1770:[2] much simpler provincial ones may be seen at the abbey of Chancelade in the Dordogne.[3] At Eu a fashionable modern pulpit was set up in 1752.[4] Many churches, such as Saint-Germain d'Auxerre, were given new choir screens of elegant ironwork; and old chapels were rejuvenated by a retable or, even more elegantly, a statue in a niche. The abbey of Saint-André at Villeneuve-sur-Avignon acquired a splendid marble abbot's throne[5] in classical style, with lions' feet, cherub arms and incurved back, with a great marble angel rising behind. Many abbey churches, too, acquired candlesticks and such-like ornaments in true classical style [*228*].

Benedictine churches were considerably enriched in the reign of Louis XV; but the work done upon them counts for little in comparison with what was done to the monastic habitations.[6] Almost every house that rebuilt its church also rebuilt its monastic quarters, and many that kept an ancient church unchanged did like-wise. Such rebuilding had little relation to the number of monks in the abbey. The monastic quarters at Fleury, for example, were reconstructed for fifty monks and a number of novices; in 1771 only eleven monks inhabited them.[7] A great block ninety metres long, eighteen wide and twenty-seven high, with seventy windows to the south, held library, guest-house and great dorter.[8] The warming-room became an orangery, a pleasant dining-room took the place of the ancient refectory, and each monk had his own comfortable room. In many monasteries the chapter-house[9] tended to become a comfortable *salon*, with good sculptured panelling, as at Saint-Martin d'Autun [*227*]. The need for models of ecclesiastical

---

[1] Now in Saintes Cathedral.   [2] See *Cong. Arch.* (1914), p. 240.

[3] Woodwork from Vézelay is now in the sacristy of Saint-Jean de Joigny; stalls from the Cistercian Abbaye de l'Épau are in the church of Savigné-l'Evêque; and forty-six choir stalls from Bonport are in that of Pont-de-l'Arche.

[4] A good eighteenth-century pulpit from the refectory of Saint-Jean-des-Vignes, Soissons, is now in the church of Oulchy-le-Château, Aisne.

[5] Now in the Collégiale; illustrated Hautecœur, II, fig. 370.

[6] An interesting list, including many now destroyed, will be found in Hautecœur, III, 328 n. 3.

[7] In that year the abbacy was united to the archbishopric of Bourges. (Chenesseau, p. 49.)

[8] Marchand, p. 87. The building was only just finished at the Revolution, when an architect bought it for demolition.   [9] See Hautecœur, III, 337.

and monastic emblems for such use was met by the engravings of such artists as Delafosse, but often enough, as at Saint-Etienne de Caen,[1] Saint-Serge d'Angers [231] and Saint-Wandrille [229] the *boiseries* were of secular design. The refectory at Saint-Etienne de Caen [230] was decorated in 1747 with charming *boiseries* carved with details of flowers, grain and fruit, with landscape paintings over the doors. The sacristy is in a similar style but with trophies of ecclesiastical ornaments. The hall-mark of such buildings was the splendid wrought iron balustrades of their staircases [248–52].

The tradition of Benedictine cloisters, however, continued with but little change [234]. Some monasteries embarked on schemes too ambitious to be completely realized. At Corbie a new abbot's lodging in the classical taste was planned in 1736 and begun in 1739. As soon as it was finished the monks proceeded to the erection of a great *ensemble* of monastic buildings on the plans of Franque. Only the monumental gateway survives [233]; much was never built, and the rest was destroyed at the Revolution.

The Benedictine style of Normandy, with its lofty round-headed windows on the ground floor, and its characteristically vaulted cloisters, is evident in several abbeys just outside the province. The greatest of them is, without question, the royal abbey of Saint-Denis. Rebuilding was decided on by the Grand Prior[2] Augustin de Loos in 1700. Plans were made by Robert de Cotte, incorporating the lodging of the head of the house, the monastic buildings, and the state apartments in a single scheme. Building began under Cotte in 1718 and was finished under Jacques Gabriel in 1752.[3]

As at Le Val-de-Grâce, the monastic buildings had a secondary royal purpose: they were intended to house the royal family at the time of the funeral of a king. Partly for this reason the buildings are, like those of Le Val-de-Grâce, more completely separated from the church than usual. The great cloister lies alongside the church, to which it is linked both by a narrow passage and a vestibule. The place where the cloister would usually be was occupied by a great semicircular courtyard[4] lined with apartments for ordinary guests.

The face of the main building towards this, originally intended for the Grand Prior's lodging [237], was later broken by a bayed pavilion in the centre. The rooms opened on to their own corridor behind the Great Cloister, fourteen bays square [232]. Not even its glazing (a part of the original plan) can make it anything but formidable in scale and proportion; it is intended not for the quiet

[1] Now the Parlour of the Lycée. The refectory at La Charité (now part of a vintner's warehouse) has a good coved ceiling, and the chapter-house *salon* off it has a charming decoration of trophies.

[2] The title of abbot had been suppressed in 1691 and the 'mense abbatiale' given to the school at Saint-Cyr.

[3] Now the Maison d'Education de la Légion d'Honneur. Plans for alterations by Lenoir 'le Romain' dated 1775 survive at the Archives Nationales (Plans, N III, Seine 166 (1–4)) together with a set for the entrance gates by Vailly (*ibid.* 167 (1–5)).

[4] Blondel's plan, published in 1771, showed a courtyard with canted corners to the street and rounded ones to the house.

meditations of a few monks, but for the cortèges of the Court of France. Externally the building is extremely simple; its pilaster buttresses are linked by a balustrade; the façade above it could hardly be more severe; the walls end in low domes, with niches holding statues [235]. At the angles of the cloister are four staircases on an oblong plan [236, 239], lit by tall windows. They, like the cloister, are on a splendid scale, but their only ornament is their wrought-iron balustrades, by a monk, Frère Denis, and the simple cartouches of the coved ceiling. A magnificent grille by the same monastic craftsman [241] is set between the cloister and the staircase to the dormitories.

The south front [238] is extremely fine, with terminal pavilions; it held the apartments intended for royal visitors, looking out on to the abbey fishpond. The Salle des Gardes, with a vaulted roof resting on consoles, has a severe square chamber at right angles to it intended as a resting-place for corpses of the royal house on their way to burial. A room beyond leads to the chapter-house, which has double apsidal ends. The refectory [240] much resembles the Salle des Gardes; externally it has buttresses of classic form terminated in urns of fire. The kitchen is if anything more richly ornamented, with great hoods over its fires. The whole forms the most splendid *ensemble* in French monastic architecture of the classical period.

The monastic buildings at Saint-Denis are half a palace, in splendour as in intention.[1] Yet even much more modest houses achieved impressive *ensembles* in the same style.[2] At Notre-Dame-de-la-Couture at Le Mans[3] the cloisters were rebuilt between 1720 and 1739, and show Norman influence in their vaulting [234]. At Saint-Martin de Séez [4] [242] the Norman Benedictine style was applied to a small monastery with good effect, between 1720 and 1739. The round-headed windows only appear on the ground floor of the central pavilion. The building is set, as a château might be, behind a curved screen and a gateway between two lodges. The interior is very simple; the refectory has a cross-vault rising from a long row of Doric columns.

The Norman Benedictine style appears in considerable splendour at Notre-Dame d'Évron,[5] of which the monastic quarters were rebuilt in 1726[6] [246].

---

[1] Little Benedictine building was done in Paris itself, but one of the cloisters and two blocks of buildings with a grand staircase and hall were rebuilt at Saint-Germain-des-Prés not long before 1736. (Piganiol de la Force, VIII, 69.)

[2] The monastic buildings at Montier-en-Der were burnt in 1735 and reconstructed in 1755 by Cardinal Ottoboni, to be again destroyed in 1850. A series of recent drawings by M. Jean Rocard attempts a reconstruction (See *Cong. Arch.* CXIII, 1957 (Troyes), 264.)

[3] Now the Préfecture.

[4] Now the Aérium de la Caisse primaire centrale de Sécurité Sociale de la région parisienne.

[5] Now the Maison Mère of the Sœurs de la Charité.

[6] The Benedictine nunnery of Neuviller was restored about 1733 by the generosity of the Bishop of Strasbourg. The buildings have disappeared. The ancient Benedictine nunnery of Chelles was also rebuilt about twenty years later, thanks to the generosity of Marie Adelaïde d'Orléans, daughter of the Regent, who entered it in 1743. For a description of the church see Piganiol de la Force, IX, 388. A little of its woodwork survives in the parish church.

Though the corridors off which the cells open are austere [243], the stair-case is on the scale that is typical of Benedictine houses in the eighteenth century,[1] and has the characteristic wrought-iron balustrades[2] [247]. The buildings at Saint-Germain d'Auxerre[3] were severe, with a cloister [274] in the grand manner. It originally had one storey of cells above it with a balustraded roof, and the pilasters of the cloister continued up to give the effect of a modest giant order.

At Le Bec-Hellouin much was rebuilt between 1732 and 1750 [244, 245, 254, 255]. The cells open off a corridor that is in itself a cloister. In the staircase that leads to them [253] the architect has been permitted more enrichments. Everywhere, however, ornament is conservative in style and restricted in scope, and the whole is of bare and solemn dignity.

Saint-Nicolas d'Angers was entirely rebuilt between 1725 and 1734, with two wings and a central block with a rounded pediment carved with the arms of the abbey and of the Congregation of Saint-Maur. Its entrance hall, with pillars elegantly carved with flowers and fruit, led by a monumental staircase to a wide corridor with cells on one side only. The fine refectory had a vault resting on angle brackets. Nothing remains.

The abbey that came nearest to rivalling Saint-Denis in size was that of Saint-Vaast d'Arras. The new buildings, designed by Contant d'Ivry in 1746, were ranged in two great quadrangles held between two immensely long ranges [256]. The first is enclosed on one side by the southern wall of the contemporary church; the second [257] has buildings on three sides, the fourth being closed by a monumental gateway, with statues of Religion and Learning [258]. This alone saves the whole from a barrack-like formality, which seems to stress the fact that at the time this immense building was erected, capable of lodging many more than a hundred monks in comfort, there were only fifty monks in the abbey. The interior still awaits its decoration, but the refectory has an elegant chimney-piece and fine panelling.

The monastic buildings at Saint-Ouen de Rouen, designed by J. P. Defrance and Le Brument and built between 1753 and 1759, are hardly less splendid than those at Arras. They differ greatly in plan, being designed as a very long range ot buildings with no attempt at a cloister or quadrangle.[4] The western façade has an important central pavilion with a colonnade and a pediment; the opposite side [259] has a very slightly projecting central feature and two pedimented terminal pavilions to break its line of twenty-three windows, in an arcaded ground floor, two upper floors and an attic. The entrance is in the centre, and leads into a

---

[1] It was begun by Béru and Fortier in 1720, and finished in 1760 by Soufflot.

[2] This, of course, finds parallels in French country houses of the time, for example, the Château de la Gataudière near Marennes.

[3] Now the hospital. The abbey of Bonneval, Eure et Loir, has monastic buildings and a cloister of 1735. It is a mental hospital and I have not been able to see the interior.

[4] The projecting wings on the west side were added at the Restoration.

splendid hall [261, 262], from which the staircase rises [263] and from which the wide corridor that serves instead of a cloister [260] opens in two directions.[1]

There are many analogies between the buildings at Saint-Ouen and those at Saint-Riquier [264] which must be of much the same date.[2] Here too an immensely long line of buildings takes the place of a quadrangular plan, though earlier blocks set at right angles to the north give the impression of a courtyard. The central pediment is sculptured with a figure of Faith accompanied by two allegorical figures and a crowd of *putti*. A building to the east, that must have been a library, has a pediment carved with globes and scrolls and the paraphernalia of learning.

The Norman Benedictine style was no less applicable to smaller houses. It appears in Normandy itself at Lessay[3] [265] in 1752; near Paris in the buildings erected about the same time at Jouarre by abbess Cathérine Henriette de Montmorin de Saint-Hérem [266]; in Burgundy at Saint-Léonard de Corbigny[4] [267]; and as far away as Provence at Saint-André de Villeneuve-lès-Avignon[5] [268]. The buildings erected at Lure between 1770 and 1789[6] [269] are a last reflection of the Norman style.

In eastern France, in the territory that had only recently become French, the Norman style was less influential. At Luxeuil much of the buildings are earlier than 1679 when it became French; a long and rather dreary façade to the garden appears to be of the mid-eighteenth century. It had one hundred and eight windows and housed twenty-five monks. The buildings of the priory of Fontaine-lès-Luxeuil are now a factory,[7] and much damaged; but what remains [270] shows a different formula. The priory at Commercy,[8] of which the buildings seem to date from 1737, has a cloister with the same flattened arch, elaborated with Ionic pilasters and lion's-head keystone [271]. The interior staircase [272] has an elegant vaulting system and the usual wrought-iron balustrade.

In central and southern France, too, the Benedictine abbeys tended to follow a less characteristic style. The year 1750[9] saw a great campaign of monastic building in Burgundy. All but one façade of the monks' lodgings at Cluny were rebuilt by Dom Dathoze.[10] The central pavilion may owe a little to the Norman

[1] The very fine sculptured sundial grotto in the garden is by P. Slodtz.

[2] They were rebuilt after a fire in 1719.

[3] Badly damaged in the Second World War but now being well repaired. Lessay had joined the Congregation of Saint-Maur in 1706.

[4] See Marillier. The buildings were only finished a few years before the Revolution. There is a fine staircase with wrought-iron balustrades in a Vitruvian scroll pattern.

[5] There is no cloister here, but its place may have been taken by the pillared pergolas of the garden.

[6] Now the Sous-Préfecture.

[7] The former chapter-house has elegant stucco decorations, ruined by the installation of machinery.

[8] Now a school.

[9] The monastic buildings of the noble Benedictine nuns of Remiremont were also rebuilt by Jennesson in this year, but it was not yet in France.

[10] Now an École d'Arts et Métiers.

tradition, but the rest is independent of it [*276*]. The cloister [*275*] is severe, with a rather low-pitched vault; the façade and the cloister-like vaulted corridor from off which the cells open are no less austere. The medieval tradition that a Cluniac church could not be too splendid[1] nor its monastic buildings too simple still held. The only enrichment is the wrought-iron work made by a monk of the abbey, Frère Placide, which adorns not only the stairways [*273*] but also the balconies of the façade. It is interesting to see how the classicism of the buildings designed in 1750 harmonizes with the classicism of the church designed in 1088. Rather plain monastic buildings were erected for the Cluniac priory at Ambierle between 1753 and 1756.[2] Saint-Pierre de Lagny acquired new monastic buildings at about this time;[3] as at Cluny, if on a much slighter scale, they have no ornaments but plain mouldings and a wrought-iron balcony[4] [*277*]. The staircase has an admirable wrought-iron balustrade.

The contemporary buildings at Saint-Wandrille [*279*] would be no less severe but for the splendid baroque sculptures of their pediments and gate[5] [*278*]. At Saint-Taurin d'Évreux, Le Monastier-Saint-Chaffre [*280, 281*] Saint-Pierre de Chartres[6] [*283*] and Notre-Dame-de-la-Daurade at Toulouse, the buildings are in their different ways curiously barrack-like, while the buildings of Valmont [*282*] are hardly less simple if more domestic in style.[7] Nothing could be plainer than the vast barrack-like block at Saint-Pé-de-Bigorre.

The buildings of Saint-Augustin de Limoges, in spite of its dedication a Benedictine house, and the almost contemporary buildings of the nuns of Notre-Dame at Troyes[8] are both curiously secular in style, and are quite unaffected by northern influences. The abbey of Lagrasse in the Aude[9] is more impressive in its modest dignity [*284, 285*]; its staircase [*286*] is in the true Benedictine tradition.

Two Benedictine buildings of this time show a fashionable curving line in the cornice. At Lavoulte-Chilhac [*289*] the line of the cloister in front of the church is incurved to give a dramatic façade: an oddity that has some justification in a dramatic site. At the nunnery of Saint-Désir de Lisieux [*287*] a line of monastic buildings with a marked central feature was framed in two separate side pavilions. The central block has a strongly incurved architrave, which is echoed in the pavilions; and everywhere—in the mansard roof, in the screen that joins the central block to the main building, and in many details—the same search for a curved line is evident.

[1] The church was enriched with sculptured stalls in the same year. They are now in the Cathedral of Lyons.
[2] Hautecœur, II, 324 n. 3. [3] Now Hôtel de Ville.
[4] They are notably more monumental than the buildings at the Cluniac priory of Paray-le-Monial.
[5] A *grand salon*, apparently intended for use as a common-room, and a chapter-house were built at the same time, and a handsome stone staircase with wrought-iron balustrade much like those at Cluny.
[6] Now barracks. It was gutted by fire in the Second World War.
[7] The buildings, gutted by fire, at Mortagne (Loire-Atlantique) are of the same kind.
[8] Now the Préfecture.
[9] Now the Préfecture; the buildings were considerably modified about 1900.

At Baume-les-Dames the buildings by Jean-Pierre Galezot were begun in 1738; progress was slow and they were never finished. The church is extremely plain externally [291], but the inside has stucchi of a feminine elegance [290]. The monastic buildings have become merged in secular dwelling-houses, to which they were never uncongenial in spirit.

The monastic quarters of the mid-eighteenth century might sometimes be barrack-like; the lodgings of the abbot or grand prior were usually far more luxurious. At Luxeuil his palace has a classical façade in two orders, like a church [288]; at Commercy, however, his lodging is like a decent manor-house.

The abbot's house at Saint-Martin de Séez [292] is a simple building like a manor-house. At Saint-Seine[1] [293] the tall arcaded front and carved rounded pediment are more monastic in style. Fécamp [295], Saint-Germain d'Auxerre[2] [294], and Saint-Valéry-sur-Somme[3] [296] achieve the dignity of a pedimented country house, but at Saint-Remi de Reims [297] the lodging,[4] designed by Durocher in 1774, is clearly influenced by the many-storeyed barrack type of conventual building. Only the elegantly curved *perron* and the armorial pediment link it with the tradition of the château.

The prior's lodging at Paray-le-Monial [298] is comparable with the cloister at Clairvaux in its style, and even the re-entrant angles of its balcony are like those of the Clairvaux staircase.[5] The prior's lodging at Souvigny [299] with splendid fluted pilasters, a triglyph and frieze, and urns, and the abbot's house at Sorèze [300, 301], full of tranquil dignity, were probably the last lodgings for a Benedictine abbot to be erected in France before the Revolution.

The great abbeys kept on building up to the very end. The grand staircase at Saint-Martin-des-Champs at Paris was splendidly rebuilt in 1786, probably to the design of Soufflot's nephew of the same name;[6] and another staircase of equal splendour was built at Marmoutier.[7] None the less the days of Benedictine activity and Benedictine life in France were ended. A full generation was to elapse before they could recommence, and then their riches were gone and their architectural tradition broken.

[1] Now a school.
[2] The entrance hall and *salon* have umbrella vaults of Gothic form, classicized in detail.
[3] The monastic buildings and church have been destroyed; some woodwork from the abbey is in the church of Pendé.
[4] Now the Museum.   [5] See below, p. 68.   [6] Hautecœur, IV, 204.
[7] In 1782, by Etienne Fournier on the designs of the Paris architect Pascal Lenot or Lesnot. It was destroyed early in the nineteenth century. (Hautecœur, IV, 183.)

CHAPTER II

THE CISTERCIANS

The Cistercian reform of the Benedictine Rule had been the first to include architectural provisions among its statutes. The twelfth-century *Carta Caritatis* forbade any curious carving, stained glass, or paintings in the church; and from the first a severe form of the contemporary Burgundian architecture was made the basis of Cistercian style. Their monastic buildings, however, were always more spacious and well built than those of their Cluniac rivals, and by the end of the Middle Ages even the abbey churches of the Order were no less splendid than those of other Benedictine houses. Many lay in sequestered corners of the countryside, and suffered severely from the depredations of the ranging armies of the fifteenth century. A few monasteries sought security within city walls: the Cistercian Abbaye-aux-Bois was transferred from near Compiègne inside Paris in 1564 and the ancient abbey of Saint-Ausone near Angoulême was brought inside the walls in 1573.

The wealth of the Order, based as it was on agricultural exploitation, recovered reasonably quickly from the ravages of the Hundred Years War. The Cistercian abbeys were soon rich enough to tempt the King to nominate commendatory abbots. The Pope forbade the practice in 1415, 1454 and 1459, but without result. The abbey of La Ferté-sur-Grosne was held *in commendam* after 1488, Pontigny after 1543, and with them most of the Cistercian houses.[1]

The continuance of the practice and all that it involved was disastrous to the Order. At the Chapter General of 1493[2] the abbot of Cîteaux—a monk—alleged three causes for the evils then affecting monasticism: the suppression of free election to the abbatiate, the impoverishment of monastic property by abbots *in commendam*, and the intrusion of secular powers into monastic affairs. Naturally he had no support from those he attacked in his proposed reforms, and the re-forming decrees issued by forty monastic abbots in the following year were never observed.[3]

The chief sixteenth-century reform of the Cistercian houses was, however, due to a commendatory abbot. The abbey of Notre-Dame-des-Feuillants, in Langue-doc, was by the middle of the century in gross disorder. Jean de la Barrière was appointed abbot *in commendam* in 1563. Ten years later he entered his abbey as a novice and was rapidly professed. He began his reform in 1577: a strict return to Bernardine monasticism, with no mattresses, no tables, no shoes, only four hours'

---

[1] Lekai, p. 101. [2] *Ibid.* p. 95.

[3] In 1577 Henri III by the Ordinance of Blois exempted La Ferté, Pontigny, Morimond and Clairvaux from rule *in commendam*.

sleep, a very austere diet, strict silence and much manual labour. Everyone left the abbey in protest except two professed monks, two novices and the abbot himself. The Cistercians as a whole did not approve the reform, considering that it was too strict, but none the less it survived and received the approval of the Pope in 1589.[1] Two years earlier Henri III had established a new house of Cistercians following the reformed Rule in the rue Saint-Honoré at Paris.[2] In 1592 Barrière was condemned and deposed for political reasons; he was exonerated in 1600, but died in that year. In 1595 the Cistercian jurisdiction over the Feuillants came to an end, and their constitutions were revised and made rather less rigorous.

Octave Arnolfini,[3] again, became commendatory abbot of La Charmoye in 1598. He retired to Clairvaux, fulfilled his novitiate, and made his profession as a Cistercian in 1602. Three years later he became abbot of Châtillon. Gradually his efforts to return to the twelfth-century austerities of his Order extended to eight abbeys beside his own.[4] The return to the Rule was not imposed from above, but was accepted by individual monks, who chose whether to join the 'abstinents' or to remain with the 'anciens'. Nicolas II Boucherat, abbot of Cîteaux, tried to secure formal recognition of the reform at the Chapter General of 1618, but failed, for the majority of the abbots present feared that its severity might bring schism into the unity of their Order. In fact it ended in disputes after the death of its promoters, and it all came to nothing but quarrels between 'anciens' and 'abstinents', until Pope Alexander VII summoned representatives of each faction to Rome. His brief *In Suprema* of April 1666 recognized the two observances, and henceforward the Cistercian abbeys of France were divided into those that followed the Strict Observance and those that followed the Common Observance, though all were united in a single Order and a single Congregation. The ensuing Chapter General of 1667 was the stormiest ever held; but by the time another was held in 1683 a measure of agreement had been secured.

Yet another reform was instituted in the Cistercian Rule. Jean Armand le Boutheillier de Rancé was appointed commendatory abbot of La Trappe, with an enormous revenue, in 1637. He lived a worldly life until 1657. Three years later he underwent a complete conversion. He disposed of his possessions, except for La Trappe; he visited it in 1662, became a monk there, and after 1663 its regular abbot. He then enforced the Cistercian Rule, with few mitigations of Bernardine austerity. He kept the medieval buildings, and even renewed the old infertile

---

[1] It had been established at the Roman house of S. Pudenziana in 1587. The Feuillants also had houses at Bordeaux, Lyons, Saint-Ouille in Normandy, Soissons, Rouen, Le Plessis-Piquet, Memin-de-Mici near Orléans, and Le Val near Beauvais. (Hélyot, *Dictionnaire*, II, 272.)

[2] The church was built between 1601 and 1608; nothing remains. It was designed by Jean II Grappin, who was followed by his son-in-law Achille le Tellier, 1602–5. Nicolas Guillain continued from 1608 to 1610, and François Mansart designed the façade in 1624. (Hautecœur, I, 548.)

[3] Lekai, p. 123; Hélyot, *Dictionnaire*, I, 946; King, *passim*.

[4] Clairvaux, La Charmoye, Longpont, Cheminon, Vauclair, Prières, L'Abbaye Blanche (Île Dieu) and Vaux de Cernay.

conflict between monastic learning and monastic austerity. Just as St Bernard had fought Cluniac art and argument, so did he (if more politely) fight the learning of the Congregation of Saint-Maur. He even went so far as to cite Bernard against Peter the Venerable on the question of the simplicity to be observed in the ornamentation of monastic churches.[1] Once again the Cistercian fold was divided, and once again victory fell neither to 'anciens' nor 'abstinents'; the reform of La Trappe continued to exist in majestic solitude.

A curiously similar drama was enacted by Dom Eustache de Beaufort, nominated abbot of the Cistercian house of Sept-Fons near Moulins, in 1654, on the recommendation of Mazarin.[2] He was nineteen years old and a regular monk, but did not take his vows seriously. In 1663 he was converted. The four monks left in his monastery were strongly against reform; he sought recruits of austerer tastes, and found them hard to find, though he built new quarters to receive them in a curiously old-fashioned style [302]. As the community gradually increased he caused it to return to a more primitive way of life, with much silence. He eventually constituted monastic buildings with five separate refectories for monks, lay brethren, retired soldier pensioners (whose charge the King had recommended to abbeys), infirm monks and guests, with a kitchen in the middle. Each monk had a separate cell to sleep in, but was forbidden to use it at other times. They worked in common in workrooms built to accommodate as many as a hundred monks. The Sept-Fons reform, however, had little influence outside the walls of its own house.

Many individual reforms were instituted, especially in Cistercian nunneries. A typical instance is the abbey of Notre-Dame-de-Tart,[3] where in the sixteenth century the nuns had led a very easy life and had cherished the wish to become a Noble Chapter. In anticipation, they wore silk dresses trimmed with gold and silver lace, earrings and pearl necklaces. Instead they were reformed. Jeanne de Courcelle de Pourlan entered the abbey in 1599; as the niece of the then abbess, she was admitted at the age of eight. Seven years later she left it to join the Order of St Clare. At twenty-five, in 1617, she was called on to succeed her aunt as abbess of Notre-Dame-de-Tart. She began to reform it gradually, on the basis of the old observance, but even so her austerities roused much opposition. When she moved to Dijon in 1623, only five of her nuns followed her. Her reforms did not receive the approval of Cîteaux and had no lasting effect. They may, however, have had some influence over the more famous reforms of Port-Royal.[4]

None of these reforms of women's houses seems to have had any architectural influence, though the connection between Port-Royal-des-Champs and the work

---

[1] De la sainteté et des devoirs de la vie monastique, II, 345.

[2] Hélyot, Dictionnaire, III, 504. The abbey is now occupied by Trappists. I reproduce an engraving from the Cabinet des Estampes top. 1860. 6160.

[3] Hélyot, Dictionnaire, III, 603.

[4] The Bernardines du Sang Précieux, Cistercian nuns who laid a special emphasis on meditation, were founded in Paris in 1653.

of Philippe de Champaigne must not be forgotten. For the most part, however, the convents involved were too poor to initiate new styles in architecture; even the buildings of Port-Royal in the Faubourg Saint-Jacques were executed without sculptures to diminish the cost.

It is not surprising that there is little record of Cistercian building in the sixteenth century. So far as I know only one abbey church was rebuilt, and that the extremely simple square edifice at remote Mercoire. The church at Barbeaux was adorned with a high altar in Renaissance style [303]. The monks of Vaux de Cernay achieved a particularly elegant and ornate cloister, almost in plateresque style[1] [304]. The nunnery of La Joie-Notre-Dame[2] acquired a charming little building [305], that may have been a guest house, and a larger block [307].

The installation of commendatory abbots in Cistercian abbeys early led to the erection of separate lodgings to receive them. At Bonneval[3] the abbot's lodging of René d'Illiers, built in 1490, survives. Like that of Jacques de Bourbon at Cluny, it is still Gothic in style, with flamboyant decoration, machicoulis, and walls in a chess-board pattern of stone, brick and flint.

Melleray was a small monastery of some twelve monks. Its rather remote situation saved it from much of the devastation of the Hundred Years War, and in 1544, when it passed in commendam, its abbot could afford a decent lodging, if a very plain one [306]. Similarly at Beaulieu (or Belloc) near Varen, lodgings were built some fifty years later, framed by two small square towers, and indistinguishable from a decent manor of the county.

Few abbot's lodgings were built in the Order during the seventeenth century, but the abbess of Port-Royal at Paris built herself a simple abode soon after the abbey was transferred there in 1637.[4] At Breuil-Benoît the abbot acquired a château-like residence much like that at La Joie, with a long range of communs [308, 309]. Perhaps the most characteristic buildings of the time are the pigeon-cotes and the ranges of farm buildings at Beaubec[5] [310] and La Garde-Dieu [311].

In the seventeenth century, however, the Order was fortunate enough in its royal patronage occasionally to undertake more ambitious schemes.[6] Louis XIII and Anne of Austria in 1614[7] gave the Feuillants at Fontaine-lès-Dijon—the birthplace of St Bernard—a charming classical chapel which still survives; its severe Doric entrance is now incorporated into a block of modern buildings. This leads to a sort of narthex of the smallest kind, from which two doors open

---

[1] It has been reset to form a hollow square round a pool. There is a Louis XIII staircase with stone balustrades and a few other features in the private house that now occupies the remains of the abbey.

[2] Near Hennebont, Morbihan. It is now a private house.

[3] Now a private mental hospital; I could not visit the interior.

[4] It survives as a part of the Maternité.

[5] Farm buildings of 1676 survive at Clairmarais, near Saint-Omer, and others at Valloires, Preuilly and Flarans. At Aubazine fresh upper storeys were built over the medieval cloister.

[6] The Abbaye de la Vallée-Honnête, near Féniers in the Creuse, was rebuilt in 1686; it is said now to be ruined.

[7] A tablet in the chapel indicates a dedication in 1619.

into the chapel. This consists in two small bays, each surmounted by a dome [312, 313] of which the pendentives descend to entablatures carved with crowns and fleurs-de-lis, resting upon paired columns of black marble with Corinthian capitals and bases. The soffits of the arches are carved with fleurs-de-lis; and the keystones of the domes are carved with the royal arms. Over the entrance doors are two little tribunes, each big enough to hold one person; they must have been intended for the prayers of the donors. The elegance and finish of the whole make the chapel a perfect example of a royal gift to a small monastery.

Anne of Austria, again, in 1662 founded a convent of reformed Cistercian nuns, the Feuillantines, at Paris [314]; it was never thought to be architecturally successful. The rather dumpy façade has the nave storey linked to the aisles by volutes that seem too delicate in scale.

The Cistercian Feuillants of Paris set a new façade designed by François Mansart, to their church[1] in 1624–9,[2] by some accounts[3] at the expense of Marie de Médicis. To judge by the engravings which alone survive [315], it was a rather clumsy affair. It was in two orders: a ground floor with four groups of fluted Ionic columns, covering nave and aisles, and an upper storey for the nave with an immense window framed by two fluted Corinthian columns on either side, supporting a rounded pediment with a baroque finial of the arms of France and Navarre. This storey was framed by the curved buttresses of the nave and counterpoised by two slender pyramids, that took the place of Gothic pinnacles. It shows, in another form, the Benedictine idea of the application of classical orders to an essentially medieval structure.[4] It was almost exactly copied to form a façade to the medieval church at the Cistercian abbey of Ourscamps.[5]

A second Cistercian nunnery rebuilt at this time bore a more famous name. The nuns of Port-Royal, a nunnery which had recently been reformed, in 1625 received permission to leave their house in the valley of the Chevreuse, as it was dangerously malarial. In 1646 Antoine Lepautre, then only twenty-five, planned new buildings for them (Fig. 3), which were erected in the next two years,[6] and survive in part as the Hôpital de la Maternité.[7] The church is completely integrated into the conventual quarters; it was entered from the side under a fine classical portico [316] which no longer exists. It is domical in plan, though crowned only by a modest low-pitched central vault. The nuns' choir is at the back of the church. Behind the apse were a parlour and other rooms intended for the clergy attached to the house. The interior of the church [317] seems always to have been

[1] There seems to be no record of the architecture of the church itself, built 1601–8, except that the nave had six chapels on either side.

[2] The façade is engraved in Blondel, *L'architecture française*, III, 95, and in Millin.

[3] Mariette's engravings.

[4] Hautecœur, II, 20, compares it with Saint Gervais (with the upper storey omitted) and with the 'ionique fleuri' of Philibert de l'Orme and Bullant, and finds some analogies with Serlio and Vignola.

[5] The second storey was destroyed at the Revolution and replaced, rather differently, at the Restoration.

[6] The first stone was laid in 1646. (Hautecœur, II, 145.)

[7] 119 Boulevard de Port-Royal.

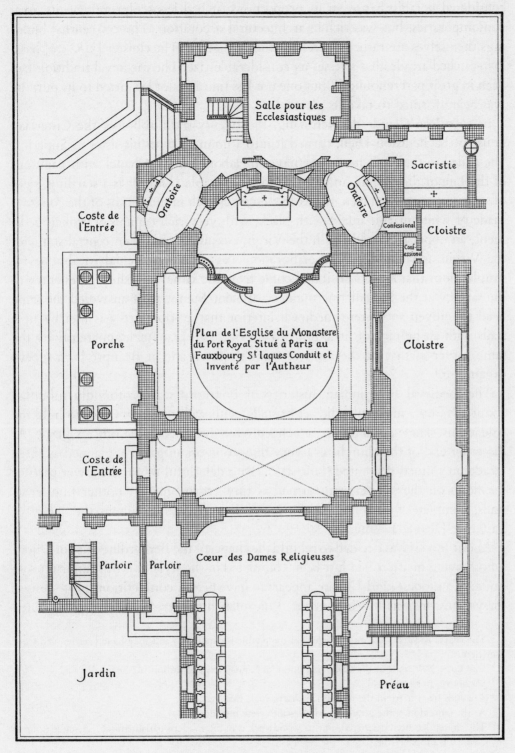

Salle pour les Ecclesiastiques

Sacristie

Oratoire

Oratoire

Coste de l'Entrée

Confessional

Cloistre

Conf-essional

Porche

Plan de l'Esglise du Monastere du Port Royal Situé à Paris au Fauxbourg St Iaques Conduit et Inventé par l'Autheur

Cloistre

Coste de l'Entrée

Cœur des Dames Religieuses

Parloir Parloir

Jardin

Préau

Fig. 3. Cistercian Nunnery of Port-Royal, Paris. Plan by
Antoine Lepautre, 1646.

considered notably happy in its proportions; it had less sculpture than its great contemporaries, but was rich in architectural decoration. The conventual buildings themselves are rather severe, but full of dignity. The cloister [318, 319] has a low-pitched arcade that stresses its considerable size. The medieval tradition had been in great part renounced, but one not less fine and not less fitted to its purpose was being formed to take its place.

In 1639 Jean-Claude de Nerestang, the twenty-sixth abbot of the Cistercian house of La Bénisson-Dieu, turned it into a nunnery with his sister as Superior. She added to the twelfth-century nave an elaborate Lady Chapel with paintings of the Life of the Virgin, and a monumental retable [320]. It is a startling piece of sophistication when seen in a Romanesque church in the depths of the country: made of white marble inlaid with black, with very rich capitals, a broken pediment, an upper tabernacle with the Virgin ascending and a fine central statue of the Virgin and Child.[1] Such elaboration was clearly congenial to abbesses; a simpler door that looks as if it had come from the same workshop gives entry to the sacristy at the Benedictine nunnery of Saint-Menoux. It answered the same need to enliven an austere medieval interior that at Bonport was met by new stalls with an infinity of little lions to adorn them[2] [321, 322], apparently by the same carver as that of the stalls at Saint-Riquier,[3] and at Beaupré by a superb organ case.[4]

The medieval Burgundian austerity of Pontigny was profoundly modified about 1675 by a most splendid set of stalls, with sculptured caryatids to hold the baldaquins. These splendours are echoed over the stalls of the officers [323]. At the other end of the church[5] is a very fine stone organ gallery, planned as three arcades in a much-decorated Ionic style. By a delightful whim the lower parts of the flutes on the pilasters are formed as tiny organ pipes. Another fine set of stalls, complete with abbot's throne and lectern, was set up in the abbey of La Grâce-Dieu at Leyme.[6]

About 1700 it was decided to rebuild the chapel of the Bernardine nuns of Dijon[7] whose living quarters had just been completed in the style of a Burgundian town house of a modest kind.[8] There appears to have been a competition for its design, for various projects for it survive. One plan by Pierre Lambert[9] [324], dated

---

[1] The chapel is dated 1644 on the exterior; the retable is dated 1637 and may have been moved from elsewhere.

[2] The Louis XIV stalls of the Cistercian house of Saint-Jean at Châtillon-sur-Seine also survive.

[3] See above, p. 22 and [76].

[4] Atlantids from it are in the Musée Départemental, Beauvais.

[5] At the same time some good ironwork grilles were introduced.

[6] The church has been destroyed, but its woodwork is in the modern parish church. A statue is dated 1678, which is probably the date of the *ensemble*.

[7] Now the Hospice Sainte-Anne.   [9] See [11].

[8] In the Bibliothèque Municipale at Dijon; I should like to express my thanks to Madame Quarré for facilitating my study of them.

[9] Now the Hôtel de France.

1707, is clearly inspired by Le Val-de-Grâce, and like its model rejects the Benedictine tradition of the long nave; there is a courtyard, however small, before the church; there is a dome; and there is a nuns' choir in the transept, and chapels in three of the piers. The plan is essentially domical; the nave is reduced to an oval 'peristyle'. Another exterior [325] is designed with a lofty lantern under the dome, and a relatively simple façade in two orders divided by a marked triglyph frieze. A second design by Pierre Lambert, also dated 1707, was that adopted. It is domical, but the nuns' choir is a rectangular continuation of the apse. The façade [326] is notable for the canted angles, each adorned with twin Corinthian pilasters, that frame the severely classical Doric doorways. The play of angle they afford is emphasized by a heavy modillion cornice surmounted by a balustrade with urns at the angles, which are repeated round the severely plain drum of the painted dome. The interior [327] is of a noble and classical simplicity; all the interest is centred in the circular centre, to which the choir seems an unimportant adjunct. The galleries and chapels round the dome are in the tradition of those of Le Val-de-Grâce.

The church of the Cistercian nunnery of Sainte-Marie-de-Battant at Besançon[1] was the work of a Benedictine architect, Dom Edme Perrot, in 1720; its façade, with a central oculus, is plain and old-fashioned; the church has four chapels set diagonally, on the model of Mansart's Church of the Visitation at Paris, under a great octagonal cupola.

None the less, it is not surprising that the eighteenth century saw few Cistercian churches built in France, and those erected as part of a general scheme of reconstruction. The Cistercian nunnery of Panthemont in Paris was rebuilt in 1747 under the direction of Contant d'Ivry; its chapel[2] was designed [328, 329] on a cross-shaped plan, with equal arms and a dome in the centre on four arches, in the French Ionic order; it is elegant if a little petty in effect. It tries to emulate Le Val-de-Grâce on too small a scale.

At Valloires the general rebuilding of the abbey,[3] that had suffered a bad fire some ninety years before, was completed by that of the church between 1750 and 1756, from the designs of Raoul Coignart. The structure is itself extremely plain, with a classically vaulted nave lit by tall high windows, a severe but noble façade and an apse almost Romanesque in its simplicity [330, 331]. The choir [332] is more or less semicircular in shape and has classical vaults. It is divided from the nave by a splendid screen of wrought iron, by Jean Baptiste Veyron. The apse is lined with elaborate *boiseries* above the stalls, centring on seats for the abbot and

---

[1] See Tournier, p. 327. The church, once a cinema, is now a school; it was not possible to visit the interior.

[2] At 106 rue de Grenelle. It is now a Protestant chapel and the monastic buildings house the Ministry of Pensions. The medieval church at Clairvaux was transformed in the modern taste about 1735-9. (King, p. 312.)

[3] See below, p. 66. It is now a sanatorium.

prior on either side of an altar with a double retable upheld by angels. The high altar [333] is of the utmost richness. Two angels kneel in adoration; and in the centre an immense branch of ironwork rises to the ceiling to hold the pyx with the host.[1] It is supported from above by an astonishing group of flying angels [334]. Fine woodwork is everywhere; even the organ has a splendid case and gallery sculptured with musician angels, children symbolizing the Manual and Fine Arts, and trophies of musical instruments. All is ascribed to Pfaffenhofen, an Austrian exile who was a friend of the commendatory abbot. By a delightful *pietas* the fourteenth-century effigies of the founders, Jean de Ponthieu and his wife Anne, still lie in the choir, framed in elaborate classical urns and pyramids.

Something of the splendour of the sanctuary of Valloires and something of the same respect for the past appear in the shrine of St Edmund Rich, erected above the high altar at Pontigny in 1749. The massive altar ends in two pedestals; on the corner of each of them stand two angels, to uphold the late medieval shrine [335].

Elsewhere a skin of classicism was laid over an older base. At Le Thoronet the choir of the medieval church was adorned with fine wrought-iron grilles, the walls were decorated with marble and stucco, and the windows were covered in to form niches for statues of St Bernard, St Laurence and the Virgin and Child.[2]

Elsewhere it was found enough to give a Cistercian church a new façade to bring it into relation with new monastic buildings. A sketch in the possession of Baron Thénard, the present owner of La Ferté-sur-Grosne, shows that when the monastic quarters were rebuilt, the early Gothic church (now destroyed) was given a classical façade with a pediment and a giant order of seven columns, with steeply roofed side pavilions to mask the buttresses. More oddly, at the house of Trois-Fontaines in the Marne, the thirteenth-century nave was repaired and given egg and dart mouldings, Corinthian capitals, and heavy classical brackets to take the vault, to modernize the Cistercian austerity of its medieval structure. At Aubazine, however, the misericords carved in 1719 are deliberate *pastiches* of the late fifteenth century even in the headgear of the persons represented. It cannot, however, be said that the Cistercians took any real part in the 'Gothick' revival that was fostered by the Benedictine architects and their abbots.

The white monks suffered like all the religious of France in the devastations of the Wars of Religion, and had to carry out a general campaign of rebuilding their living quarters comparable with that of the other Benedictines, even if they did so at a slower pace and on a smaller scale. A typical instance is Fontmorigny, which was renovated at this time.[3] The abbot was first provided in mid-century

---

[1] The only surviving parallel known to me is a crozier-like support for a pyx now in the sacristy of the Benedictine church at Beaulieu, Corrèze.

[2] This group is now in the parish church of Lorgues.

[3] When I visited it (1955) it was in process of being destroyed piecemeal by the proprietor; in 1939 the buildings were still perfect.

with a handsome lodging. Then the medieval church was given a classical entrance door [336], and a fine cloister and monastic quarters were added. The cloister [337] is notably severe and very dignified. At La Grâce-Dieu[1] the monastic buildings were re-erected, again in a very plain and institutional style, in the second half of the sixteenth century.

In the seventeenth century conditions were easier. At Mortemer [338, 339] a good range of buildings arose in a Benedictine style comparable with Saint-Riquier; at Le Pin [341] a larger building is of severer effect in a setting as beautiful as that of Rievaulx. At Notre-Dame-de-Boisgroland the Cistercians of the Strict Observance built a small monastery in an agreeable manor style [340].

In 1666 Pope Alexander VI authorized the division of dorters into cells in Cistercian houses, and this permission, combined with Colbert's edict of the same year,[2] ordering that the capital of religious houses was to be spent in rebuilding cloisters, abbot's lodgings and monastic quarters, provided a stimulus to building. In the following year the Feuillants in the rue Saint Honoré erected a splendid entrance designed by François Mansart [342] and the Cistercians of Clairvaux a great cloister, glazed for warmth.[3] At about the same time the Cistercians of Boulbonne erected a great building[4] all of warm pink Toulousain brick [343-8]. A very simple exterior, with tower-like projections at the angles, masks a great cloister which is as classical as any structure all of brick can be [343, 344]. None the less the walks still have Gothic vaults. A fine gateway [346], likewise of brick, is dated 1738; and the elegant rococo decorations of the refectory [347, 348] seem to be of much the same date.

At La Ferté-sur-Grosne a fine range of buildings, in the style of a small Louis XIV château, was erected in 1682 [349]. At Fontaine-Daniel[5] plain and dignified blocks were erected together with a notably austere cloister that seems to have been built on medieval foundations. At Pontigny a classical cloister was fitted into the north aisle of the long medieval nave; the heavy buttresses in alternate bays have something medieval about them, but the carved brackets that take the vaulting are entirely classical [350, 351]. At about the same time the entrance was dignified with lodges and a gate [352].

A number of Cistercian nunneries were rebuilt at this time. The sisters known as the Filles du Précieux Sang rebuilt their Paris house in 1659.[6] A typical nunnery of the time is that of the Bernardine house at Dijon [353] which, like a medieval Cistercian abbey, adapts contemporary Burgundian secular style to its own use. Secular style reappears in an even simpler form in the Abbaye de Beauvoir, near Marmagne, rebuilt in 1624 by the Abbess Marie de Chauvelin de Richemont. At

---

[1] Now a mental hospital. [2] See above, p. 29.

[3] Hautecœur, II, 856. It does not appear to survive; but parts of the Louis XIV buildings of the abbey are now devoted to housing criminal lunatics, and cannot be visited.

[4] Half of it was destroyed at the Revolution, together with the church, except for one tower.

[5] Now a factory. [6] Piganiol de la Force, VII, 276.

Orgelet the buildings of the Cistercian nunnery,[1] which date from between 1708 and 1718, are said to be due to Dom Vincent Duchesne. The façade of the chapel is set high, with twin staircases rising to the outer of its arcade of three arches. Set back behind the arcade is a simple façade with an oculus [354]. The very plain façade of the nuns' buildings is relieved only by a handsome doorway. The cloister is austere, with a second arcade of wood above [355]; it may be an addition but appears to be an original part of a very utilitarian design.

The Feuillantine nuns in the rue Saint-Jacques at Paris rebuilt their quarters about 1713.[2] Little remains unmodified of the house of Bernardines at Dôle;[3] most of it may date from before the cession of the city to France. What remains of the nuns' quarters of Sainte-Marie-de-Battant at Besançon, dating from 1739, has a good wrought-iron balustrade in a Vitruvian scroll pattern.

A metropolitan scheme, with pilastered end pavilions, was designed by Contant d'Ivry for the Paris nunnery of Panthemont in 1747[4] [356-9]. The Bernardine nuns of Marseilles rebuilt their convent[5] between 1746 and 1751, with fine court-yards surrounded by simple cloisters, in part on two floors.

This wave of rebuilding reached even the remotest Cistercian houses. In 1765 the 'bête du Gévaudan'—an enormous wolf that killed women and children tending their sheep on the hill pastures of the remote nunnery at Mercoire in the Massif Central—was killed and an officer of the abbey took its skin and its skeleton to Louis XV at Versailles. There, it would seem, an unusual contact with the court made the emissary conscious that the future of the monasteries was uncertain. At all events, very soon afterwards the abbey's capital was hurriedly employed in building. The result was a very plain edifice with wings at right angles, without a cloister, in the backward architectural style one might expect in such a site[6] [361]. The only architectural feature is the central pediment; this never received its destined heraldic sculpture.

The most splendid Cistercian nunnery of the eighteenth century is the royal abbey of Saint-Antoine-des-Champs, near the Paris Bastille[7] [360]. It was rebuilt by Lenoir 'le Romain' in 1767, as two fine long buildings joined by a lesser construction. The general style, plain but noble, with wide plain pilasters and pediments, is rather English in its squareness and simplicity, and like the contemporary English style is inspired by direct study of classical Roman architecture. Far more than most French monastic buildings, it recalls an English college; a common inspiration has for once produced a common style.

Few of the Cistercian nunneries were wealthy and many made ends meet by

[1] Now Caserne de Gendarmerie and Collège.
[2] See Blondel, *L'architecture française*, II, plate 200.   [3] Now flats.
[4] Designs for the cloister and for the woodwork of the choir survive in Arch. Nat., Plans N III, Seine 86 (5) and 7. The latter is dated 1743.
[5] Now the Lycée. The church is domed; I was not able to see the interior.
[6] The buildings are now a farm and a post office.
[7] Now the Hôpital Saint-Antoine. The Nunnery survives at Stape Hill near Wimborne.

taking in ladies as boarders, sometimes in separate buildings designed for the purpose.[1] The Paris Feuillantines, for example, built pavilions for boarders in their garden early in the seventeenth century.

The Cistercian Rule had always permitted the inclusion of lay brethren in the Order, who did most of the heavy work of the abbey farms. A good many of the country monasteries rebuilt their lay brethren's quarters in the last quarter of the seventeenth century, perhaps under the stimulus of Colbert's edict. The monastic quarters built by Henri de Briqueville de la Luzerne, bishop of Cahors, at La Garde-Dieu, which he held *in commendam*, are little more than good farm buildings and incorporate many medieval walls. Subsidiary buildings sometimes survive when more splendid edifices have vanished, for they easily adapt themselves to farm use. It is, moreover, easy to imagine that the needs of many small priories and remote abbeys with hardly any monks could be met by a range of buildings for lay brethren or secular farm labourers, quarters for three or four monks, perhaps in some patched-up medieval building, and a modest lodging where the commendatory abbot or his land agent could stay when they came on a tour of inspection.

Nearly all the Cistercian rebuildings of the late seventeenth and early eighteenth centuries survive, if they survive at all, in a sad state of decay. At Val-des-Choux near Vorlaines in the Côte-d'Or—an abbey once flourishing enough to have dependent houses in Scotland—a large quadrangle survives as stables and barns [362, 363]; it is still entered by a plain gateway surmounted by a statue of St Bernard. In the living quarters to the left of the gateway some battered chimney-pieces and stuccos remain as testimony to a former elegance. At Morimond—one of the four elder daughters of Cîteaux—little remains but a huddle of farm-buildings in which two arcades of the cloister can still be discerned [365] and the battered remains of a splendid baroque gateway [364]. At Cherlieu, another abbey famous in Cistercian history, two groups of buildings remain, of which one bears the date 1708 [366, 367]. The arcades of the simple cloister have been blocked up to make a stable.[2]

At Coët-Malouen church and monastic buildings erected about 1709 by Languet, archbishop of Sens and titular abbot, alike stand roofless and ruined [368, 369]. They already begin to show a measure of influence from the Benedictine revival of building. At La Grâce-Dieu in the Doubs (now a Cistercian nunnery) a good deal remains of the buildings erected between 1720 and 1726 [370]. Everything is of a notable simplicity; even the chapter-house has a plain coved ceiling rising from two Doric columns without adornment. At Langonnet the noble arches of the cloister give style to a building no less essentially simple [372]. At Acey in the Jura[3] the buildings were also begun in 1720 and were

[1] Hautecœur, I, 555.
[2] The abbey of La Chalade in the Meuse acquired simple countrified living quarters in brick and stone at about the same time.   [3] It is once more a Cistercian house.

finished in 1746.[1] There is a great quadrangle, with a cloister[2] that has been modified and three tangential blocks. All are more or less uniform in style [371]; they are very simple, yet are not lacking in dignity or in calculated architectural effect. It would not be at all surprising to discover that they were by a Benedictine architect.

Yet the Cistercians remained outside the Congregation of Saint-Maur, and the impetus to build was less continuous and its results less systematic than with the Benedictines. The most splendid Cistercian buildings of the time were those of the royal abbey of Chaalis, designed in 1736 by Jean Aubert, the architect of the stables at Chantilly. They were begun in the following year[3] [373, 374]. In spite of the originality of much of their architect's work elsewhere, these show the influence of the Norman Benedictine style[4] in their arcaded ground floor and their heavy rustication. The cloister, of which only one walk was erected, is equally Benedictine in style. They aroused the critical faculties of the Abbé Lebeuf, who wrote concerning them[5] in the *Mercure de France*: 'Il saute aux yeux que les édifices du douzième et du treizième siècle sont ravissants par leur délicatesse, tandis que ce qu'on élève depuis cinquante ou soixante ans, en fait de cloître et de réfectoire, est massif et grossier. Qu'on dise tant qu'on voudra, que ceux qui n'aiment pas ces grosses masses de pierre, ces immenses piliers quarrés ont le goût dépravé.' Funds ran out; the plan was never completed; and in 1785 the King closed the abbey because it was heavily in debt.

The destroyed Cistercian house of Signy-l'Abbaye in the Ardennes was, like Chaalis, built under Norman Benedictine influences[6] [375]. It affords a comparison with the two great ranges of buildings at Ourscamp [376] with a pedimented centre and a terminal pavilion, built on either side of the church which had already been given a classical façade.[7]

In 1738 the rebuilding of Valloires[8] was begun, after a bad fire which destroyed the earlier buildings. Here, too, the Norman Benedictine style inspires the whole, yet the projection of the pavilions gives the façades a more secular air [377, 378]. The main buildings are in a rectangle round a rather plain cloister, some forty metres square, with the abbot's quarters to the west. Each monk had a nice little wainscoted cell, with a closet on either side of the alcove, and a fireplace. The refectory, however, is of medieval simplicity. The chapter-house still has its elegant carved panelling, with portraits of the titular abbot and the prior. The gateway is the centre of a semicircle of 'communs', as at Saint-Denis.[9] The same

[1] The main gate is dated 1780 on its ironwork.
[2] The abbot kindly stated that the old cloister was burnt in 1683 and reconstructed in 1720; but this building has been glazed in.
[3] The buildings now house the Musée Jacquemart André. The cloister has been glazed.
[4] See above, p. 33.   [5] Cited Hautecœur, III, 344.
[6] My thanks are due to the Archiviste-en-Chef of the Ardennes for finding the drawing for me.
[7] The left wing of the façade was built by Cardinal de Gesvres, elected abbot in 1750; the other appears to be the earlier.
[8] See above, p. 61.   [9] See above, p. 48.

plan is followed in the abbey of Cercamp[1] [379–82] which is yet more Norman Benedictine in its long unbroken façades. It does not include a cloister and it is not easy to see how one could have been fitted in, though the west end of the block seems unfinished; it must in any event have been amply spacious for the nine monks who occupied it in 1768.[2]

At Trois-Fontaines[3] a good deal of building was done between 1737 and 1741. A spectacular outer gate [383], with every horizontal line curvilinear, leads to a vast courtyard, bounded to north and south by high walls, and to the east by a screen with a gate in the centre, running between two pavilions, which are linked by a passage behind its balustrades [385, 386]. Beyond the gate the screen wall is revealed as arcaded to form a cloister; and one of the pavilions is seen to be extended by a long wing of monastic quarters at right angles. The second pavilion has no such appendage, and was presumably the abbot's lodging. The staircase in the monastic block has stone balustrades [384] with a splendid stone finial.

Another east French house that was rebuilt in the middle of the century is Auberive, which has been reoccupied by the Cistercians since 1954. It follows the general scheme of Chaalis and Ourscamps, but with a minimum of the rounded Norman Benedictine windows—two to stress the central pavilion—and less emphasis than usual on the end pavilions [388]. The spacious cloister [387] achieves old-fashioned elegance by the Ionic pilaster strips above the rusticated buttresses. Within, the stairs [390] and corridors are simple; the fine entrance gate [389] was given by Carvillon de Vandeul, son-in-law of Diderot.[4] There are remains of a mill. The thirteenth-century chapter-house is incorporated in the later building.

The great northern abbey at Loos rebuilt its monastic quarters between 1752 and 1757.[5] Its plan[6] [391] shows how the new buildings were arranged to include the medieval church, lengthened by a Lady Chapel, in a cloister with projecting wings. The central pavilion of stone with a richly sculptured pediment and a balcony [393] has the Norman Benedictine windows, but the rest of the building is in the local brick and is rather conservative in style [394]. The original gateway[7] [392] was a monumental one in Doric style. The late eighteenth-century monastic buildings of the Bernardines at Neufchatel-en-Bray are extremely bleak and rectilinear.[8]

The Cistercian mother-house at Cîteaux had its monastic quarters rebuilt in 1760; they are now once more occupied by the Cistercians. The original designs

---

[1] Now a school.   [2] Lekai, p. 327.   [3] Now occupied by the army.

[4] It seems originally to have been at Beaulieu near Faye-Billot, Haute-Marne. I owe this information to the kindness of the abbot.

[5] Now a men's prison. I am greatly indebted to Monsieur de Saint-Aubin, the Chief Archivist of the Nord, for his kindness in making the old photographs and the plan available.

[6] Archives du Nord, 27 H 279.

[7] Destroyed in the First World War. The other buildings were damaged in both wars and are now being restored.

[8] The Cistercian house at Flarans, near Condom, has two long ranges of modest pretensions dating from 1759.

for them by Lenoir 'le Romain' survive in the Municipal library at Dijon; they show [395, 396] an immense quadrangular building, with two very long sides, 237 metres long, broken by a central feature and four pavilions, and two shorter with a central and terminal pavilions. The convention of a uniform façade is here renounced; the effect must have been extremely splendid, but palatial rather than monastic. There were only forty monks in the house at the time. Only one block was finished; it survives, with a lofty cloister [397] of great austerity, a very plain vaulted refectory and the usual splendid stair [398]. The church, destroyed at the Revolution, was given a new façade to bring it into the scheme.

The work at Cîteaux seems to have had an influence on the great central block at the Cistercian abbey of Bégard[1] [399–401] and on a guests' wing at the back. The buildings at La Valasse[2] [405, 406] seem to owe something to the same inspiration; their noble ranges were occupied by only ten monks. The same pedimented style is carried out in brick in the abbey of Sainte-Colombe at Blendecques[3] [407, 408], which has a fine gateway. At Melleray in 1761 [404] the pediments crown the end pavilions; the central block is marked by heavy coigns and a balustrade. This sophisticated exterior is belied by an austere interior, once again in Cistercian occupation, old-fashioned even in its stone balustrades.

Five years after Cîteaux, in 1765, the great Cistercian house of Clairvaux[4] was likewise rebuilt, on designs sometimes ascribed to de Carpentier.[5] Though there were fifty-four monks in the community it was never as palatial as Cîteaux, but its long range of façade [403] must once have rivalled the mother-house. The rusticated entrance door [402] with its two adjacent pavilions, is more austere and even more monumental than that at Saint-Wandrille. The cloister [409] and the staircase [410] with its odd re-entrant angles combine elegance with dignity. The central feature of the cloister walks recalls the entrance at Blendecques. The refectory had elegant *boiseries* with a picture at the head of each panel.

Even the remote Cistercian abbey of Sénanque (which then boasted only four monks) acquired a modest block in the style of Cîteaux with a single wrought-iron balcony. Only in the planning of the Provençal house of Bonpas [411] did local style prove stronger than Cistercian tradition. In 1775 the Feuillants of Paris started to rebuild their monastic quarters to the design of J. D. Antoine,[6] with a fine plain façade to the Place Vendôme centred by a pedimented pavilion framed by Corinthian pilasters with a garlanded doorway with a relief above the lintel.

The Cistercian house of Bon-Repos in Brittany must once have been little less

[1] Now the Institution du Bon Sauveur.   [2] Now a private house.
[3] Now the offices of a factory.
[4] Now a central prison. The chapel has a pleasing rococo door, and a fine iron gateway leads to the garden.
[5] Hautecœur, III, 327. See also King, p. 315.
[6] Hautecœur, IV, 255, fig. 130. They included houses for letting in their plan; some survive in nos. 229–35 rue Saint-Honoré.

elegant than La Melleray, but now it is a picture of utter dereliction. The building has been burnt out; ivy covers it and threatens to bring it down; the keystones are dropping from the arches and trees grow between the flagstones of the cloister.[1] At Le Relec nearby all the buildings have vanished, but the piers and fountains of the abbot's gardens survive in the farmyard [412].

The Cistercians continued their unhappy tradition of quarrelsomeness into the eighteenth century. After 1738 royal commissioners were sent to sit at the Chapters General and came to play a more and more important part in their deliberations. Perhaps because of this, the Cistercians were exempted from the dissolution of small monasteries ordered by the commission of 1766. At the Chapter General of 1783 the commissioners threatened, however, to suppress all Cistercian houses with less than nine monks.

Even when a house was rich enough to secure continuance, it might go on in a strange fashion. Soon after 1750[2] only two monks were left at the Cistercian house of Noirlac. The cells were redivided to form larger rooms, with alcoves, large windows and balconies, for the abbot's guests, and the monks themselves were housed, very comfortably, in the old guest-house. Fontenay, that had made a good recovery from the Hundred Years War, had begun to decline after it fell *in commendam* in 1557. By 1745 its buildings were in such a bad state that repair seemed useless, and the refectory was pulled down.

The Cistercian houses were rich in subsidiary buildings, to house lay brethren, guests and other dependants. Few can be definitely identified; at Royaumont a decent secular building appears to have been the guest-house [413]. At Lille the abbey of Loos rebuilt its 'Refuge'[3] as an elegant town house [414]. Naturally the Cistercian abbots and abbesses continued to require lodgings of considerable dignity, however few the number of their religious, and a number were erected in the eighteenth century. About 1700 the abbot of Preuilly erected a lodging like a decent manor house, as did his brother of Montpeyroux. At Pontigny Jacques Gabriel Grillot, abbot from 1742 to 1764, built himself a splendid residence like a château.[4] At the ancient Cistercian house of La Ferté-sur-Grosne the block of monastic buildings erected by Claude Petit in 1682[5] was broken about 1777[6] by a new central pavilion [349] to provide a château-like habitation for the abbot Antoine de la Cerve. Its splendid ironwork balustrade [415] is monastic enough, but the hall that served him as a cloister [416] (though it has Gothic reminiscences in the vault) and his *petit salon* with trophies of the arts [417, 418] are well calculated to make a gentleman feel at home. His bedroom was done up with biblical

---

[1] What appears to be Robert de Cotte's design for the abbot's lodgings will be found in the Cabinet des Estampes, Hal 8 fol. 400.

[2] *Cong. Arch.* 1931 (Bourges). At the moment of the Revolution the number of monks had risen to five.

[3] See above, p. 7.   [4] Hautecœur, II, 887.

[5] King, p. 142.

[6] Commune of Puy-Guillaume, Puy-de-Dôme. Now a country house.

scenes elegantly painted in *camaieu bleu*, and discreet trophies of books. Brieux's *Art de Bâtir* shows the comparable work undertaken at Saint-Just-en-Picardie,[1] yet more elaborate, with urns between the windows and curved pediments to the terminal pavilions.

At Longpont a great Louis XVI *salon* remains with decorations of reliefs of the sciences and the liberal arts. At Royaumont the commendatory abbot, Monsieur de Balivière (chiefly famous as a gambler) in 1785 engaged Louis le Masson to design him a new lodging [419]. It was a strange massive cubical building in the style of Ledoux, with *œils-de-bœuf* and lunette windows, and great flights of steps up to the entrance doors. One of these, to the north, was classical; but the triple arcade of that to the west is almost Arab in feeling. The Revolution came too quickly for the design to be executed. For once one feels few regrets.

[1] Now destroyed.

CHAPTER III

THE AUGUSTINIANS

I. TRADITION AND REFORM

The easier Augustinian Rule, by which the clergy of a cathedral church lived as a community, had been extended by the synod of 1059 to other religious who wished to work in common. It had undergone various reforms in the early Middle Ages under Benedictine influence, some of which imposed a common dorter in place of the single room allowed by the Rule. As a result of these reforms there were in the fifteenth century not only Augustinian canons, living in independent communities, but also the Orders of Grandmont, Fontevrault and the Premonstratensians, who followed an Augustinian Rule.

Devoted work was done, as always, by Augustinian nurses and teachers, yet in many of the wealthier houses life was as easy and aimless as in an unintellectual English college in the eighteenth century. Since Augustinian houses were generally in towns[1] they suffered less than the Benedictines did in the Hundred Years War; and since they were less obviously rich their life was less changed by the rapaciousness of royal nominees. Independence, too, sometimes helped to keep a house in being since amalgamation with another house was less easy. Saint-Amand-de-Coly, near Perigueux, for example, had had all its monastic buildings destroyed by the English, but even in the eighteenth century four regular canons continued to serve in an enormous, deserted and half-ruined church.

None the less various reforms were instituted in houses of Augustinian canons, and the acceptance of such a reform by several abbeys tended to the formation of a congregation, if less closely knit than the Congrégation de Saint-Maur. The Grands Augustins, sometimes called the Vieux Augustins, owned ninety-three houses in France. The Petits Augustins, who followed a reformed Rule instituted at Bourges, had thirty-one convents. The Discalced Augustinians or Petits Pères, members of a reform which reached France from Grenoble, had thirty-six. Marguérite de Valois established them in 1609 in what is now 14 rue Bonaparte; they moved to Montmartre in 1612 and in 1628 to what is now the Place des Petits Pères. They were replaced in their original home by Petits Augustins.

Another reform, with a wider scope, was that which resulted in the Augustinian Congrégation de France. The old foundation of the Canons of Chancelade had been ruined by the Calvinists; in 1617 the community consisted only in an abbot and three canons, who spent their time in hunting and dicing.[2] Alain de

---

[1] A few houses outside the walls, such as the abbey of Saint-Ruf at Valence, came within the gates in the sixteenth century. [2] Hélyot, *Dictionnaire*, I, 751.

71

Solmignac became commendatory abbot in that year, at the age of twenty-two, in succession to his uncle. He studied in Paris under Jesuit influences, and returned in 1622 to reform the community. He rebuilt, with himself as architect and clerk of the works, the monastic quarters, revaulted the ruined church, and pierced the Romanesque walls with windows in flamboyant style. The few old brethren opposed his reform, but he sent them away to the abbey livings and secured new novices, on whom he imposed strict vows of poverty, and a Jesuit discipline of mental prayer. In 1629 the 'commende' was removed by the King, who reappointed Solmignac abbot on the recommendation of the community. The abbot became administrator and reformed five other Augustinian houses.

In 1624 Cardinal de la Rochefoucauld called upon Père Charles Faure, an Augustinian of Saint-Vincent de Senlis, to reform the monastery of Sainte-Geneviève at Paris.[1] He turned it into a congregation of canons, commonly called Génofévains, from the name of their patron saint. By the time of his death in 1644, more than fifty houses had been reformed by him. They were then amalgamated with the reformed Congregation of Chancelade to form the Congrégation de France.

The houses of Augustinian nuns who were not nursing sisters and did not belong to an Order or Congregation increased little in the seventeenth and eighteenth centuries. The English canonesses of Notre-Dame de Sion were founded in Paris in 1634,[2] and the Chanoinesses regulières de Saint Augustin were founded in the rue de Picpus in 1640, and transferred to Notre-Dame des Victoires in 1647.[3] Other houses of canonesses were founded by great ladies. Madame de Maintenon, reconverted to Catholicism under Ursuline influence, in 1682 had a house at Rueil where fifty young girls were educated by an Ursuline. In 1684 it was enlarged and transferred to Noisy-le-Sec; in 1686 it was finally moved to Saint-Cyr, where two hundred girls were educated in fine buildings designed by Mansart.[4] In 1692 Saint-Cyr was reorganized as a convent of the Dames religieuses de Saint Louis, following the Augustinian Rule. The ladies wore a uniform secular dress of black until 1707, when they took the monastic habit.

One would hardly expect the Augustinians to have shared in the Maurist interest in medieval monasticism;[5] yet a most interesting collection of drawings by several hands of houses belonging to the Congrégation de France made about 1690[6] includes drawings of a number of Romanesque and Gothic churches executed with even more loving care than those of their relatively modern monastic buildings; and when the Génofévains rebuilt their church at Celles-sur-

---

[1] Hélyot, *Dictionnaire*, II, 378.

[2] They were transferred to what is now the rue du Cardinal Lemoisne in 1638; nothing remains of their buildings.

[3] See below, p. 75.   [4] See below, p. 75.

[5] *The Nouveau Traité de toute l'architecture, ou l'art de bien bâtir*, published at Paris in 1714 by the Chanoine de Cordemoy of Saint-Jean-des-Vignes at Soissons, is conventionally classical.

[6] Bib. Nat. Est. Ve 20.

Belle[1] between 1670 and 1680 they engaged François Leduc de Toscane to design it in Gothic style.

There was a long tradition of luxury in the conventual buildings of the Augustinians, whose Rule was deliberately planned to be less austere than that of the Benedictines. Such magnificence was naturally most apparent in the abbot's lodging. Robert Richardson, 'Richardinus', who was living in Paris when he published his book on the Rule of St Augustine in 1530, declared 'Video hisce temporibus nonnullos Abbates sedes magnifice et regio more construere, quibus nobilibus gratificentur, in his enim aedibus isti splendide excipiuntur. Religiosorum uero aedes, ac templa deorum interea labascunt, et prae uetustate corroduntur, ne semel quidem a praefectis restitutae.'[2]

An abbot's lodging of the date of his publication still remains: the manor built by Abbé Pierre Kernévenoy at the Abbaye de Sainte-Croix near Guingamp. It is protected by two hexagonal turrets and is quite secular in style. The early Gothic church remains in ruins.

The Augustinian buildings of the sixteenth and early seventeenth century were equally modest.[3] At their house at Saint-Jean-de-Côle, for example, already enriched by a sixteenth-century cloister in which Gothic arches and Renaissance pilasters are combined [420] and by an abbot's lodging of much the same date in secular style, the Augustinians linked the two by a wing with an arcade beneath its formal bays [421]. At Lannion the Augustinian nuns built themselves not undignified quarters in the simple Renaissance style of their province [423] and the monks of the same Order in the same place followed a little later with even simpler buildings.[4] The Regular Augustinian nuns of the well-named house of Val-Paradis near Espagnac in the Lot rebuilt their quarters too, in a very simple and almost farm-like style.

The small Augustinian house at Toulouse had its little cloister built in 1626[5] of brick, with stucco pilasters surmounted by stucco statues. The spaces over the arcade were originally ornamented with rectangular paintings of the story of David. The collection of drawings, already mentioned, made for the Congrégation de France, includes one of Notre-Dame-de-Livry-en-l'Aulnoy[6]—now destroyed [424]—which shows a stumpy cloister of the same kind, as well as a fine block between two projecting wings, each ending in a pavilion. It looks as if it might date from 1637, when the abbey became Génofévain. A careful drawing[7]

---

[1] It had been destroyed by the Huguenots in 1569. [2] Ed. Coulton, pp. 54–5.

[3] The *Répertoire*, Bib. Nat. Est., Ve 20, fol. 11, represents good simple buildings which appear to be of about 1600 at Saint-Cheron de Chartres, and rather dull ones (fol. 33) at Saint-Pierre de Rillé.

[4] The remains of the little cloister at Saint-Jean-des-Vignes, Soissons, are still Gothic in arch and tracery, but the spandrels and frieze have Renaissance medallions.

[5] Hautecœur, I, 557.

[6] The abbey was founded from Saint-Vincent de Senlis in 1186; it was near Gonesse, Seine et Oise. Bib. Nat. Est. Ve 20, fol. 5. Another of Notre-Dame d'Eu (*ibid.* fol. 10) shows a good Louis XIII building abutting on to the medieval church.

[7] *Ibid.* fol. 56.

[426] of the buildings at Saint-Acheul, just outside Amiens, shows a château-like block in two sections joined by a domed pavilion, all in a country version of Le Mercier's style. The remaining two sides of the cloister (the medieval church forms the fourth) are very much simpler, and presumably held the monastic quarters. A simple seventeenth-century quadrangle, with pavilions projecting to east and west, is shown in the drawing of the priory of Mont-aux-Malades[1] [425]; this looks some forty years earlier than its entry into the Génofévain congregation in 1669. It bears a fairly close resemblance to the pleasantly countrified house, like a large manor house, which the Augustinians of Saint-Ambroix de Bourges built themselves [427].[2] Their other house at Bourges[3] [428] is much more monastic in style, with its heavily arcaded cloister, but is a little less plain. The building closely resembles the drawing of the Augustinian abbey of Le Val-des-Ecoliers in the Bibliothèque Nationale.[4] The same collection includes a drawing [429] of the Augustinian priory of Château-l'Hermitage, near Pontvallain,[5] which shows a fine quadrangle with a projecting wing very much in the style of the monastic quarters at Saint-Wandrille, built in 1636. The cloister is in the same style as that of Saint-Symphorien d'Autun in the same collection[6] [430] and the end pavilions show variations on the same theme. Simple but charming cloisters of the same kind survive at Crémieu[7] [431] and La Rochelle [432].

A small but particularly charming Augustinian abbey is that of Saint-Martin-ès-Aires[8] just outside Troyes, built, probably, soon after it was reformed by the Génofévains. It stands round three sides of the cloister with a balustraded wall on the fourth side [433]. Its elegant proportions, its careful balance between brick and stone, its modest scale and its perfect homogeneity, make it a little masterpiece among the monastic buildings of the reign of Louis XIII.[9] The cloister has its arcades resting on heavy piers; the vaults are still medieval in form, but the cloister is not an annexe of the building but an essential part of it. The abbey is entered through a good classical gateway [434].

The large Génofévain house at Châtillon-sur-Sèvre is planned as a long building with projecting wings [435]; the use of quoins and stone panelling is clever enough,

[1] Now destroyed; it was near Mont-Saint-Aignan, Maromme, Seine-Maritime. Bib. Nat. Est., Ve 20, fol. 58. The buildings of a hospice (Saint-Jean d'Aquafort) just outside Le Mans look Augustinian, but I have not been able to discover anything of its history.

[2] Now a private house. Little remains of the apsidal church with fluted pilasters built in the middle of the eighteenth century.

[3] Now workshops and tenements.   [4] Bib. Nat. Est., Ve 20, fol. 55.

[5] The monastic buildings are destroyed but there are some remains of the medieval church.

[6] The abbey, originally Benedictine, became Augustinian in 1656. It looks as if the cloister had been rebuilt soon afterwards.

[7] The buildings, now a college, have been greatly modified.

[8] Now a hospice for old ladies. A drawing of its buildings made c. 1715 will be found in the Cabinet des Estampes, Ve 20, p. 18.

[9] The abbey of Saint-Ausony, an ancient foundation destroyed in turn by the English and the Calvinists, was rebuilt in a faubourg of the city at this time. It was again rebuilt by the redoubtable Abadie in 1864-9. (Migne, *Dictionnaire des Abbayes*, col. 68.)

but the general effect suggests economy. The abbot's lodging appears to have had its upper part rebuilt; originally it must have seemed like a small Louis XIII manor. A slightly grander secular air is given to the abbess's lodging at Beau-repaire[1] [436] by Ionic pilasters and a pediment with her arms.

The style of the monastic buildings of Châtillon-sur-Sèvre seems to have also been followed at the abbey of Notre-Dame de Chatrices-en-Argonne, now known to us only by a drawing.[2] This too was planned as a long block with projecting wings, but its garden front was more important than at Châtillon, with an additional storey and end pavilions.

The age of Louis XIV brought greater splendours to Augustinian as to Benedictine houses. Madame de Maintenon's educational foundation at Saint-Cyr followed the Rule and, however exceptional, must count as an Augustinian house. Her magnificent buildings[3] [437–41], designed by J. H. Mansart in 1685, were planned as a long block with three courts on one side and the church at the end. The central court was closed on one side only by a low wall; the two others were true quadrangles. The left-hand courtyard was the only one directly accessible from the outside, and contained the bakery and workmen's quarters on the ground floor, lodgings for the Visitor (the bishop of Chartres) and the Intendant on the first floor, and rooms and a small chapel for visiting priests above. It was extremely simple in elevation, with a central pediment. The other courts were a little richer, with carved trophies. Their ground floor was taken up by refectory, parlours, and the Directress's rooms; the classrooms were above, and the cells for the mistresses and the pupils on the second floor.

The influence of contemporary Benedictine architecture is evident in the buildings of the Augustinian abbey at Beaugency [442], reconstructed after it was taken over by the Congrégation de France in 1642. At that time grass grew in the nave of the medieval church as in a field; the Congregation repaired it but did not rebuild it. It affords a close parallel with the drawing[4] of the Génofévain abbey of Sainte-Madeleine-de-Géneston[5] where a classical cloister was surrounded by buildings on two sides. A yet more marked influence of the Norman Benedictine style is evident in the later buildings at Saint-Acheul, near Amiens[6] [444, 445]; the long round-headed windows are in the Tremblaye style, though outside the cloister they are oddly divided.

Several Augustinian houses rebuilt their canons' quarters about the time of the passing of Colbert's edict. At Thouars the Augustinians built themselves a seemly house [446] rather secular in style.[7] At Saint-Quentin-lès-Beauvais a similar architecture was created on a larger scale [448]. The Augustinians of Montmorillon

---

[1] Now a miners' welfare centre. [2] Bib. Nat. Est., Ve 20, fol. 51.
[3] Terribly damaged in 1940. See Hautecœur, ii, 563. [4] Bib. Nat. Est. Ve 20, fol. 29.
[5] Monbert-Géneston, Loire-Atlantique; now destroyed; it became Génofévain in 1656.
[6] Now barracks. For the earlier buildings, see p. 74.
[7] Now municipal offices. Good buildings of c. 1680 at Château-Remy are represented in Bib. Nat. Est., Ve 20, fol. 3; and others at Saint-Jean de Sens (fol. 17) and Saint-Jacques de Montfort (fol. 30).

built a great deal in a barrack-like style that almost defies dating; it appears to be of the last years of the seventeenth century. The Génofévain house at Celles-sur-Belle, rebuilt by François Leduc de Toscane between 1670 and 1680 [443], is a notably severe building of stone; no one would mistake it for anything but a monastery.

Elsewhere the Augustinians showed themselves conservative and even backward in their architecture. The left wing of the Augustinian nunnery at Hazebrouck was built in 1718 in Flemish style, with stepped gables [449]; the nuns of Châteauroux reconstructed theirs in 1741[1] [447] in a style that might be a century older. A few unimportant houses, such as Notre-Dame-de-la-Roche at Lévy-Saint-Nom,[2] Graville-Saint-Honorine[3] and Saint-Etienne de Rennes, were rebuilt. At Saint-Pierre de Châtillon-sur-Seine[4] the medieval church was given a fine new entrance [450] and the monastery a gate [452].

At Sainte-Geneviève at Paris royal generosity caused the monastic buildings[5] to be considerably modified, with a well-proportioned cloister [454, 455], a central rotunda with elaborate columns formed as flower-wreathed palm trees, a library with elegant rococo *boiseries* and plaster-work, and fine wrought-iron balustrades to the staircases.

In a few rich provincial houses building was undertaken on a grand scale. At Sablonceaux the abbot's lodging was rebuilt with a delightful balustraded loggia on the first floor [456], and the lesser buildings and the gateway were likewise rebuilt in seemly fashion. The gateway [457] was clearly intended to bear the arms of the abbey and its abbot, but in 1788 the shields were completed with the inscriptions 'La Loi' and 'La Constitution'. The Augustinian house of La Couronne near Angoulême had suffered badly in the wars; its buildings had been patched up and the west side of the cloister rebuilt in 1599. About the middle of the century its monastic quarters were rebuilt in a most elegant if rather provincial style, with an entrance gateway and courtyard [453] with an elaborately framed fountain and a highly civilized lodging for the abbot [458]. The church was not altered.

The great wave of Benedictine building in the middle of the eighteenth century found an echo among the Augustinians. The fine but rather barrack-like block at Saint-Loup de Troyes[6] [451] is paralleled in Soufflot's splendid buildings[7] for the Génofévains, Saint-Irénée de Lyon [459].

The most splendid Augustinian buildings of the mid-eighteenth century are

[1] Now Lycée.
[2] Now an orphanage. Bib. Nat. Est., V 20, fol. 6 has an elevation of the Augustinians at Meaux, dated 1712, which shows the dorter on a ground floor of pointed Gothic arches without capitals. This, however, may represent an earlier building.
[3] Now destroyed. Little remains of the Augustinian house at Chinon, now the Sous-Préfecture.
[4] Now a hospital.   [5] Now the Lycée Henri IV.   [6] Now the library.
[7] The upper storey in the central block has been added. The chapel was rebuilt after the Revolution but seems still to have some elements of Soufflot's design in its façade.

those of Saint-Vincent de Senlis.[1] They date from 1759 and comprise an immense square block [460] enclosing a cloister, with secondary cloisters of simple arcades to the south and west, and a second plainer block detached from it [461]. The central cloister [462, 463] is of particular elegance, with rusticated piers between its coupled columns and an ornamental vault; its style is followed in the adjacent refectory. In comparison the elaborate façade, with four storeys under a rounded pediment and a meaningless central feature, seems curiously weak and hesitating. One of the latest Augustinian conventual buildings is that at Wissembourg[2] [464], built in the style of a town house in 1784, when the future of the Order was already menaced.

The independent Augustinians had been less homogeneous than the Benedictines or the Cistercians, and in the Middle Ages had never achieved a really characteristic art or architecture, though their churches were usually richly furnished by the generosity of individuals. The Augustinian churches of the classical period are no less disparate. At Auxerre the Augustinian abbey church of Saint-Père-en-Vallée,[3] that had been destroyed in the wars, was rebuilt about 1575, in a rather old-fashioned style [465, 466]. The basic conception is late Gothic, though the heavy pillars with their classical capitals recapture something of Romanesque majesty. As at Valmont[4] the arcade of the apse seems purely Romanesque in its inspiration, though the windows and vault above it are completely Flamboyant. The façade, begun in 1630 by Blaise Chéreau, and finished in 1658 by F. Laligne,[5] shows a no less typical alliance between Gothic form and Renaissance decoration. The door and two storeys of windows are each framed by two pairs of fluted columns, the lower Ionic, the two upper Corinthian. The composition is weighted by a heavy cornice and an œil-de-bœuf framed in scrolls and surmounted by a modest pediment. The line of the flying buttresses is echoed in the lines of the side of the façade, marking the aisles; the whole is framed in the two massive classicized buttresses. Again the basic conception is Gothic, though all the swags and bucrania and niches, with which the façade is loaded with Mannerist generosity, are as classical as a Burgundian architect of 1630 could make them. His most elegant achievement, indeed, is the side door to the cloister, which contrives to be a good deal more Metropolitan than the façade. The splendid if battered gateway has couchant statues in the tympanum labelled Ceres and Noah, perhaps in allusion to the abbey's riches in corn and wine.

In the early seventeenth century it was only under royal patronage that Augustinian churches in the true classical style could be built. Marguérite de Valois gave her protection to the Discalced Augustinians or Petits Pères, and established them in Paris near her palace in 1609, with a chapel on a hexagonal

[1] Now a school. [2] Now the Sous-Préfecture.
[3] It became Génofévain in 1635. See Cong. Arch. (Auxerre), 1958, p. 76.
[4] See above, p. 12.
[5] Hautecœur, I, 649. The façade provides an interesting comparison with that of the parish church of Saint-Étienne-du-Mont at Paris, begun in 1610.

plan.[1] Her permanent foundation for them was at Notre-Dame-des-Victoires, of which the first stone was laid in 1629.[2] It was a thank-offering for the King's victory over the Protestants at La Rochelle. The church was not finished until 1656, and was considerably modified between 1737 and 1740.[3] It was designed by François Galoppin[4] and carried out by le Muet, Libéral Bruant and Gabriel Le Duc successively, the last adding tribunes in the four great piers of the crossing. The three chapels on each side were dedicated to St Augustine, Our Lady of the Seven Sorrows, St John the Baptist, the Holy Ghost (no doubt by allusion to the Order of the Saint Esprit) and Notre-Dame de la Savonne.[5]

Notre-Dame-des-Victoires remains the most splendid of the surviving Augustinian churches in classical style [467]. It retains the long nave and narrow aisles of the medieval Augustinian churches. The scheme is Ionic, with a heavy cornice and a lofty vault; the retro-choir has a three-sided apse. The boiseries are excellent [469]. Yet it is fair to say that, like the Augustinian churches of the Middle Ages, it is rich rather than noble. The façade, designed by Cartaud in 1739 [468], remains in the tradition of the Feuillants' church of 1678. Nothing survives of the conventual buildings, but Piganiol de la Force[6] records that they were quadrangular, with four dorters each composed of many cells communicating on the same level. The cloister was on two floors, the upper glazed and hung with many large pictures by Olivet. The refectory opened off one walk of the lower cloister; it was ninety-one feet long, twenty-six feet broad and twenty-seven feet high, with twelve large windows and a coved plaster ceiling.

After the middle of the century Augustinian churches in the cities of France began to aim at a greater splendour. The portal of the church of the Augustins of Poitiers[7] built in 1671 by one of the brothers Girouard, is of a conventional magnificence of a Louis XIII kind, a little belated; fluted Corinthian columns, rich scrolling foliage on frieze and mouldings, elaborately carved doors: everything is very splendid and a little out of date. Something of the same provincial search after richness and fashion is evident in the endimanché façade of the Génofévain church of Saint-Léger at Soissons [470], and in the stone retable of La Couronne.

A new façade was added to the Augustinian abbey of Saint-Etienne at Dijon towards the end of the century.[8] The two-storeyed elevation, with its Ionic and Corinthian half-columns, is Parisian in style. The Augustinian church at Sens[9] has a great plain gable, an Ionic central door and Tuscan side doors. The Augustinian church of Saint-Martin-ès-Vignes at Troyes, said to have been designed by one of

---

[1] Some remains are in the buildings of the École des Beaux Arts.

[2] Lebeuf (ed. Cocheris), I, 258. The stone had four emblematic medallions: see Piganiol de la Force, III, 85.

[3] The façade, designed in 1739 was not completed until 1759.

[4] See Hautecœur, I, 549. [5] Piganiol de la Force, III, 86.

[6] III, 109 ff. [7] Now the entrance to the Musée des Augustins.

[8] Now the Chambre de Commerce. [9] Now the chapel of the Hospice.

its canons named Maillet in 1681,[1] is curiously amateurish in design: a very high plain lower storey, broken only by a string course and a great arch, is surmounted by a pediment and a peristyle clearly taken from an engraving of the Temple of Jupitor Stator at Rome. Some nine years later another canon, Père Claude Paul de Creil, designed a Doric portal and a great staircase for the Paris Génofévains.[2]

Elsewhere, like the poorer Benedictine houses, the Augustinians had to content themselves with adding a new door or a new façade to an ancient building. The modest decoration of the country church of Génofévains at Saint-Jean-de-Côle still displays an effort of the same kind in a medieval interior. The small choir, enough to hold the dozen monks of the house, has elaborate late seventeenth-century *boiseries* enriched with pictures of saints.

An uncorrelated magnificence, as typical as its medieval counterpart, was beginning to creep into the richer Augustinian houses, especially in the metropolis. The high altar of the Grands Augustins at Paris[3] was in 1675–8 framed in a semicircular peristyle with flattened ends; all the eight columns were of violet breccia. The half-dome above was filled with a relief of God the Father and angels, by Charles le Brun; statues of St Augustine and St Monica stood on either side on the lofty stylobate. Piganiol de la Force, again,[4] describes a splendid washing fountain in the Augustinian house of Sainte-Croix-de-la-Bretonnerie at Paris. 'Dans le vestibule qui conduit au réfectoire est un lavoir, ou fontaine d'architecture, en forme de demi-cupole, dont les colonnes et tous les autres ornemens sont de différens marbres, et de metal doré. Ce morceau est plus beau qu'il ne convient, et seroit mieux placé dans quelques bosquets des jardins de Versailles que dans une maison religieuse.'

The series of Augustinian churches continues into the eighteenth century. Saint-Étienne at Rennes was rebuilt in 1700; two niches on the façade contain statues of St Augustine and the patron saint. The interior is classical and even elegant. At Châtillon-sur-Sèvre the influence of Benedictine historians makes itself felt in an interior that is half classical, half-Gothic; a wholly modern note is struck, however, in the splendid baldaquin of the altar [471]. The ancient abbey of Saint Ruf at Valence was rebuilt in a severe style, with a façade designed only with a door, two windows and an oculus. The interior[5] is more ornate, with moulded panels between Corinthian pilasters [472].

The greatest Augustinian church built at the time was that of Sainte-Geneviève at Paris,[6] which had long been ruinous. At the end of the seventeenth century[7] Claude Perrault had designed a splendid church for the Génofévains, with a façade of which the regular hexastyle portico was far more truly classical than

[1] Hautecœur, II, 733, fig. 565. [2] Now destroyed. *Ibid.* p. 716.
[3] Millin, III, 62. [4] IV, 303.
[5] Now a Protestant church. The house next to it looks as if it had been part of the monastic buildings.
[6] Now the Panthéon. (See Hautecœur, IV, 188.)
[7] Before 1697. See M. Petzet, 'Un projet de Perrault pour l'église Saint Geneviève à Paris', *Bull. Mon.* CXV (1957), 81.

most of the buildings of the time. The regular columns of the very long nave were exceptionally designed, with true classical feeling, to support not an arcade but an architrave; the general effect is of one of the great early basilicas of Rome. Had the design ever been executed, it would have been a landmark in the history of French architecture; but there was not money enough for the foundations.

In 1756 Louis XV lay ill at Metz, and made a vow to rebuild Sainte-Geneviève. A competition was instituted, which Soufflot won. His design of 1757 was a domed Greek cross with equal arms; within this plan the colonnade supports an architrave. He had to modify it to hold a larger congregation by adding a bay to the nave, covered by an oval cupola, and then for symmetry added a similar bay to the choir.[1] The short arms of the cross were covered by cupolas on arches rising from columns at the corners [473]. The dome itself was extremely daring [474]; it is clearly inspired by that of London's St Paul's in plan.[2] It is over sixty-two feet in diameter and height, with triangular piers to carry the drum.[3] It was originally planned that it should be surmounted by a pedestal with figures of Religion and the four Evangelists, and that statues of the eight Fathers of the Church should stand round the drum.[4] On the exterior it towers like St Paul's above the pedimented peristyle [475].

Even when the main part of a medieval church was preserved, it was sometimes masked by a late classical façade. About 1770 the process was effected at Saint-Amable de Riom [476] with a fine front of Volvic stone carved with ecclesiastical trophies and garlands of flowers.

Even now there were houses that did not heed the presages of politics. Coyze-en-l'Argentière had since its foundation in 1273 been a house of noble ladies,[5] following a much mitigated Benedictine Rule. In 1777 it reformed itself, with still more exact requirements of noble birth, and still easier vows, as a house of noble canonesses. Each canoness had her own house, which she might share with a real or adopted niece. An engraving survives [477] which shows the agreeable if secular dignity of the buildings, with a modest chapel as their centre, as designed at this time by Desarnod but never executed.

2. THE OLD ORDERS

The medieval Orders of Grandmont, Fontevrault and Prémontré all followed versions of the Augustinian Rule. The houses of all of them suffered even more heavily in the wars than the urban Augustinians, since they were often out in the open countryside.

[1] The basement was finished in 1764 and the dome begun in 1778, and the church was incomplete when Soufflot died in 1780. The lantern was put up in 1790. See Damiron.

[2] Rather later Avril, in *Temples anciens et modernes*, writes at length on St Paul's.

[3] For a section see Ward, II, 457; for other plates, Blomfield, II, plates CLXXVI ff.

[4] Dargenville, I, 484-5. The pediment was filled by sculptures of the Triumph of the Faith by Coustou, which were removed at the Revolution.

[5] See Evans in *Arch. Journ.* XCVIII (1942), 82.

The Order of Grandmont had fallen into decay when about 1630 the Abbé de Tautal attempted a reform and restored the buildings of the mother-house. The abbey had many small dependent houses, which had suffered much in the wars, and the reform could only be slowly extended. In 1643 Dom Georges Barnay, his successor as abbot of Grandmont, summoned a Chapter General to restore the regular observance.[1] Fresh statutes were passed,[2] but a second reform had to be attempted by the prior Dom Charles Frémont, about 1650, with a doctrinal emphasis on the Trinity and on the hidden life of Jesus at Nazareth. By the end of the century it had been accepted by five houses.

By 1732 the church and abbey buildings of Grandmont were in a bad state of repair, and a complete rebuilding of the monastic quarters was planned, and that of the church completed in 1768; it followed the plan of Sainte-Geneviève, cruciform with a central cupola.[3] In 1768 the Government demanded a fresh reform, or the closure of the Order. In fact the abbot decided in 1769 to refuse to take in further novices, and the Grandmontains gradually disappeared. Its last abbot died in 1787, when only five monks were left, and the relics of the abbey treasury were given to the churches of the neighbouring parishes, where for the most part they still remain. I have failed to find any of their buildings that survive;[4] a fine seventeenth-century altar from Grandmont with a large sculptured panel of the Supper at Emmaeus remains in the church of Saint-Junien.

The Order of Fontevrault had fallen on evil days in the fifteenth century, and various attempts at reform had failed. In 1502 a new and stricter Rule was imposed by Renée de Bourbon. At her death in 1534 there were a hundred and sixty nuns in the abbey (and a hundred and fifty monks in the brother-house, for it was a 'double' monastery) and thirty-four reformed houses in the Order. Some of these were sacked later by the Huguenots, and Fontevrault, after a long siege, fell in 1562. None the less, the monastery and the Order survived, thanks to the continuance of royal patronage; at the end of the eighteenth century Fontevrault could still boast two hundred and thirty nuns and sixty monks.

At Fontevrault the chapter-house was rebuilt in the years following 1540,[5] in two aisles of three bays with a vaulted ceiling with lantern finials. Its rich decoration incorporates the interlaced LL of the abbess Louise de Bourbon. There are reliefs of St Benedict and St Scholastica, in memory of Fontevrault's partly Benedictine past, of St Nicolas and of the emblems of Francis I. The walls were painted between 1565 and 1570 with frescoes of the Passion of Christ, by Thomas

[1] Hélyot, *Dictionnaire*, II, 422. The church of Mailhac, Haute-Vienne, has an arm reliquary of St Apollinaire with the arms of Abbé Barnay.

[2] They decreed that there must be a porch or narthex to the church where the monks could speak to strangers.

[3] It was destroyed at the Revolution.

[4] The sixteenth-century stalls from the Grandmontain house of La Haie-aux-Bons-Hommes still survive in the church of Saint-Maurille at Les Ponts-de-Cé.

[5] Some sculptures are dated 1541 and some 1547; the pavement bears the date 1543.

Pot, to which portraits of abbesses have later been added. A splendidly sculptured doorway [478] leads to the cloister, of which all but the south walk is also of the time of Louise de Bourbon [480]. It has a lierne vault in the Gothic taste, combined with round arches on classical pilasters. The buttresses are formed as twin Ionic columns on a high stylobate. The washing fountain, now destroyed, was adorned with five leaden figures representing the baptism of Christ. The dorter and the novitiate above were planned with a series of rooms each holding five beds. Externally the building is an early and interesting attempt to integrate a cloister into a Renaissance façade [483, 484], with an archway and a decorated *lucarne* to centre it.

Once again in the eighteenth century royal influence encouraged building at Fontevrault. In 1738 the arrival of the daughters of Louis XV as pupils necessitated some new building;[1] it is very simple, but has a fine ironwork balustrade to the stairs. The Order, like many others, embarked upon fresh building in the middle of the eighteenth century. The whole *enceinte* was rebuilt, doubtless to house the lay servants, with various handsome gateways and a main door [481, 482]. New buildings were erected inside [485] and the whole was completed by a most elegant lodging for the last abbess [486].

The reformed Augustinian Order of Prémontré survived the wars better than most, doubtless because its houses were concentrated on the eastern side of France. Even the Premonstratensians, however, had to be reformed in Lorraine about 1617,[2] and offered some resistance to the process. Their wealth was notorious, and they suffered as much as the Benedictines from the King's nomination of commendatory abbots. By 1770 sixty of the ninety-two Premonstratensian houses in France were given *in commendam*, and only twenty-five had abbots and priors elected from and by the community.

It is significant that the remaining Premonstratensian churches are none of them of sixteenth-century date. In the seventeenth century the Premonstratensian house of Saint-Martin at Laon was to some extent modernized by the addition of Louis XIV panelling that winds in and out of its medieval chapels and round the medieval choir [487]. The early foundation of Laval-Dieu in the Ardennes was drastically modernized towards the end of the seventeenth century. A fairly simple façade in brick was added to the church, with a gable framed in volutes; a fine gateway was set up, together with a classical cloister that survives only in part; and the choir [488] and sacristy were enriched with good *boiseries*.

Far away near the Spanish frontier the Premonstratensians built Sarrance, in a wild and lovely site. It was, and is, a pilgrimage church on the road to Spain, and it seems likely that the rebuilding may date from the years after 1659, when the

[1] Bossebœuf, p. 85.
[2] Hélyot, *Dictionnaire*, III, 277. The reformed Premonstratensians were installed in Paris in 1662. Some remains of their buildings will be found in the right-hand court of 11 rue de Sèvres, but the doorway, which existed till recently, has now disappeared.

Peace of the Pyrenees gave a new importance to the route. The church has an unusual western tower [487] with six incurved sides each with two niches, surmounted by a lantern. Inside, the richly decorated nave, veneered with Pyrenean marble, is dominated by a fine baldaquin over the high altar [490]. The cloister [491], a haven of peace in the wild mountains, is simply designed but is unusual in being on two floors.

The church of Saint-Jean-des-Prémontrés at Amiens was rebuilt in 1714. It stood gutted but upright in 1944;[1] nothing now remains.

The great Premonstratensian church in the Faubourg Saint-Honoré was built at the expense of Anne of Austria in 1661, but was rebuilt in 1719.[2] It had been designed by Dorbay for a different site and was never considered successful. The façade was more like the central pavilion of a château than the entrance to a church. A Doric door had niches for statues on either side; the next storey had bas-reliefs on either side of a central trophy.

A few Premonstratensian monastic buildings of the early Renaissance survive. The sixteenth-century Premonstratensian house at Ardenne in Normandy is extremely simple, in the Northern manner, with a curved slate roof; the entrance arch is vaulted with a tardy Gothic vault. Nicolas le Saige, Prior of the Premonstratensian house of Saint-Martin-de-Laon between 1613 and 1645, built himself a lodging, with a little pavilion in the garden [492]—a lodging that is charming yet not magnificent. At Prémontré a block of buildings, pilastered and pedimented [494] and a gateway [495] look as if they belonged to the years following Colbert's decree; they are certainly earlier than 1734, when they were illustrated in Hugo's *Annales*.[3]

The buildings of the important Premonstratensian house at Verdun[4] were badly damaged in the Second World War. In the course of their restoration by the Commission des Monuments Historiques a leaden plaque came to light recording that their rebuilding had been undertaken in 1686 on the designs of Thomas Mordillac.[5] A room, probably the chapter-house, that, in spite of its Louis XIV panelling, has a rib vault of an early sixteenth-century type, is dated 1698. The buildings form a delightfully complete Premonstratensian ensemble of the end of the seventeenth century [496, 497]. The cloister [500] had had its arcades blocked by later windows; its arcade is low pitched; to the courtyard it has rusticated piers and spandrels. The refectory [501] maintains the tradition of a central line of columns. The monks' quarters on the first floor, approached by a handsome staircase with a rather severe wrought-iron balustrade, survive to give a pleasant idea of the circumstances of monastic life about 1700 [498, 499]. The Abbot's lodging[6] is unexpectedly simple.

---

[1] Methuen, p. 121. He also notes two cloisters of the same date.
[2] Hautecœur, III, 121, 735 and fig. 568.   [3] Vol. I, plate not numbered.
[4] Now Palais de Justice and Préfecture.
[5] I owe this information to the Société Philomathique de Verdun.   [6] Now a hotel.

In the eighteenth century the Order of Prémontré began to rival the Benedictines in splendid buildings, and like the Benedictines boasted architects among its members. Père Nicolas Pierson was both architect and painter. The abbey of Sainte-Marie-Majeure at Pont-à-Mousson[1] was built under his direction in 1711, a few years before the province became French.[2] The church is remarkable for the great height of its Corinthian pillars, which take a high rounded vault. The very narrow aisles, lit by a great window in each bay, are nearly as high as the nave. The rounded apse has three great windows. The showy façade is still Mannerist in style; its lofty attic masks the two towers behind. The library, some fifty feet long, is finely panelled, with a wrought-iron gallery, a decorated ceiling, and a marquetry floor, all rather in the Swiss or Austrian style. The parlour has a vault rising from ornamental brackets; in its decoration, as in that of the refectory, there are rocaille elements. The staircase has a fine balustrade [493]. Père Pierson also designed the convent of Jean d'Heurs, in the Meuse, between 1731 and 1742.[3] This is a magnificent building planned as a long block with a central staircase, with two projecting wings [502]; the longer contains the chapel (now altogether spoilt) and the sacristy, between the main block and a pavilion that was probably the abbot's lodging. The whole inner face is arcaded to form a glazed cloister [504]. The north side is centred by a pediment; the *piano nobile* has a good wrought-iron balustrade. Relief is given to the façade by terminal pavilions that achieve a giant order of Doric pilasters. The bay nearest the entrance has a carved keystone with the Holy Spirit in clouds and rays. The entrance hall is nobly colonnaded [503]; the staircase is enriched with splendid wrought-iron balustrades and gates [506]. The woodwork of the sacristy and the adjacent passage is notably rich [505].

Pierson is also credited with the façade of the church of Étival in the Vosges, an ambitious composition with two towers in four storeys of superimposed orders, Doric, Ionic, Corinthian and Composite. They were never finished. The medieval nave was not replaced, but its rib vaults were strangely bedizened with ornamental plasterwork and a classical frieze of stucco was put in below the clerestory.

Another Premonstratensian architect and painter was Père Eustache Restout. He became prior of the abbey of Mondaye, which he completely rebuilt [507]. The rich and elegant chapel has its choir, rather atavistic in style, adorned with oval paintings of Old Testament subjects and large statues of the Evangelists. The nave arcade has oval medallions in the spandrels, that have never been filled [509]. The great feature of the interior is the splendid decoration of its altars. The façade [508] recalls that of Saint-Thomas-d'Aquin at Paris; the rest of the exterior is of an almost Romanesque simplicity [512, 513].

---

[1] Now the hospital.

[2] The Premonstratensian house of Saint-Joseph at Nancy (not then French) rebuilt its monastic quarters between 1723 and 1758; a monk, Père Louis Hugo, supervised the work, with the advice of Mique, a professional architect. The rounded pediment reappears, but the *ensemble* lacks elegance.

[3] Hautecœur, III, 326 gives 1742; but the sacristy is dated 1731.

His monastic buildings betray the influence of the Norman Benedictine style. The cloister[1] [510], which seems always to have been intended for glazing, has flat pilasters and heavy archivolts on the outside. The exterior of the main block of monastic buildings has a notably lofty windowed arcade on the ground floor [514]. The great double staircase is noble in its simple lines and its rich balustrade of scrolling ironwork[2] [511]. Restout may also have advised on the remodelling of the buildings at La Lucerne and have designed buildings for the Benedictine nuns of Cordillon, near Balleroy.[3]

In 1719 splendid buildings were designed for the mother-house of Prémontré at the order of the abbot Lucas de Marin.[4] They are designed as three sides of an oblong quadrangle, but do not touch at the angles; the western block has a wing at right angles to the north[5] [515]. The central block, containing the abbot's own quarters, has a great bowed projection in the centre,[6] surmounted by a curved pediment [516]. It is in fact the smallest block, but is greatly prolonged by wings on either side. The side blocks, at right angles to this, are nearly identical but differ a little in the design of their pediments [517, 518]. All three blocks have giant Ionic pilasters through their three storeys, with high-pitched roofs. The abbot's block is notable for its use of the traditional Benedictine high arcade on the ground floor; it here shelters two tiers of windows. A fine staircase with a wrought-iron balustrade rises in a great unsupported spiral in an oval cage. This splendid *ensemble* was completed by Marin's successor with an elaborate grille right round the front of the abbey, running from one urn-surmounted pier to another, and completing the resemblance of the whole to a monastic Versailles. Only in 1757 did the abbot begin to think about rebuilding the church[7] and then it was too late.

Already the Augustinians other than nursing sisters were doomed. In 1771 they were ordered by the Commission to reform. The Premonstratensians none the less continued to build, and erected the nave of the church and two pavilions at Licques, near Boulogne, as late as 1783. The church has an extremely plain interior, astonishingly adorned with Gothic rib vaults; the pavilions look like the *communs* of a small château.

[1] One side has disappeared.
[2] Its double form may be compared with that of the Hôtel Salé at Paris, 1656; illustrated Hautecœur, II, 128. Lenôtre, p. 34, says that the Paris convent of Prémontrés, destroyed in 1889, also had a fine staircase with a wrought-iron balustrade, and one of about 1760 survives in the buildings of Saint-Martin de Laon.
[3] Hautecœur, II, 717 n. 1. They no longer exist.
[4] *Ibid.* III, 324. Prémontré is now a lunatic asylum.
[5] The library wing, with cells above, was destroyed at the Revolution.
[6] It offers a comparison with the Hôtel de Beaumont at Valognes: Hautecœur, III, 207, fig. 158.
[7] The old church was destroyed at the Revolution.

3. THE NEW ORDERS: NURSING

The new life that flowed through the Church of France in the seventeenth century tended to develop in the direction of learning, of contemplation, or of active service to the community in nursing or teaching, or in the care of orphans and penitent women. A number of communities of nursing sisters, following the Augustinian Rule, were founded in the seventeenth century.[1] The most famous, the Sisters of Charity, founded by St Vincent de Paul at Châtillon-lès-Dombes, and established at Paris in 1633, was a society that gradually became a community and grew to be a Congregation, with four hundred and twenty-six houses in France at the Revolution.[2] Their work was so useful that the Consulate recognized their Order as early as 1801, but they spent little on art and architecture.[3]

A second Order inspired by St Vincent de Paul, the Servantes des Pauvres Malades, or Sœurs Grises, has left even fewer visible memorials.

The Hospitalières de Saint-Alexis at Limoges were founded in 1657, and continued their work even after the Revolution.[4] The Hospitalières de Dijon et de Langres were founded by a canon of Saint-Étienne de Dijon in 1688[5] and the Augustines du Saint Cœur de Marie d'Angers took over the hospital at Saumur about 1700.[6] The Brothers Hospitallers of St John of God,[7] a Portuguese Order, were given a house in Paris by Marie de Médicis in 1601; they are remembered in history not for the beauty of their buildings but because they insisted on each patient having a room to himself and being kept clean. Their chapel, rebuilt in 1613–21, has been destroyed. Their Hôpital-de-la-Charité was rebuilt in 1733 by Cotte; some of his buildings remain.[8]

At the same time some ancient nursing communities were given new life by reform. The ancient Order of Nuns Hospitallers of St John of Jerusalem in France[9] was reformed by one of their members in 1618 and was able to found two new houses. Choir nuns had to prove their nobility of descent and to provide a thousand crowns of dowry, but the Order had the support of a 'noble' community of men, the Knights of Malta. A more ordinary community reformed at the time was that of the Sœurs de la Charité de Nevers, an old foundation devoted to nursing the sick,[10] which was reformed under Oratorian inspiration in the years after 1680. By 1725 they had seventy establishments all over France and in 1789 were planning to rebuild the mother-house on a grand scale.

---

[1] The Council of Trent had renewed the ancient precepts affirming the duty of bishops to provide for the poor and to supervise hospitals, and several of these Orders came into being under episcopal encouragement. For a general account of nursing architecture see Hautecœur, I, 564 ff.

[2] Hélyot, *Dictionnaire*, I, 810.

[3] Their Paris house has been destroyed; their house at Évron [243, 246, 247] was originally Benedictine.

[4] Hélyot, *Dictionnaire*, IV, 91.   [5] *Ibid.* II, 29.   [6] *Ibid.* IV, 105.   [7] *Ibid.* IV, 614.

[8] The Augustinian 'Frères de la Mort', founded in 1620 with two classes of monasteries, one urban, of which the members tended the sick and prisoners and buried the dead, and one rural, composed of hermits, were suppressed by the Pope in 1633 (*ibid.* III, 252).

[9] *Ibid.*   [10] Hélyot, *Dictionnaire*, IV, 232.

The tendency to group monasteries into Congregations exerted an influence even on the communities serving a single hospital, which tended to develop affiliations. The Hospitalières de la Charité-Notre-Dame, for instance, founded at Nancy in 1624 to serve and nurse poor women, spread to cover no less than eleven provincial towns, together with two Paris houses.[1] Similarly, the Hospitalières de la Miséricorde de Jésus of Dieppe, an early Augustinian foundation, after their reform in 1627 increased to seventeen houses in France.[2] The Sœurs Hospitalières de Saint-Thomas de Villeneuve, founded in Brittany in 1661, became the mother-house of an Order in 1711, with thirteen Breton houses and a fourteenth in Paris.[3]

Sometimes such an increase led to a change of Rule; the Religieuses Hospitalières de Loches, founded early in the seventeenth century, about 1629 became an enclosed Order, with thirteen houses in central and southern France.[4] Exceptionally the Augustines of Laon, who founded a Paris house in the rue du Cherche-Midi in 1634 became affiliated to the Benedictines in 1669 through the influence of Marie de Rohan, abbess of Malnoue.

A number of new foundations combined the work of nursing with that of teaching,[5] and others were formed to look after orphans.[6] Most of them seem to have followed a version of the Augustinian Rule. The Sœurs de Notre-Dame de Charité de la Refuge,[7] founded at Caen for the care of penitent women in 1641, had a house in Paris[8] and three branch houses in Brittany. They followed the Augustinian Rule, and were closely linked with the Visitandines. Early in the eighteenth century they established a house next to the hospital at Besançon.[9] Its elegant chapel survives [519, 520]. It was designed by Nicole and erected between 1739 and 1745. It is on an oval plan; the façade of the nuns' quarters is curved to provide a graceful approach. The oval nave is surmounted by an elaborate dome with painted medallions; the detail of the architectural decoration, of the trophies on the walls and of the organ loft is all so good as to suggest a noble or even a princely donor. Most of these minor foundations, indeed, depended on external inspiration; the Filles du Bon Pasteur, founded in 1688 in the rue du Cherche-Midi to help penitent women, was under strong Sulpician

[1] *Ibid.* I, 823. Nancy was of course not French at this date. [2] *Ibid.* IV, 568.

[3] *Ibid.* III, 909. The Paris house was not shut at the Revolution because of the value of its work.

[4] *Ibid.* II, 783.

[5] For example, the Sisters of St Charles, founded at Le Puy in 1624 by Just de Serres, bishop of Le Puy; the Hospitalières de Saint Joseph, founded at Le Puy by Père Médaille in 1650; the Sisters of the Cross, founded there in 1673; the Sisters of St Charles, founded at Lyons by the Abbé Démis in 1680; the Sisters of St Paul, founded at Chartres at the end of the seventeenth century; and the Sisters of Notre-Dame-de-Fourvières, founded in 1732 at Usson.

[6] For example, the Paris Filles-Orphelines founded by Mme Cossart in the rue Notre-Dame-des-Champs in 1658, and the Communauté des Orphelines du Saint-Enfant Jésus, founded in the rue Rabaud about 1700.

[7] Hélyot, *Dictionnaire*, II, 1137.

[8] *Ibid.* II, 812. It became a kind of prison for women of dissolute life.

[9] See Tournier, p. 326.

influence and the Sisters of Providence of Évreux were inspired by the Eudistes. The Madelonnettes, or Filles-Repenties, founded at Paris in 1618 under Salesian influence, were allied with the Visitandines from 1629 to 1671; then lived under Benedictine influence until 1677; then under Ursuline inspiration; and then were allied with the Hospitalières de l'Ordre de la Miséricorde de Jésus. In 1720 the house was reformed from an Augustinian nunnery at Tréguier; and then in 1743 was taken over by the Augustinian Dames de Saint-Michel, until the Revolution brought it to an end. Their church—now destroyed—was built in 1680; it had a chapel built on the model of the Holy House of Loretto.[1] The church held a picture of the Descent from the Cross painted by Le Brun.[2] So little remains of the buildings of these Orders—in any case not rich and devoted to service—that no consecutive account of their art and architecture is now possible.

4. THE NEW ORDERS: TEACHING

The Church recognized in the sixteenth century that one of the duties of its religious Orders was teaching, and this became one of the great tasks of the Society of Jesus.[3] The Jesuits were not alone in their work, but their chief co-adjutors, the Brothers of the Christian Doctrine, were members of a congregation not under vows. Another teaching Order, the Frères des Ecoles Chrétiennes, was founded in 1680 by a canon. Its members did not teach Latin, but chiefly occupied themselves with free elementary schools for boys. They had a house in Paris after 1688[4] and after 1705 one at Saint Yon in Rouen. Nothing of their buildings survives.

The Jesuits did not teach girls, but inspired a number of Orders of nuns, mostly following the Augustinian Rule, to undertake the work. The first teaching Order of women was that of the Ursulines, founded in Italy by St Angela de Merici. The work began as a lay enterprise, but was undertaken in community in 1535; statutes, based on the Augustinian Rule, were approved in 1540. The Ursulines were at first not enclosed, but accepted the cloister in 1574.

The Order was introduced into Avignon by Mère Françoise de Bermond in 1574,[5] but her teachers did not form a community until 1596, under the influence of the founder of the Pères de la Doctrine Chrétienne.[6] The Ursulines quickly spread all over France; each house was independent, though under the visitation of the bishop of the diocese. They were grouped in the Congregations of Paris, Arles, Lyons, Bordeaux, Dijon and Tulle. By the end of the eighteenth century there were more than eighty houses in the Paris Congregation; eight in that of Arles, over a hundred in that of Bordeaux, including a few houses in Flanders and

[1] Piganiol de la Force, IV, 60. [2] Jouin, p. 480. [3] See below, p. 124.

[4] At first near Saint Sulpice; after 1722 in the rue Notre-Dame-des-Champs.

[5] Hélyot, *Dictionnaire*, III, 757.

[6] Their friendly relations with the Jesuits are attested by a design for their Dinan house by Martellange. (See Moisy in *Bull. de la Soc. de l'hist. de l'art français*, 1850, p. 73.)

Canada; seventy-four in the Congregation of Lyons; twenty-seven in that of Dijon, twenty in the Congregation of Toulouse and seven in that of Tulle.

Three Ursuline convents still show remains of architecture earlier or little later than 1600: Auxerre, Brive and Espalion.[1] They already show the characteristic of Ursuline architecture: an extreme simplicity dictated by economy. Any display that was found possible was concentrated on the chapel. At Auxerre the tympanum over the door represents a familiar medieval theme modified to their use; the Virgin stands with outspread arms with the nuns of the community sheltering beneath her cloak. At Espalion[2] [521] two doors are rich enough, but the arms upon them commemorate a wealthy benefactor, though the device of the pierced heart above the outer pillars is Ursuline. At Vesoul their chapel served as a theatre after the Revolution; it was damaged during the war and has lately been demolished. The school survives: a modest building round a courtyard [522, 523] that offers to the outside world only the niches round its door to distinguish it from an ordinary town house.

The Order was brought to Paris by Blessed Marie de l'Incarnation (Madame Acarie)[3] in 1612, because she realized that women who had no vocation for the contemplative life of the Carmelites might none the less do good work as teachers. A little remained until lately of the nuns' quarters[4] of the house she founded, but nothing of the church, built in 1627. Of the house of Ursulines founded at Langres in 1614 nothing remains but some walls of the nave of the chapel and the lower part of the façade. This had double Corinthian columns on either side of the door, supporting a rather heavy entablature. At Eu only a gateway remains [524] in Flemish style. At Quimper the Ursuline buildings of 1621 survive as a part of the barracks;[5] the church has been destroyed. The stone buildings have three floors and an attic in the high-pitched roof; they are simple, dignified, and some thirty years out of date.

The Ursuline cloister at Montpezat,[6] dating from 1631 [525] is of a monumental simplicity. That at Château-Gontier [526–9], a house founded in 1630,[7] is much more elegant, with amusing detail in the Ionic capitals of its pilasters; it is, however, traditionally modest in the timber vaults of the cloister. It was never quite completed. The church (dedicated to the Trinity) is no less elegant, with rusticated pilasters on the façade, a statue of the Virgin in a richly garlanded niche over the door, and instruments of the Passion sculptured in the gable. The

[1] Their house at Bourg-Saint-Andéol, now the Hôtel de Ville, has to all intents and purposes been rebuilt, as has that at Montbrison. There are said to be some remains of their house at Vézelay, built in 1624, but I have not been able to identify them.

[2] M. Bousquet, Archiviste en Chef of the Rouergue, kindly tells me that the church was blessed by the Vicar-General Thomas Regnoust in 1674: it looks to be rather earlier. The church, rib-vaulted with chapels with transverse vaults, was destroyed in 1953.

[3] Piganiol de la Force, VI, 134.

[4] On the site of the Musée Pédagogique.

[5] Because of this I was forbidden to photograph them, on grounds of security.

[6] Now the Collège.   [7] Still belonging to the Ursulines.

interior has an elaborate coved vault, partly in *trompe l'œil*, and rich sculptured decoration.

The rusticated pilasters reappear on the façade of the Ursuline chapel at Abbeville, built in 1642 and gutted in the last war [530]. Like the door at Espalion, it bears the Ursuline device of the pierced heart; it appears above the two niches of the façade. The Ursuline convent built at Bar-sur-Aube in 1643[1] is extremely plain. It has no cloister, but an arcade between the two wings that project at right angles to the main block. The staircase has elaborate stone balustrades in the Mansart manner;[2] the wings are shut off by handsome iron grilles.

A similar stair recurs at Bollène[3] [532]; it is, indeed, as characteristic of Ursuline houses as balustrades of wrought iron are of Benedictine monasteries. The buildings at Bollène are extremely simple but for two good entrance doors [531]. At Aix-en-Provence the familiar staircase reappears under a finely decorated plaster ceiling. The church, dating from 1647, has an unusually rich façade [534]. The simple conventual buildings are set back behind a curtain wall and gateway [533]; the cloister is low pitched, with heavy ribbed vaults. Their church survives at Angers a good deal modified; its door seems to be a stock piece by a local sculptor [535]. At Luçon their chapel has an arcaded outer wall [537]. Inside, it is like a tunnel, relying for effect on a painted wooden vault, now much faded, and a fine retable.

The convent at Quimperlé[4] dates from 1652 [539, 540]. It is again designed as a long block with projecting wings, with a cloister on the inner side.[5] The chapel [536] sticks out to the east; it is small and simple, with a façade in two storeys linked by volute buttresses. The glazed cloister has a simple coved ceiling.

The remains of the Ursulines' house at Pontivy[6] offer no feature of interest but the widely spaced windows of the cloister, which suggest its use as an indoor recreation room.

The Ursuline house at Avallon, dating from just after the middle of the century, is on the street side like any provincial town house, and resembles one but for the statue under a pediment in the attic. To the garden it presents a long terrace and a monotonous long block of buildings: perfectly fitted to its purpose, but without distinction.

At Poligny their church, of 1678, has been destroyed, but their cloister of 1673 [538] remains, with its small windows, its high roof and its Tuscan columns, as the archetype of a poor but honourable women's house. There is a clumsy Virgin and Child in a touchingly elaborate niche over the entrance. At Selles-sur-Cher

[1] Now the Hôtel de Ville, theatre and post office.
[2] Cf. the staircase at Maisons (Blunt, *Art and Architecture*, plates 97 and 100). The Ursuline house at Eymoutiers, Haute-Vienne, always plain, is now greatly modified.
[3] Now the hospice.   [4] Now the Ecole primaire supérieure de Jeunes Filles.
[5] The large but much modernized Ursuline buildings outside Charlieu seem originally to have been in the same style.
[6] Now part of the Collège.

the Ursulines' house[1] is not much more pretentious, but includes an earlier church which they took over and renovated. Their house at Saulieu,[2] much altered, seems always to have been plain and domestic, with a high-pitched roof in the local style; that nearby at Semur-en-Auxois[3] is no less plain; the cloisters are vaulted, but the walls are perfectly plain but for a very simple wall-fountain. At Bayeux the building[4] [541] is a little more ambitious; it might be taken for that of a small Benedictine house. The convent of the Ursulines of Beaune[5] built in 1697 [542] followed the usual plan of a three-sided cloistered building; the cloister and the buildings over it are of notable simplicity. At Flavigny the stone buildings contain a cloister and a little chapel, forty-eight cells, infirmary, children's quarters, common rooms and guest rooms; there is no library.[6] Everything is simple and domesticated.

The Ursuline house at Gournay-en-Bray, built in 1683, has a sharp gable of patterned bricks like the neighbouring houses; there is nothing, indeed, to distinguish it from a private residence. Even a country convent like that at Charlieu tended to the same simplicity, without any pretensions towards looking like a château; while the larger town convents, like those at Montferrand[7] and Saint-Hippolyte[8] [543–5] achieve a barrack-like austerity. Recent remodelling as a Cité Administrative has left hardly anything of the large convent of the Ursulines at Dijon, but a plan,[9] by its architect Guillaume Tabourot, of 1643 [546] shows its quadrangular form, and indicates that in a teaching Order the church was apt to be much smaller than in other convents.[10]

The Ursulines were conscious that their role in the field of girls' education was analogous with that of the Jesuits, and sometimes Jesuit influence brought richness even into Ursuline architecture. At Vannes their chapel, built between 1688 and 1690[11] [547] has a façade much like that of the Jesuit church in the same town, with the inscription: 'Sacrae Familiae, 1690.'

The earliest surviving Ursuline chapel in the grand style is that at Bourges[12] designed by Mansart in 1695[13] in the Ionic order, with a central dome, a nave of two bays, a shallow transept and a semicircular apse: a reduced version of Notre-Dame-des-Victoires [548, 549].

[1] Now a hospital. [2] Now cornmarket and Salle des Fêtes.

[3] Now École d'Apprentissage.

[4] Now the Collège and said to be threatened with rebuilding. There is a good plain barrel-vaulted chapel; the nave has Ionic pilasters, the apse Ionic columns. [5] Now Hôtel de Ville.

[6] Plans for the very plain Ursuline house at Loches (Arch. Nat., Plans N III, Indre-et-Loire 33) are interesting since they name the purpose of each room.

[7] Now the Gendarmerie. It follows the usual three-sided plan, with a screen to the street.

[8] Now Gendarmerie and École communale. A foundation stone gives the date 1700.

[9] In the Bibliothèque Municipale. Designs for the decoration of the chapel ceiling survive in the Archives départementales. (See H. Ronot, in *Bull. de la Soc. de l'hist. de l'art français*, 1956, p. 90.)

[10] At Auxonne, too, the Ursulines' convent has been drastically remodelled and little is left but some furnishings in the chapel. [11] Now part of the Collège François-Xavier.

[12] Now the Salle des Pas Perdus of the Law Courts.

[13] A plan will be found in Deshoulières, p. 54.

Ursuline building continued in the eighteenth century. At Langres their house[1] was rebuilt after the fire of 1746, and was not yet finished in 1762. The lower part of the façade of the church survives [551]; it looks as if it had never been completed. The residential quarters are plain and dignified [552]. Their chapel at Arbois in the Jura, designed by Attiret in 1764,[2] is a good example of a chapel that retains dignity with a minimal emphasis on its pediment [553].

At Quimper[3] [550] there seems never to have been a cloister; the buildings, in two storeys with an attic, are extremely simple but well proportioned. At Dinan the buildings[4] are lower and no less plain; a pediment is, indeed, their only adornment. The chapel survives in part as the theatre. At Seurre their chapel[5] [554], which dates from 1776, is even more modest; as at Arbois it is architecturally integrated into the scholastic quarters.

Their most important foundation of the time was the 'Couvent de la Reine'[6] which Queen Marie Leczinska founded at Versailles for the education of the daughters of the nobility, after the death of her father had left her with a heritage. She invited Ursulines from a house in Lorraine founded by an *aumônier* of her father King Stanislas, and established them temporarily at Compiègne. She summoned Richard Mique, the famous architect of King Stanislas at Nancy, to Versailles in 1766, expressly to design the convent.[7] The Queen died in 1768, before the building was far advanced, but the work was completed by her daughter Madame Adélaïde. It was opened by Louis XV in September 1772.

The essential of the plan is the setting back of the convent from the road, behind a great central court. This has houses (presumably for *pensionnaires*) on either side of a one-storeyed screen to the street, with a handsome gateway on to the road [555]. At the end of the court is the chapel, a Palladian building[8] planned as a Greek cross with three apses and a peristyle [556, 557], with a complicated roof combining an ovoid dome and three half-domes. The four Ionic columns of the front are crowned by a pediment with a group representing Charity. The wall under the colonnade has to the left a statue of St Chrysostom, surmounted by an oval medallion of Fénélon, and to the right a statue of St Augustine and a medallion of Bossuet. Over the door a relief by Deschamps shows the Queen and her daughters receiving the little girls whom their mothers bring to them. In the interior, the semicircular halls on either side of the choir were intended one for the nuns, and one for their pupils. The interior is very rich, with a coffered ceiling.

---

[1] Now the Collège Diderot. [2] Now the Syndicat d'Initiative and Hôtel de Ville.
[3] Still a girls' school. [4] Now the Justice de Paix.
[5] Now a school, and divided into two floors. [6] Now the Lycée Hoche.
[7] He submitted three schemes. The first was very modest, for a limited number of boarders only. This was extended to include a chapel with an oval choir and classrooms for day-girls. Finally, the present plan was adopted; it included quarters for the Queen like those of Marie de Médicis at Le Val-de-Grâce, but even simpler.
[8] See Hautecœur, IV, 78.

On either side of the chapel is a courtyard with a projecting forepart that frames the chapel and held the parlours. Behind this are three courts, that on the right intended for the nuns, that on the left for the boarders, and the central one for classrooms. All the riches of the building are concentrated on the chapel; the conventual and scholastic quarters [558, 559] have an elegance of proportion but are otherwise extremely simple. Even the cloisters and galleries have no ornament whatever, and the stairs have plain balustrades. A three-sided court with a cloister lies on either side of the chapel and behind these are the true cloisters.

The Versailles house was the last fine Ursuline building to be erected in France; it is fitting that it still fufils an educational purpose.

The next teaching Order of women to be founded, the Dames de l'Assomption,[1] did not increase beyond their original convent. In 1622 a community of poor widows, founded in 1264, was reformed under the Augustinian Rule, and united with another Augustinian house in the rue Saint Honoré at Paris, to direct a school and to organize retreats. They had only a small chapel until 1670 when a new one was designed for them by Charles Errard, Director of the French school at Rome[2] [560, 561], whence he sent the plans.[3] It was carried out in his absence by a contractor who made some modifications in the plan (Fig. 4); in the result Piganiol de la Force[4] found the proportions bad and the details incorrect. The church, which still survives, is entirely dominated by a great dome on a drum, borne on four arches with coupled Corinthian columns. Round the dome are four recesses in the arches, with sham and real windows. The entrance is framed by three columns in a peristyle on either side of the door, with a pediment above. The influence of the Pantheon is evident, but Errard did hardly enough to adapt it to the needs of a nunnery, beyond including the hanging garlands that the age of Louis XIV thought appropriate to feminine use.

The modest Augustinian Order of the Filles de la Croix,[5] founded as a secular congregation at Roye in 1625 to teach girls dressmaking, became monastic and enclosed in 1642. It had a Paris house and about a dozen houses in the provinces. The Ordre du Verbe-Incarné, again, grew out of a small society of friends in Lyons, and formally became an Order devoted to teaching in 1633.[6] It had six houses, but flourished little after the seventeenth century.

The Filles de la Présentation were founded by Nicolas Sanguin, Bishop of Senlis, in 1626, and were recognized in 1630. Jesuit influence had much to do with their foundation; they followed the Augustinian Rule. A part of their Senlis convent survives.[7]

---

[1] Sometimes called the 'Nouvelles Haudriettes'. (See Hélyot, *Dictionnaire*, II, 447.)

[2] See Blomfield, pp. 105 ff. Hautecœur (I, 506) says that their cloister was built in 1632 by Louis Métazeau.

[3] A set of plans survives in Arch. Nat., Plans N III, Seine 387 (1–8).

[4] III, 17.   [5] Hélyot, *Dictionnaire*, p. 1170.

[6] It was one of the Orders to which the King sent Protestant women for imprisonment.

[7] Now part of the Collège Saint-Vincent.

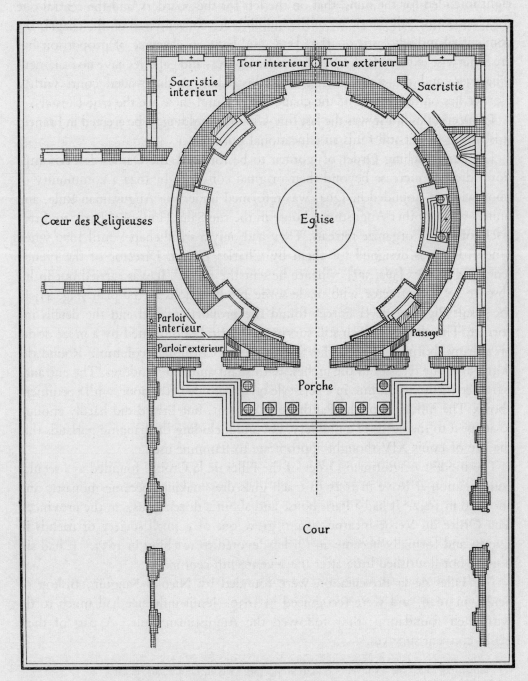

Fig. 4. Church of the Dames de l'Assomption, Paris.
Plan of church, by Charles Errard, 1670. (After Blondel.)

The Filles de la Providence, again, founded in 1638 for the education of female orphans, spread, and had seven houses; the nuns were not enclosed.[1] Of few of the minor Orders[2] are there now any visible remains. The Filles de Sainte-Geneviève, an Order devoted to teaching poor girls, commonly called Mira-miones, after their part-foundress Madame de Miramion, are still represented by the south façade and the staircase at 47 rue de Pontoise, Paris, where they came in 1691. The Communauté de Sainte-Aure, founded in Paris in 1687, moved at the end of the century to the rue Neuve-Sainte-Geneviève, where Madame du Barry was educated under their care; their house, 27 rue Lhomond,[3] has a good façade on to the court [562], that shows the influence that the buildings of Saint-Denis might have even on a small nunnery.

5. THE NEW ORDERS: CONTEMPLATIVE

The practice of mystical devotion was one of the springs of life in the French church in the seventeenth century, and inspired the foundation of a number of Contemplative Orders of women. Several of these followed versions of the Augustinian Rule, which, since it demanded fewer hours in choir than that of St Benedict, and did not necessarily require manual labour, left more time free for meditation. The cult of the Perpetual Adoration of the Sacrament, first officially recognized in France in 1592, inspired the Sœurs de l'Adoration Perpétuelle du Saint-Sacrement,[4] established in 1659 near Toulouse. Their founder was a Dominican monk, but the sisters followed the Augustinian Rule. Again we know nothing of their buildings or their devotional art.

A second Contemplative Order, that of the Visitation,[5] was founded in 1610 at Annecy in the Duchy of Savoy by St François de Sales, Bishop of Geneva, and Ste Jeanne de Chantal. The Order was intended for women unfitted to endure physical austerity. It was at first meant to be a Congregation; after a year's training in the cloister its members were to visit the sick poor and to follow the contemplative life. In 1616, at the request of the Archbishop of Lyons, it became an enclosed religious Order, following a mitigated version of the Augustinian Rule.[6] The Constitutions of 1616, drawn up by St François de Sales, admit every reasonable relaxation; there is to be no rising at night, no sleeping on hard surfaces, no perpetual abstinence nor prolonged fast. On the other hand the

---

[1] The Paris house specialized in boarding elderly ladies; Madame de Montespan retired there in 1681 and Madame du Deffand about 1755.

[2] Others were the Filles de l'Institution Chrétienne of Paris, founded in 1657; the Sœurs de l'Instruction de l'Enfant Jésus, founded at Le Puy in 1667 by the Sulpician Tronson; and the Sœurs des Ecoles Charitables du Saint Enfant-Jésus (Hélyot, *Dictionnaire*, IV, 423), founded at Rouen by Père Nicolas Barré. It later had a teachers' training college in Paris.

[3] Now the Institution Lhomond.   [4] Hélyot, *Dictionnaire*, IV, 58.

[5] It should not be confused with the small Contemplative Order of the Sisters of the Visitation of St Mary, founded at Le Mans in 1634. This also had a house at Le Puy founded in 1659.

[6] The visitation of the sick had to be given up, as it was not compatible with enclosure.

possessive instinct is sternly mortified. There is to be a strict vow of poverty, and every sister is to change her room and bed, her medals, crosses, rosary and pictures every year, so that there may be nothing that she considers her own. Every minute of the day, but for two hours' recreation spent in common, is to be filled by work or spiritual exercises. The Mother Superior may hold office for two terms of three years, but is then ineligible for further office.

The writings of Ste Jeanne de Chantal, including her letters, seem to show her, for all her competence and good sense, totally uninterested in buildings. Her first and second houses at Annecy (not then in France), were, however, both of considerable dignity; the chapel of the first, built between 1614 and 1618, has a façade in two storeys, the upper framed in volutes which are echoed in the buttresses of the aisled nave. The second (of which the chapel has been rebuilt) has an unusual plan with a circular foyer under a dome in front. The Order seems quickly to have arrived at a formula congruous with its aims: an ideal of monastic buildings of an extreme simplicity allied with a church attractive enough externally to induce the passer-by to enter, and calm and austere enough within to encourage meditative devotion in him as in the nuns who worshipped there. The stress lay on individual devotion, and there was no great need for a large nave.[1]

The Order spread rapidly into France. It reached Lyons in 1615, Moulins in 1616, and Bourges in 1618, to reach Paris in the following year. By the death of Ste Jeanne de Chantal in 1641 it included eighty-six houses; at the centenary of its foundation in 1710, a hundred and forty-seven.

The earliest surviving French Visitandine house is that of Sainte-Marie-d'en-Haut at Grenoble, dating from 1622. Its site on the slope of a hill did not encourage an ambitious scheme, and the building is of a devastating plainness. The chapel is hardly richer externally,[2] though it has a pair of carved wooden doors [563] with some decorative pretensions. The Visitandine house at Saumur still has its chapel, with a charming Renaissance door [564] and a dome resting on Corinthian pilasters that frame plaster figures of the Evangelists inside the church. The conventual buildings are simple but well proportioned. They may be compared with those of the original quadrangle at Tours[3] [565] later completed and enclosed by more splendid buildings. The chapel has vanished; it was designed by a Feuillant, Dom Bernard Louis, in 1656.

The Order first achieved architectural splendour at its Paris house, designed by François Mansart and erected between 1632 and 1634 at the expense of the Commandeur de Sillery. Nothing remains of the conventual buildings, but the chapel, dedicated to Notre-Dame-des-Anges, remains as a Protestant church [566]. The dome rests on four arches, between which are Corinthian pilasters supporting

---

[1] The chapel of the Visitandines at Avignon (not then part of France) was designed by des Noyers de la Valfenière in 1631-8. It has a charming façade, and a wall arcade in the interior in place of lateral chapels. The nuns' choir was in the transept. (Hautecœur, I, 634.)

[2] I have not been able to enter it.   [3] Now the Préfecture. (See Hautecœur, II, 716.)

the cornice: a plan said to have been inspired by Santa Maria della Rotonda at Rome. The dome is surrounded by one large apse, lit by an oval lighting dome in the Roman manner, and decorated with handsome and heavy plasterwork, and three lesser apses, with galleries for the nuns. The whole occupies an almost square site with the choir to the west; the apsidal chapels are at a higher level than the central space.

In the same year of 1632 Mansart designed the residential buildings for a lesser Visitandine house at 193 rue Denfert Rochereau, built by the same benefactor.[1] It was designed in two great blocks with pediments as their only adornment. Nothing remains. Destruction has likewise fallen upon their house founded in 1651 by Queen Henrietta Maria on the site of the present Palais de Chaillot.[2] Both the church, begun in 1687, finished only in 1704, and the monastic buildings were planned by Dorbay and revised by Jacques II Gabriel. The church[3] was planned with a nave of only one bay and a circular choir, off which the chapel of St François de Sales, which served as the private chapel of the English royal family, opened on one side, and the nuns' choir, preceded by a transept bigger than the nave, on the other.

The Visitandine house, founded by Ste Jeanne de Chantal at Moulins[4] and built after 1634 and before 1655[5] by a widowed Duchess of Montmorency, retains some of its ancient glories, including a fine crystal reliquary given by St François de Sales. Yet the general impression is one of great austerity. The double pilasters of the chapel façade rise to a plain pediment: the walls are of brick worked in chequers [567]. The chapel is Jesuit in plan if not in style, with two side chapels on either side, a very shallow transept, and a separate nuns' choir. The Doric cloister is plain and heavy [568]. The rather later cloister in their house at Nantes is equally plain; it has a wooden roof and a rather squat arcade on octagonal pillars.

A similar note of austerity, expressed in the local architectural idiom, is evident in the Visitandine house in the rue de la Dalbade at Toulouse [569]. The façade gives entrance through a little courtyard in red brick to the very plain Doric colonnade that masks the entrance to the chapel.[6] The Visitandine chapel at Caen, built between 1636 and 1668, was unusually designed as a Greek cross;[7] it does not survive.

The Moulins buildings afford a striking contrast with what remains of the house of Visitandines at Nevers [571] (though this too has Burgundian lozenged brickwork): a contrast that indicates the independence of the houses within the Order prescribed by the Constitution. The Nevers house was built between 1639 and 1649. The façade strangely combines a certain Baroque massiveness of

[1] Hautecœur, II, 21.
[2] See Vauthier. Bossuet's *Oraison Funèbre* for her was made here in 1669.
[3] Hautecœur, II, 721.   [4] Now the Lycée Banville.
[5] Hautecœur ascribes it to Claude Collignon, 1648, and says it was finished by Joseph Lingré in 1676.
[6] Considerably altered.   [7] Hautecœur, II, 721 n. 7.

proportion and relief with a complication of delicate and rather out-moded ornament. The whole, indeed, suggests the work of a Flemish architect, influenced perhaps by the Jesuit Novitiate at Paris. We are reminded that it was the nuns of this house who inspired Gresset to write:

> Les petits soins, les attentions fines,
> Sont nés, dit-on, chez les Visitandines.

The nuns' quarters at Nevers have been destroyed,[1] but others of much the same date survive at Avallon [570] which do not appear to be much later than the foundation of the house by Hélène de Chastellux in 1646. They follow the Ursuline three-sided plan. The Visitandines at Paray-le-Monial inhabited a rather similar building, with a very plain cloister [573]; it is famous as the home of Blessed Marguérite Alacoque.

The Visitandines of Rennes built their chapel between 1659 and 1661 with an interesting façade. The buildings and cloister of the Visitandines of Rouen, built between 1681 and 1691, survive[2] with many modifications. The cloister was notably plain, and the nuns' quarters are, as at Moulins, in the simple contemporary style of town architecture. The Tulle house still has buildings[3] of the late seventeenth century, with a bell-cote over the curved central pediment. Their house at Montbrison,[4] built between 1700 and 1702, has a domed chapel on a cruciform plan: it is clearly modelled on Mansart's Paris church in its façade and dome [572]. The conventual buildings,[5] now gendarmerie and prison, are of slight architectural pretensions.

The conventual buildings at Mamers[6] are in secular style and resemble any fine Breton town house; they seem to date from the second half of the century.

The house at Le Mans,[7] erected between 1730 and 1737, was designed and planned by a Visitandine nun, Sœur Anne-Victoire Pillon. The monastic buildings are extremely plain;[8] the church is unusually rich. The façade [574] is elaborate and Corinthian; it is definitely an applied 'frontispiece' rather than an integral part of the building. The interior has a system of Corinthian pilasters and a high narrow gallery with a good ironwork balustrade that recalls that in the Cathedral of Angers. The roof has cross-vaults in bays. The apse is a rectangle with slightly rounded corners and very elegant plaster decorations [575]; the western end is filled with a charming singing gallery. Sœur Anne-Victoire Pillon must have been a gifted amateur; the interior, indeed, is a remarkable work to be designed by anyone not a professional; perhaps she had good advice.

[1] The Visitandine house at Montpellier, built by J. Bonassier between 1650 and 1656 (Hautecœur, II, 881), has also perished.

[2] Now the Musée des Antiquités.   [3] Now the hospice.

[4] Now the Palais de Justice. (See Hautecœur, II, 721 n. 4.)

[5] The room for the jury has Louis XV decorations.   [6] See *Cong. Arch.* (1910), I, 291.

[7] They survive with some modification as the Palais de Justice.

[8] Now mairie, library and gendarmerie.

At Auxerre the Visitandine church survives [576]; its fine façade is massive in form and extremely delicate in detail. It contrasts with that at Limoges[1] [577], which is an Ionic building with twin pilasters on either side of the door, a heavy rosette and triglyph frieze, and a garlanded pediment. It is domed within. Their chapel at Montbrison[2] is equally domed. A parlour in the house has good Louis XV decoration.

The last convent built by the Visitandines before the Revolution was the great one at Nancy,[3] built between 1780 and 1783 by J. D. Antoine. Pavilions and central block are both pedimented, and there is a great porch to the street. The chapel is a domed rotunda with a pedimented façade and a richly ornamented door.

The Visitandine house of the Faubourg Saint-Antoine in Paris was near the Bastille. On 14 July 1789 the surging mob that had captured the prison broke into the convent while the community was gathered together in adoration of the Sacrament. The Superior sent the nuns into the cloister and faced the mob alone. In face of such quiet and helpless courage the Revolutionaries were disarmed, and the Visitandines remained undisturbed, save for a few official visits, through the first Saturnalia of the Revolution.

[1] Now a barracks.
[2] The chapel is now the Palais de Justice; the monastic buildings serve as gendarmerie and prison.
[3] Now the Lycée.

CHAPTER IV

THE CARTHUSIANS

Charterhouses, dedicated to the contemplative life, tended to be set in quiet countrysides, or, at their most urban, outside the gates of cities. Consequently they suffered severely in the endless warfare of the fifteenth and sixteenth centuries. At Laon, indeed—that city of monastic Refuges—the Carthusians of Val-Saint-Pierre built a Refuge of their own; the earlier part is a handsome town house of about 1540, the later a plainer building dated 1613 [578].

In spite of the tribulations of war, the Carthusians—who have never needed reform in their long history—maintained their discipline. A third compilation of their statutes, with some stricter liturgical rules, was published in 1509, and a fourth in 1581.

There was a little Carthusian building in the sixteenth century; since their members had always occupied single cells, there was no shift from dorters to individual lodgings to be provided for. The Charterhouse of Gaillon was founded by Cardinal Georges d'Amboise in the sixteenth century. The great cloister had four walks each with fifty small arches; the lesser had windows of stained glass. Nothing remains.[1]

The Charterhouse of Notre-Dame-des-Prés, at Neufville near Montreuil, was so poor that at the end of the Middle Ages the monks lived on a pittance of bread and water.[2] The house was badly damaged in the war between Henry VIII and Francis I, but was restored in 1571, and a little later an elaborate entrance was erected between two pavilions joined by a shell-headed doorway; such a doorway, that emphasized the seclusion of the monks from the world, became a characteristic of the later Charterhouses.

The Carthusians, the oldest Order devoted to the contemplative life, took on new energy in the mystical atmosphere of seventeenth-century France. New houses were founded and old ones rebuilt,[3] and in several cases built with a certain splendour.

The monks of the ancient Charterhouse of Castres had moved to Toulouse in 1569, and their church (now Saint Pierre) was begun in 1602 and consecrated, unfinished, in 1612. It was the first church in Toulouse to have a dome. The interior was planned with six chapels in the nave entered from a plain arcade on piers and joined by a narrow passage. The cloister is of stuccoed brick, with plain stumpy pillars and a tiled penthouse roof [579, 580].

---

[1] A stone Entombment group from the church is now in Notre-Dame-des-Andelys.
[2] I. A. Lefebvre, p. 116 et passim.
[3] By the middle of the eighteenth century there were some seventy-five Charterhouses in France. (Hélyot, *Dictionnaire*, I, 863.)

The Carthusians of Villefranche-de-Rouergue[1] enjoyed the use of one of the largest Gothic cloisters in France, and had little need to build; but about 1600 the brethren built a pavilion like a manor with a steep-pitched roof, and a richly carved door; it looks as if it had been intended as a Prior's residence.

The Carthusian tradition of handsome entrance gates was maintained at the Charterhouse of Val-Bénite at Villeneuve-lès-Avignon, which had two: one [581] of 1649 and another, a little lighter in style, of the second half of the century [582].[2] Charles des Brosses described the house at the height of its beauty: 'On entre dans la Chartreuse par un portail d'ordre composite, d'une bonne architecture: une allée composée de quatre rangs de colonnes et de grands mûriers entremêlés ensemble, conduit à la maison.... Les cloîtres sont gais et propres. Dans un coin, une perspective représentant une chapelle, où un chartreux dit son bréviaire, mérite d'être remarquée.'[3] A massive temple-like building, that housed the cloister fountain, survives; it is said to have been designed by the des Noyers de la Valfenière.[4] Nothing remains of the church but the splendid altar, now in the Collégiale of the town [584], with a relief below the altar of Christ in the tomb.

The buildings of the Paris Charterhouse were mostly medieval, but the great cloister was rebuilt between 1649 and 1652, and the church was given new *boiseries* in Ionic style about 1680.[5] Their type may perhaps be imagined from the pulpit of 1681 from the Chartreuse of Val-Saint-Pierre in Thiérache now in the cathedral of Laon [583].

Notre-Dame-des-Prés had its great cloister and cells rebuilt in 1667, with a chapter-house, Chapelle des Morts, refectory, kitchens, library, parlour, bishop's rooms, guest-houses and apartments for the prior, procurator and coadjutor.[6] All were rather secular in style, of brick with stone quoins and ornaments. The little cloister was rebuilt in the same style in 1726, and in 1742 the rebuilding of the church was begun, with a façade in brick and stone and a great open porch.

The most splendid Carthusian *ensemble* of the seventeenth century must once have been that of Saint-Bruno de Bordeaux, built in 1665. The entrance gate [585] is particularly elegant in its proportion. The same lofty elegance character-izes the façade [586]: a heavy line divides the lower storey, which is broken by six flat pilasters with Corinthian columns, irregularly grouped; a very plain pilastered storey then plays the part of a giant frieze. The gable that masks the high roof continues the pilasters to twist into richly foliated volutes and swags at the top. The buttresses are each formed as a pedimented wall. The whole is elegant and unusual. The interior is tunnel-like; the *trompe-l'œil* architectural

---

[1] Now a hospice and hospital, which when I went to it did not welcome visitors.
[2] Charvet, *Les des Noyers*, p. 143.   [3] *Lettres d'Italie*, letter II, 1739.
[4] The family of amateur architects, the des Noyers de la Valfenière, came from Avignon to work at the Charterhouse from 1643 to 1646, but their designs for the façade were not executed. (Charvet, *op. cit.* p. 143.)
[5] Piganiol de la Force, VII, 223.   [6] I. A. Lefebvre, p. 162.

paintings of its wooden barrel roof are now too faded to be effective, but the apse is still noble with the marbles and sculpture of extremely high quality set up in 1672 [587].

So splendid a Charterhouse,[1] even if it chiefly survives in records, provides a striking contrast with such a modest one as that of Apponay [588], now a farm. The chapel is medieval, but the living quarters were rebuilt late in the seventeenth century. The monks were housed in cells off a corridor. The prior's room is hardly distinguishable from the rest. There is no suggestion of luxury anywhere. The stair is of solid logs of wood, with squarish wooden balusters.

The Charterhouse of Vaucluse in the Jura[2] has a fine gateway [593] but the buildings round its courtyard are of the utmost simplicity [589]. No more was needed on so superb a site, high up on the bank of the river, with sheltering arms of forest behind.

The Charterhouse of Montrieux in the Var[3] still has its two cloisters. The great cloister is like that of the many Benedictine houses, with quadrangular piers and a groined vault. The lesser cloister is more unusual with elegant Ionic columns to support the heavy beams of the roof.

We know little of the Charterhouse of Saint-Julien de Rouen save that when it was rebuilt in 1686 the monks invited a Protestant architect, Nicolas le Genevois, to design it, and continued to employ him even after the revocation of the Edict of Nantes.[4]

At the Charterhouse of Le Liget the steep descent to the monastic buildings was made the excuse for a whole series of gates: first a splendid entrance [592], with a relief of St Bruno on one side and one of Christ in the wilderness on the other; then, after a courtyard of outhouses, another [590] leading to parallel groups of buildings, perhaps for visitors; and finally to the Charterhouse itself [591] and its medieval church.

The Carthusian Order retained its vitality in the eighteenth century, and expressed it in much building.[5] Even the splendid chapel given by the dukes of Burgundy to the Charterhouse of Champmol near Dijon[6] had its walls in 1762 stuccoed in classical style up to the windows, with Corinthian pilasters between niches. The old great cloister of the fourteenth century was pulled down and replaced by one in heavy classical style. A new library was built in 1775, and a new lesser cloister begun in 1787, but it was pulled down before it was finished. All that remains is a range of simple buildings.

The greatest surviving Carthusian church of the eighteenth century is that of

---

[1] Fine stalls and woodwork of about 1700 also survive from the Charterhouse of Val-Dieu near Mortagne, in the churches of Notre-Dame de Mortagne and Loisy, and very good bookcases and cupboards from the house are in the municipal library of Alençon.

[2] Now a private house. [3] Much was rebuilt in 1843. [4] Hautecœur, II, 718.

[5] The Charterhouse of Bosserville, Meurthe-et-Moselle, was built just before the province became French.

[6] Monget, II, 380. It is now a lunatic asylum.

Saint-Bruno-des-Chartreux at Lyons,[1] with decorations executed in the main by
Frère Delamonce. It was built between 1733 and 1736.[2] The central dome [594]
was designed by Soufflot a year or two later. The nave and choir are of almost
equal length. The heavy metope frieze of the interior [595] is adorned with roses
and doves and heads of angels like those of the first chapel at Versailles. There are
angels, garlands, scrolls and shells on the vaults and on the frames of the altar-
pictures, to give a rhetorical flourish in the Jesuit manner. The choir is far more
austere [597]; its richness lies in the stalls by Van der Heyden and Marc Chabry,
carved between 1744 and 1747 [596, 599], with royal emblems to recall the foundation of the monastery by Henri III, and delightful cherubs. It is narrower than
the nave, with the sacristy fitted in on one side and the cloister on the other. The
altar [598], designed by Soufflot between 1743 and 1749, is double-faced in the
Carthusian manner, with one side towards the nave and one to the choir. Even
the sacristy has noble woodwork and a fine altar-piece.

The Charterhouse of Auray in the Morbihan[3] [602] is less rich and less urban,
but is none the less a fine building. The chapel of 1730 [603] is finely adorned with
Louis XIV *boiseries*; the cloister [600, 601] is decorated with copies, made in 1742
by a local artist, of the famous paintings of the life of St Bruno in the Carthusian
cloister at Paris. The furnishing is rich, with a good wooden screen and an altar
on either side of its door, each with a pedimented retable. The high altar in the
choir has an elaborate baldaquin with a curved frieze broken by a great glory.
The Charterhouse of Rodez was rebuilt in 1749; at the Revolution it was turned
into a stud-farm, as which it still serves. All has been gravely disfigured; the
portal remains, surmounted by a shell-headed niche.

An additional richness was given to the earlier church of Saint-Pierre-des-
Chartreux at Toulouse [605, 606, 608] by the decoration of the crossing by Cammas
late in the eighteenth century in pale yellow marble and many tones of grey
and white [604], and by the splendid double high altar [607] erected in 1785.

The Carthusians, indeed, lived through the eighteenth century with less dis-
turbance than other Orders, since in 1766 the Charterhouses were exempted from
the compulsory dissolution of small monasteries.

The Charterhouse of Gaillon was destroyed by fire in 1764, and was rebuilt by
Hélin, a Paris architect, in time for the church to be dedicated in 1776. An
engraving [610] shows a traditional two-storeyed façade to the church, only en-
livened by an improbably spindle-shaped spire and two blocks of monastic buildings of the severest kind, ending in two equally austere pavilions. This was, so

---

[1] The history of its plans is complicated. The first were by Jean Magnan. After his death in 1640
Martellange seems to have taken over. (See Bib. Nat. Est., Ubqa, fo. 120; Bouchot, 'Martellange',
p. 30.) Then Delamonce took over; his drawings are in Archives Dep. du Rhône, fond des Chartreux,
tiroir 79. Soufflot seems to have been invoked at the last moment.

[2] Plan in *Cong. Arch.* (Lyons) 1935, p. 152; Hautecœur, III, 373.

[3] Now an orphanage. The fine stalls from the chapel are now in the chapel of the nuns of the Père
Eternel at Auray.

far as I know, the last Charterhouse to be rebuilt, but new buildings at Le Liget were at least planned in 1787.

The Carthusians, for all their monastic humility, struck the onlooker as men of breeding. Marmontel, writing in 1788[1] said 'Les Chartreux ont parmi les moines l'air de grands Seigneurs. Leur orgueil est poli, tandis que l'orgueil d'un Bénédictine est prononcé'. Such airs did nothing to help them when Revolution came. Chateaubriand has left a description of the Charterhouse of Paris after the Revolution.

I saw a church of which the roof had fallen in, of which the lead had been torn from the windows and the doors barred with planks. Most of the rest of the monastic buildings no longer existed. For a long time I walked among the black marble tombstones, thrown down haphazard; some were broken to pieces, others still showed the remains of epitaphs. I went into the inner cloister; two sloe-trees grew therein among tall grass and broken stone. On the walls were paintings of the life of St Bruno, half effaced; a sundial remained on one of the gables of the church; and in its sanctuary instead of that hymn of peace that there used to rise in honour of the dead, I heard the shriek of the saw which a workman was using to saw up the tombstones.[2]

[1] XII, 43.   [2] *Le Génie du Christianisme*, Bk v, chap. 3. I translate.

CHAPTER V

THE CARMELITES

A second important Order, mainly contemplative in intention, that had many important houses in post-medieval France was that of the Carmelites. The Order suffered a good deal in the wars of the early fifteenth century and had to be reformed in 1466. A certain number of independent houses survived but they were poor and built comparatively little in no very distinguished way. Among their few surviving monuments of the sixteenth century are a double door at Saint-Amand-Montrond [611] that charmingly combines Gothic and Renaissance elements, and the bell tower at Pont-l'Abbé in Brittany.

In 1502 a new Carmelite Congregation was formed with its centre at Albi, under an Italian prior. This contained only four or five houses; they suffered in the Wars of Religion and the Congregation was dissolved by the Holy See in 1584.

It seemed as if the history of the French province of the Order was at an end, but it was not so. The influence of St Teresa of Avila brought so much new life to the Carmelites, both men and women, that the Order was rejuvenated even outside Spain. Madame Acarie (Blessed Marie de l'Incarnation) read the life of St Teresa in 1601, and, after having a vision, introduced a version of her reformed Rule at 'Le Carmel Reformé' in the rue Saint Jacques in 1602, with the help of some Spanish nuns. A house at Pontoise was founded in 1605, one at Tours in 1608, one at Rouen in 1609 and one at Bordeaux in 1610. At her death in 1618 they had fourteen houses.

The Discalced Carmelites of the reform of St Teresa (followers of a rule as essentially eremetic as that of the Chartreux) were introduced into France in the women's house of Notre-Dame-des-Champs in 1604, which was quickly followed by houses for men at Tours and Nantes in 1610.[1] It eventually had sixty houses for men and sixty-nine for women in France. A third reform, that of the Observant Carmelites, also on the model of St Teresa, was started at Rennes in 1604, with some help from the Discalced Carmelites. One reform was accepted by about twenty-five houses of men, four of women and two hospices.[2] They included five houses in Paris: one in the Place Maubert and one in the ancient convent of the Billettes [615, 616].[3]

Notre-Dame-des-Champs owned the Gothic church of a priory of Marmoutier, from whom they acquired the site and buildings. They built a heavy classical

---

[1] Hélyot, *Dictionnaire*, I, 660, 661. Nothing remains of the last two.
[2] *Ibid.* I, 700.
[3] Originally that of the Frères de la Charité.

porch to precede it, and remodelled the church in 1613[1] with side chapels, each separated from the next by a little oratory. There was no true transept; a small choir preceded the altar and retable, behind which lay the nuns' choir.[2]

Their convent has been altogether rebuilt but for the prior's house, of which the heavy Doric entrance door remains.[3] All the buildings were low and simple,[4] but the church was once one of the most brilliant in Paris.

The church of the slightly later house of Saint-Joseph-des-Carmes at Vaugirard, built between 1628 and 1630,[5] survives [612–14]. It was one of the earliest domed churches in Paris; the dome is still tentative and clumsy. The façade, which has been considerably modified, is best studied in Marot's engraving. The interior is dark and gloomy, in spite of its extremely rich decoration in the Spanish style. The door to the choir may stand as an example [614]. The monastic buildings,[6] begun in 1613 and finished in 1616,[7] were, on the other hand, very plain.

Of the Carmel of the Incarnation, near Le Val-de-Grâce, the house to which Louise de la Vallière retired from the world in 1674, nothing remains but a bay of the cloister in a coal yard [623]. Its church, destroyed in 1797, had been richly decorated soon after 1604 by the Prioress Mère Madeleine de Saint-Joseph,[8] under the inspiration of her devotion to the Holy Sacrament. Its central feature was a magnificent high altar; Marie de Médicis ordered Guido Reni to paint an Annunciation to hang above it.[9]

Meanwhile the provincial houses of Carmelites[10] were acquiring buildings of considerable splendour.[11] The convent at Ploërmel was rebuilt, after its destruction by the Huguenots in 1592, in the opening years of the seventeenth century.[12] The chapel has been rebuilt in the nineteenth century; the cloister of 1604 is very simple, with round arches on columns [617]. A second cloister, rather later in date, has classical pilasters and a frieze that seem to betray the influence of the Norman Benedictine style [618]. A drawing by Martellange, dated 1616,[13] shows the cloister of the Carmelites at Lyons as having walks in no less than three storeys, two arcaded and one plain.

In 1622 the first stone of the chapel of the Carmelites at Toulouse[14] was laid by Louis XIII and Anne of Austria [619]. It keeps the memory of Gothic vaulting in

[1] Hautecœur, I, fig. 447.
[2] Hautecœur, I, 557, says that plans were sent from Spain according to the Teresan formula.
[3] 24 rue Denfert Rochereau.   [4] Erlau, pp. 57 ff.
[5] Hautecœur, I, 670. Plans of the Carmelite house in the rue Chapon, dedicated in 1625, survive in Arch. Nat., Plans N III, Seine 292 (1–11).
[6] Parts survive in the Institut Catholique.   [7] Piganiol de la Force, VII, 277.
[8] See Vanuxem, p. 57.   [9] The picture is now in the Louvre.
[10] I have found nothing remaining of the houses at Saintes and Bordeaux, both established before 1620.
[11] The house at Nancy, not then French, was built in 1626; it was notable for its rich decoration (Pointel, II, 277). The Carmelite church at Dôle, Jura, also appears earlier than its cession to France.
[12] It is now a school.
[13] Bib. Nat. Est., Ub 9a, p. 119.
[14] Now a Museum of casts in the École des Beaux Arts.

the roof. The whole was transformed between 1746 and 1750 by paintings that cover both walls and vault. The fine red brick cloister is typical of Toulousain rather than Carmelite style.

A vision of St Anne appeared several times to a pious villager at Auray in 1624–5, and ordered him to rebuild the ancient chapel in the village. In 1627 the Observant Carmelites took it over, and it was greatly enriched by Anne of Austria and Louis XIII. The church has been rebuilt, but the delightful cloister remains [620, 621]. Its deep walks are completely amalgamated in the façade, which has a broken pediment to centre it on every side. The angles are bridged by pavilions with rounded pediments. The Carmelites of Vannes[1] rebuilt their cloister in 1632, with an arcade on massive square pillars [622]; the same scheme was followed at Beaune.[2] The chapel there[3] [624] has an agreeable gabled façade with a rusticated ground floor, a triglyph frieze and an elegant central window between decorated niches. Their Dijon house[4] has a fine baroque portal of 1630, with a statue of the Virgin and three saints in niches. A far simpler version of the theme exists in a battered state at Dieppe,[5] in the Carmelite chapel built in 1636.

The 'Grands Carmes' of Marseilles transformed their late Gothic church in the seventeenth century by installing in its side chapels grotto-like sculptural compositions of the Adoration of the Magi, the Crucifixion, and the Baptism of Christ. The general effect is of an aquarium.[6] At the same time a new entrance was erected, with a heavily rusticated arch surmounted by a niche with a pleasing statue of the Virgin and Child [625].

The Carmelite church at Conflans[7] has an elaborate façade with a classical base surmounted by a plain storey with a great lunette window over the door, sweeping up into a semicircular head that rises into the roof. At Rennes only the entrance remains; at Carpentras only a door.[8] At Poitiers [626] the façade centres on a round window, as it does again at Auch[9] [627]. At Chartres[10] [628] the oculus has been changed into a round-headed window. The Discalced Carmelites of Arles had a chapel begun in 1673, that relied for its elegance upon its richly sculptured friezes in the Provençal style [630, 631].[11] It might be mistaken for a Jesuit church.

[1] See *Cong. Arch.* (1914), p. 49. It is now a sports centre.
[2] Now a timber yard. It may be compared with the former cloister of the Carmelites at Mâcon. (See Rozet, plate 14.)
[3] Now École Communale.   [4] Now the Caserne Brune.
[5] Now a Protestant chapel; I was unable to visit the interior.
[6] It has so far proved impossible to get satisfactory photographs, which I much regret.
[7] Hautecœur, I, fig. 606.
[8] Now in the wall of the Palais de Justice.
[9] Now the library.
[10] Now the Cour d'Assises.
[11] They may be compared with those in the Jesuit church in the city. Of the Carmelite chapel only the façade and side walls remain, as a storehouse of the Ponts et Chaussées. The cloister and refectory built in 1750 have disappeared. I owe my thanks to Monsieur Rouquette, Keeper of the Musée Réattu, for this information.

The Carmelites of Rouen had their church of Saint-Romain built between 1676 and 1730 [629] with a traditional use of niches on either side the door. The interior is remarkable for its use of coloured marble to give an effect of shrine-like splendour.

At La Rochelle only the entrance to the church survives; its splendid and unusual shell above the door [632] suggests that a remarkable building has been destroyed. The cloister [633] is also unusual in style and proportion. Both now serve as part of the fish-market. Another Carmelite building of this time is that of the Discalced Carmelites' church at Tulle[1] [634] designed as an octagon with three chapels on either side the apse, with two smaller chapels on either side the entrance. The octagonal cupola is surmounted by a lantern; the façade maintains the niche tradition. At Besançon the monastery of Carmelites, rebuilt between 1685 and 1695, eleven years after it had become French, has been destroyed but for its splendid sad cloister[2] in the Tuscan style [635].

Meanwhile the chapels of the Carmelites were being rebuilt or beautified. The Paris house in the Place Maubert was enriched in 1683 by a grand high altar designed by Jacquin, formed of an angular peristyle of four groups of rich marble columns, to enshrine statues of the Transfiguration.[3]

Carmelite building continued in the eighteenth century. Their church of Saint-André at Lille [637], built in 1702, combines Ionic and Corinthian orders on its two-storeyed façade, with statues of St Peter and St Andrew in niches. The interior barrel vault rests on plain columns with Corinthian capitals; the choir is Ionic, and richly decorated with sculpture. An amazing baroque pulpit [636] betrays the nearness of the Flemish frontier.

In 1720 the Discalced Carmelites of Clermont-Ferrand built an elegant little church,[4] planned as a rotunda with four hemi-cyclic chapels. The lofty drum of the dome rises above the façade [640]. It is notably more elegant than the chapel built at Vannes between 1734 and 1737[5] [638, 639].

The church of the Observant Carmelites in the rue des Archives at Paris, built by Frère Claude in 1755, survives as a Protestant chapel.[6] Its rather flat façade, framed in Doric pilasters, is of a stock type; its interior is remarkable for the substitution of a colonnade of Ionic pilasters for an arcade; it is continued round the apse. There is a single balustraded gallery round the nave. Piganiol de la Force[7] thought it so badly designed and proportioned that it made him regret its Gothic predecessor. The oval choir particularly shocked him.

The last important Carmelite building before the Revolution was that at Saint-Denis[8] [641] designed by Mique in 1767 to the orders of Madame Louise,

---

[1] Now the Passage des Carmes. [2] Millin, IV, 22. [3] Hautecœur, II, 724.
[4] *Cong. Arch.* (1924), p. 60. It is near the Michelin works, in which it may soon be absorbed.
[5] *Ibid.* (1914), p. 419.
[6] The house on the right of it has a stair with a good ironwork balustrade that looks conventual.
[7] IV, 315. It had formerly been the church of the Billettes.
[8] Now Justice de Paix.

daughter of Louis XV, who made her profession there and became its prioress. It is basilican in plan but aisleless, with a fine cupola 'à rosaces' on four Ionic columns, and a nave with a denticulated frieze on Ionic columns. The peristyle of the façade is also Ionic, and has a sculptured pediment. When it was erected the good days of the Order were already over. J. B. Blondel, writing in 1771,[1] recommended that all the houses of the Order should be united in one convent. The churches of the others should become parochial, and squares and markets should be built on their gardens.

[1] *Cours d'architecture*, II, 324.

CHAPTER VI

THE DOMINICANS

The Order of Friars Preachers flourished in the sixteenth and seventeenth centuries, for it was able to make up in the Americas for what it lost in Europe. Their French houses, nearly all within cities, suffered less in the Wars of Religion than the Benedictines in the country, and the Franciscans just outside the city walls. The Order had fewer houses and perhaps carried less weight in France than in Spain or Italy, but it maintained the high standard of academic scholarship that it had reached in the later Middle Ages. Jean Baptiste Gonet, a Dominican of Toulouse, was one of the most brilliant of the neo-Thomist philosophers; and Jacques Goar, of the Dominican convent of the Annunciation in the rue Saint-Honoré, was one of the greatest of the French Hellenists. Joseph Galien, a Dominican of Avignon and Le Puy, was a distinguished meteorologist, physicist and writer on aeronautics; the Montgolfiers seem to have derived much of their inspiration from his work.

The Order, more united than the Franciscans, had been reformed at the end of the fourteenth century, and was divided on small points of discipline into the Dominicans proper and the reform 'de l'Étroite Observance' of the Jacobins; both, however, accepted the same Rule. The Order included a certain number of convents of women in France; of these Poissy, Aix-en-Provence (Saint-Barthé-lemy), and Montfleury in the Viennois were 'noble' houses and only admitted women who could prove their noble descent for several generations. In the seventeenth century two small Orders of Dominican nuns were added to them. The Congrégation du Saint Sacrement or Sacramentines[1] was instituted by Père Antoine le Quien in 1635, as a Dominican reform towards poverty and the strict observance of the ancient Rule. They began at Avignon, and acquired five houses in Provence.[2] The Filles de Saint-Thomas were called to Paris in 1626 by the Duchesse de Fronsac, and established in 1642 in what is now the Place de la Bourse. The convent of the Filles de la Croix, established in 1641 in the rue de Charonne, was their only daughter-house.

The medieval tradition of the Dominicans remained unbroken, but in their work of preaching to the cities they found fresh rivals in the new Orders of the sixteenth century, and most of all in the Society of Jesus. As a consequence the Dominican Order increased little, and was not under the necessity of undertaking much building.

The Dominicans were rather slow to adopt the Renaissance style in their

---

[1] Hélyot, *Dictionnaire*, III, 425. They were broken up at the Revolution, but survived secretly and re-appeared under Napoleon.   [2] Thirteen nuns from their convent at Bollène were executed in 1794.

architecture. Their church of Saint-Cannat in Marseilles, built about 1528, has a Gothic nave. They do not, indeed, seem to have built much in the sixteenth century;[1] the Wars of Religion were hard on the provincial cities that were their stronghold. The house of Dominican nuns at Pont-l'Évêque rebuilt their monastic quarters in the most rustic Norman style[2] [642].

By the seventeenth century, however, the Order had a few architects among its members.[3] Père Alexandre Richard from 1658 to 1660 directed the construction of the Lyons house, designed by Lepautre; Père François Romain built several churches, though not for Dominican convents.

The house of Saint-Laurent at Le Puy was rebuilt early in the century, but what survives is undistinguished. The Dominicans of Saint-Sever-sur-l'Adour rebuilt their monastic quarters at this time[4] [643]. They are unusual in being of brick, only relieved by brackets and a few details of sculptured stone, but they follow the same tradition in their proportions and pilasters as those of other cloisters of the time. At Pamiers their house[5] was rebuilt after its destruction by Calvinists; the chapel has been greatly modified, but the cloister survives [645].

The seventeenth century saw activity in the Paris houses of Dominicans. The Jacobins built a house in what is now the rue du Marché-Saint-Honoré in 1611. The entrance[6] had a central arch and two lesser ones for foot passengers, surmounted by statues of St Dominic and St Catherine of Siena. The church was notable for its simplicity; externally the façade had no decoration but an *œil-de-bœuf*, and the sides nothing but a cornice and a row of windows, with dormers in the roof. Another house, in the rue Saint-Dominique in the Faubourg Saint-Germain, was set up in 1631, with a small temporary chapel, and, as has been said, three houses of Dominican nuns were built. Nothing remains of any of these buildings.

The Dominicans in the Faubourg Saint-Germain rebuilt their church of Saint-Thomas-d'Aquin on the designs of Pierre Bullet in 1682-3, to serve as that of the Novitiate General of the Order.[7] The church, aisled and cruciform, is richly designed with Corinthian pilasters, but is not especially distinguished. The choir was rebuilt in 1722[8] and the façade only in 1770, on the designs of the Dominican Frère Claude [646, 647]. Blondel[9] severely criticized it as being in two storeys of much the same height. A part of the cloister [648] and two lofty and austere staircases with wrought-iron balustrades remain.[10]

[1] *Gallia Dominicana*, I, 15, mentions the stalls of their Amiens house set up in 1594; they do not appear to survive.
[2] The Dominican church of Barcelonnette dates from the seventeenth century but is in Gothic style.
[3] Hautecœur, II, 718.
[4] Now a School of Agriculture. Part of the church is now a garage.   [5] Lenôtre, p. 294.
[6] Now the Maison des Œuvres. At Farjeaux, also in the Aude, the buildings are of various dates and much modified. Only a couple of doorways have any architectural pretensions.
[7] Plan in Hautecœur, II, fig. 549.
[8] The fine high altar by Martin was demolished to use its marbles in the chapel of the Rosary and a new high altar *à la Romaine* was set up. Piganiol de la Force, VIII, 138.
[9] *Cours d'architecture*, IV, 344.   [10] The buildings, much modified, are now the Musée de l'Artillerie.

A second important Dominican church in classical style survives in Notre-Dame de Bordeaux, which was begun in 1684, on the designs of Michel du Plessy and the Dominicans Jean Maupéou and Jean Fontaine. The façade [650] is sculpturally conceived in the round, as are few French churches of that date; the elements—Corinthian pilasters and columns, volutes and a pediment—are commonplace enough, but they are combined into a whole that is original and, in France, unique. The interior gives an effect of unusual breadth. Like the medieval Dominican churches it is clearly designed for preaching; the wide nave can hold a large congregation, and the pulpit dominates it. The side chapels are cross-vaulted; the aisle arches are each surmounted by an empty oculus.

A similar breadth and greater height mark the splendid Dominican church of St Mary Magdalene at Aix-en-Provence, built in 1703 [649]. Its piers of Corinthian pilasters, and the imposts above them, have multiple mouldings in the Provençal manner, yet even these fail to impair the majesty of the whole. At Nîmes, however, the Dominican church[1] is much less characteristic of the Order. Its façade [651] is in the Provençal style of the third quarter of the eighteenth century, and within it has galleries in the Jesuit manner.

These remain the most important Dominican churches of the classical period.[2] A few minor churches survive, such as that of the Jacobins at Auch [652]; the interior is extremely plain but for a fine retable filling the whole east end.

Many Dominican convents were content, like that at Avignon,[3] to enrich a medieval building with new stalls, altars and retables; or like that of Saint-Cannat de Marseilles, to put a classical façade on a Gothic church [653]. The church of Saint-Maximin in the Var was in the years after 1683 enriched with splendid stalls [654] of carved wood, marble and terracotta reliefs, iron grilles, and many paintings. The pulpit [655], carved by Louis Gudet, a Dominican of the house,[4] with scenes of the life of St Mary Magdalene, is a fine piece of rhetoric. At Montauban the very plain church is ennobled by a dignified classical baldaquin over the altar.

The difficulties of the time are exemplified by the case of the noble Dominican nunnery of Poissy.[5] Their medieval church was nearly destroyed by lightning in 1700. Mansart was sent to inspect it, and said that its restoration would cost 180,000 livres. Nothing was done until 1705, when the King offered to find 300,000 livres for a new church on condition that the Pope granted him the right

[1] Now the Grand Temple Protestant.
[2] Parts of the Dominican buildings of the end of the seventeenth century survive at Semur-en-Auxois; they are plain and unremarkable. Very little remains of their house at Bergerac, rebuilt in the middle of the seventeenth century. Their church at Lyons was pulled down in 1860 and that at Millau in 1861, but I have not been able to find engravings of either. The house of Jacobins at Tours (in recent years the Manutention Militaire) was destroyed in the war.
[3] See *Cong. Arch.* (1909), II, 307.
[4] Another Dominican sculptor was Omer Danvin, who carved the pulpit of Notre-Dame de Saint-Omer in 1714. A fine pulpit from their church at Dinan is now in the church of Saint Malo.
[5] Blomfield, II, 43.

to nominate the abbess. To this the Pope agreed. The King failed to produce the money, but authorized the abbess to raise it by a lottery. This produced 96,000 *livres* and the work was begun. Robert de Cotte designed it in a Gothic style to harmonize with the conventual building[1] [*656*]. By 1718 over 300,000 *livres* had been expended and the work was not finished. Antin, the superintendent of the King's works, wrote to Cotte to say that the work must be completed. Cotte went to Poissy and told the abbess that in these hard times she must expect less.[2] The work was not complete at the Revolution when all was destroyed.[3]

It was probably similar difficulties which caused the paucity of rebuilding of Dominican living quarters in the seventeenth and eighteenth centuries. The Jacobins of Rennes built themselves plain and dignified quarters towards the end of the seventeenth century.[4] They have been much modified by the military authorities who occupy them, but the cloister [*644*] still shows an unusual and provincially classical frieze with projecting metopes. Their plain but handsome buildings at Poligny, built in 1715 on the plans of Amondry[5] [*658*] have a rather unusual staircase and retain at least one good chimney-piece [*659, 660*].

The Dominican nuns of the reformed Third Order of St Catherine of Siena built new quarters for their house at Dinan, founded in 1625, on the designs of the architect Poussin,[6] between 1661 and 1664 [*657*]. The church has a classical façade with pairs of Doric columns; the buildings, of considerable extent, are of the local rubble masonry with stone quoins. The finest surviving monastic buildings are those at Bordeaux[7] [*661*] which seem but little later than the church, and those at Saint-Maximin [*662*]; the entrance leads to a staircase with a wrought-iron balustrade in the Benedictine manner, dramatically set.

The house of Dominican nuns at Murat was rebuilt after a fire in 1771;[8] it is of archaic simplicity, and might well be dated much earlier. In the following year the Toulousain architect Iche completed their buildings in that city. Much has been modified, but the staircase survives; it looks as though the elaborate wrought-iron balustrade had never been completed below the upper floor.

The latest Dominican house to survive is that at Lisieux, built between 1775 and 1777. The chapel has been destroyed. There is a good classical gateway, and a long residential building, with nothing to distinguish it from any large dwelling-house on the outskirts of a country town.

---

[1] Some of his designs survive in the Cabinet des Estampes, Va 953.

[2] His report suggests that an exact restoration of the Gothic church had been attempted.

[3] Hautecœur (II, 853) says that the convent of the Dominican nuns of the Cross at Charonne was a plain building of the barrack type. Their buildings of 1773 at Toulouse were practically reconstructed in 1872.

[4] Now in military occupation and inaccessible. My thanks are due to M. Raymond Cornou, Architecte des Monuments historiques at Rennes, for photographs and information. The façade to the street has been a good deal modified but still has attics with alternate angular and rounded pediments to its windows.

[5] Now the Sous-Préfecture. The chapel, which is earlier, is now a warehouse.

[6] Now the hospice. My thanks are due to the Archiviste-en-Chef at Saint-Brieuc for this information.

[7] It is now the library.   [8] It is now the Tribunal.

CHAPTER VII

THE FRANCISCANS

I. THE CORDELIERS

It might well have been thought that the Order of St Francis, vowed to poverty and devoted to evangelism among the citizens of the towns, would have found great spheres of work in the crowded cities of France in the sixteenth, seventeenth and eighteenth centuries. In fact, the Order was already beginning to decline when it was tried by the wars of the fifteenth century; and though it achieved a measure of recovery it was no longer fecund. It had acquired riches and had lost its inspiration. It is not unfitting that the most famous French Franciscan of the sixteenth century should be François Rabelais.[1]

Attempts to reform the Order in the fifteenth century had led only to dissension. In 1517 a *capitulum generalissimum* was summoned to meet in Rome, to unite the factions. As a result they were divided into two groups, the Conventuals and the Observants.[2] The Conventuals hardly existed in France; the Observants, generally known as Cordeliers, who adhered more closely to the founder's Rule, had some two hundred and fifty houses there, divided into eight provinces.[3]

The Cordeliers were endowed with several new buildings at the turn of the century, but they were built in a gabled late Gothic style.[4] Before the end of the sixteenth century their church at Laval was given a classical door with heavy rusticated stonework and an elaborate oculus,[5] and rather later a great marble retable in the style of that at La Bénisson-Dieu.[6]

Much of the great Paris house was destroyed by fire in 1580, and rebuilt by Henri III between 1582 and 1606.[7] Nothing of this building remains. The church was one of the largest in Paris, three hundred and twenty feet long and ninety

[1] He began his education with the Benedictines and finished it with the Franciscans in a house near Angers. He became a Franciscan in the convent of Fontenay-le-Comte and remained there for fifteen years. He then left it; after receiving pardon he entered the Cluniac abbey of Maillezais; he left it in 1530 and never returned to conventual life.

[2] The new 'Observants' based their Rule on the observance of 1380.

[3] Hélyot, *Dictionnaire*, III, 55.

[4] For example, the Paris house given by Anne of Brittany, which survives as the Musée Dupuytren, and the church at Guingamp, built between 1507 and 1521 by Guy de Bretagne. Similarly, their church at Aurillac, Notre-Dame-des-Neiges, though built about 1600, is entirely Gothic in style.

[5] An early surviving fragment of their Renaissance architecture is the door of their house at Dôle (now the Palais de Justice) with angels reclining on the slopes of a pediment, of which the architrave is broken to enshrine a niche. It dates from 1572; Dôle became French in 1636.

[6] See above, p. 60.

[7] The choir was rebuilt at the cost of Henri III and the Knights of the Saint Esprit; the nave and aisles by members of the family of Le Thou.

wide. The arcade was on columns; the church was not vaulted but had a ceiling of dark wood. The chapter-house,[1] with an open arcade to the cloister, had one wall decorated in *trompe-l'œil* as the interior of a church. Above the panelling on the others was a frieze with small square portraits of the heads of the Cardinals, Patriarchs, Generals and Saints of the Order. The rebuilding was accompanied by a great effort by Francesco Gonzaga, General from 1579 to 1587, to restore the keeping of the vow of poverty and to bring back the pursuit of learning to the Paris convent,[2] which was the French centre of study for the Order. A number of his successors were Spaniards, and could do nothing to maintain the reform of the Observants in a France that was increasingly conscious of its nationhood. In 1673, indeed, and again in 1745, the French Observants obtained papal briefs which allowed them to retain real estate and vested incomes.

The Cordeliers of Chartres rebuilt their convent early in the seventeenth century. The cloister and several ranges of buildings remain [*663, 664*].[3] There was once a door[4] decorated with trophies of arms in relief, with two inscriptions: one in Greek, Μὴ ὑψηλοφρόνη ἄλλα φοβοῦ. I. M.,[5] and the other in Hebrew, 'My house shall be called a house of prayer',[6] but this has now disappeared. The Cordeliers' house at Châtillon-sur-Seine was rebuilt about the same time, as a quadrangle round a courtyard [*667, 668*]; its low buildings and simple cloister do not seem incongruous now that it is a farm. A fine door survives that once formed the entrance to the house at Carpentras erected early in the seventeenth century and another survives in that of the Cordeliers at Châlons-sur-Marne [*665*].

The Cordeliers of Autun rebuilt their house[7] towards the end of the century with a simple and elegant doorway[8] [*666, 669*]. The cloister itself is very plain [*670*], with rectangular panelled piers and a cross-vault; it may be compared with that at Montbrison. The cells above have an attractive high-shouldered roof with attic dormers.[9] The cloister of the Paris house was built between 1673 and 1683; its arches were closed by ornamental iron grilles wrought with the arms of benefactors.[10]

The eighteenth century witnessed a marked decline among the Cordeliers. Recruiting to the Order was poor, and the great Paris house was far from full.[11]

[1] Piganiol de la Force, VII, 6.   [2] *Ibid.* VII, 38.

[3] François Feuardent, 1539–1610, was a great Franciscan preacher of the time, and in his old age restored the Bayeux house and gave it a library.

[4] See *Cong. Arch.* (*Chartres*), 1900, p. 164; *Bull. Mon.* LXVI (1902), 30. I failed to find it in 1958.

[5] Romans xi. 20.   [6] Isaiah lvi. 7.

[7] Now part of the Hôpital Saint Gabriel.

[8] Another of about the same date remains in the Collège of Soissons, once the Cordeliers.

[9] The cloister of the Dijon house is now part of a Dominican convent and cannot be visited.

[10] Piganiol de la Force, VII, 6. The cloister was destroyed in 1877. The remains of the Cordeliers' buildings at Montbrison are now defaced, but look as if they had never been beautiful. The Observant Franciscans of Carpentras have left some unimportant remains; their church has been largely rebuilt but keeps their eighteenth-century altar. The seventeenth-century buildings of the Cordeliers of Amboise were destroyed in the last war; those of Aubeterre survive as a private house.

[11] Lenôtre, p. 317.

The chief activity lay on the south-eastern frontier of France. At Lons-le-Saunier the church [671] was rebuilt between 1714 and 1731 and the gate and cloister[1] between 1737 and 1747. At Dôle the Cordeliers rebuilt their house[2] on the designs of Père Nicole between 1731 and 1760 [672]; the cloister is remarkable for its two tiers of arcades on one side [673]. One or two rooms retain their vaulted ceilings [674]. The house at Vic-Fezensac was reconstructed in 1752.[3] It is on the most modest scale with no features but a staircase with a wrought-iron balustrade.

In 1766 the Commission des Réguliers, under Cardinal de Brienne, inquired into the affairs of the Franciscan Order. A reform was ordered in 1770[4] and in 1771 the French Observants were united with the international congregation of the Conventuals. Five years later it was proposed to pull down half the great Paris church and to turn the rest to parochial use; but instead it was taken over by the Revolutionaries. It is a measure of the want of respect in which the Observant Franciscans were held that few of their churches survived the Revolution; once the apostles of poverty, they had come to stand for wealth, influence and privilege, not always wisely or unselfishly used.

The women Franciscans, under the patronage of the Saint's sister, Ste Clare, were after the reform of Urban VIII divided into two groups: the Filles de Sainte Claire or de l'Ave Maria followed a stricter Rule than the Clarisses Mitigées or Urbanistes. The Filles de l'Ave Maria had a house at Paris, built about the middle of the seventeenth century. Nothing remains, and no other buildings of the Order have been recognized.

The Clarisses of Aubeterre rebuilt their house in 1608, in a rustic and conservative style, with a machicolated gateway [675, 676].[5] An interesting house of Clarisses survives at Sarlat[6] with an unusual cloister on two floors [677]. The simple chapel has a single arcaded aisle; the apse has a plain Doric colonnade with niches for two statues and a good wrought-iron communion rail. At Poligny their convent, founded by Ste Colette, is entered by a doorway of 1680 of some architectural pretensions [678]; their chapel appears to be of the nineteenth century.[7] The 'noble' house of Clarisses at Montigny-lès-Vesoul is sited on a lofty hill. Its chapel[8] [679] and its buildings are of an extreme plainness without; there is hardly anything to distinguish the little houses of the noble ladies from a row of cottages. Inside, a modest wrought-iron balustrade [680] survives in one of them to show that they aimed at a Benedictine decency.

Their house at Aigueperse[9] [682] appears to date from the last third of the seventeenth century. It is divided from the street by a low screen wall with a

---

[1] Now houses.
[2] The monastic buildings are now the Palais de Justice and what is left of the church a huge garage.
[3] Now the hospital. [4] Prat, p. 215.
[5] It is now a private house.
[6] Now a girls' school, the Institution Sainte-Claire.
[7] Their near-by house at Salins (now the École Voltaire) dates from 1658, before the town was French.
[8] Now a barn. [9] Now the Hôtel de Ville.

belfry over the gate [681]. Inside the court a long block with projecting wings has a plain cloister under the building on the three inner sides. There is a marked absence of decoration; the stairs have a stone balustrade. The chapel has disappeared. A long block of the building of the Clarisses survives at Pertuis in Provence; it is indistinguishable from an ordinary good town house of the region. The church survives with rich ironwork and *boiseries*. Their conventual buildings at Toulouse[1] have been considerably modified but retain their austere three storeys above a simple cloister [684]. The house of Franciscan nuns at Arras offers a simple frontage to the narrow street; the chapel has a plainish classical façade and a charming interior, still sanctified by the devotion of nuns [683]. The Paris house, near Saint-Germain, known as the Petites Cordelières, occupied the Hôtel de Beauvais and turned the ballroom into a chapel.[2] They did not prosper and were suppressed in 1749.

The penitential Order of the Annonciades, founded by Jeanne de Valois at Bourges in 1500, was also under Franciscan jurisdiction. It was dedicated to the virtues of the Virgin, and the church of its mother-house at Bourges bore the initials of these virtues. Their nuns came to Paris, in the rue de Sèvres, in 1630, and acquired another house in the rue Popincourt in 1638; these were united in 1654, but nothing remains. Their house at Saint-Denis was designed by J. H. Mansart, with a chapel of the Ionic order; its dome was built by d'Aviler in 1681.[3] Their chapel at Boulogne-sur-Mer and their eighteenth-century chapel at Vesoul survived until the 1939 war.[4]

2. THE RECOLLETS

When Francesco Gonzaga tried to reanimate Franciscanism in the sixteenth century[5] he set up 'Houses of Recollection' to revive the spiritual life of the Friars. The Recollets arose out of an Observant reform of 1532. The Order was introduced into France in 1592[6] by a house of Italian friars founded by the Gonzaga Duke of Nevers. The first entirely French houses were a second house at Nevers, founded in 1597, and houses at La Charité in 1602, Paris in 1603 and Saint-Denis in 1608. By 1606 the Recollets had enough houses in France to be organized in provinces.[7] They did most of the work of chaplains to the Army, and sent many missionaries to Canada.[8] The Order was particularly strong in southern France.

The Recollets early took over the convent of Notre-Dame-des-Anges, founded by Anne of Brittany at Aber-Wrac'h in 1507; little remains but a picturesque

---

[1] Now the Institut Catholique.   [2] Piganiol de la Force, VIII, 103.

[3] Hautecœur, II, 647 and 682.

[4] Now the museum. Their church at Pontarlier dates from before it was French.

[5] See above, p. 115.   [6] H. Lefebvre, p. 33.

[7] The Province of Brittany had eleven convents and one hospice; Provence, thirty convents and three hospices; Aquitaine, twenty-nine convents and one hospice; Anjou, eighteen convents; Lyons, thirty convents and two hospices, and Toulouse, twenty-nine convents. (Hélyot, *Dictionnaire*, III, 333.)

[8] Joseph le Caron, professed in Paris in 1611, sailed for Canada in 1615 and became the evangelist of the Hurons as Chrestien Leclercq did of the Micmacs.

courtyard. About 1630 their Paris house in the Faubourg Saint-Martin erected a chapel of considerable splendour; three of its chapels, the tabernacle, the high altar and many pictures were paid for by private benefactors.[1] It survives rather denuded in the Hôpital Villemin, where two splendid later ranges of buildings also remain to attest the importance of the house: one, of the Norman Benedictine style, of about 1685 [685], and one, with pilasters, that appears to be of about 1730. The Recollets were not amalgamated with the rest of the Friars by the Commission des Réguliers in 1771, but continued to have a separate existence until the Revolution. The women who followed their Rule, known as Recollettes, had a house in the rue du Bac; nothing remains of it.

Few houses of Recollets have survived the Revolution. At Saint-Céré in the Lot their chapel, built in 1662, shows a rather lumpy classical façade [686] adorned with reliefs of St Francis with a banner and of another Saint, probably Francesco Gonzaga. Beneath these reliefs are niches with statues of St Joseph and St Anne. The façade of the church is integrated into a long line of buildings, now tenements, which must once have formed the monastic quarters. Their buildings at Sézanne survive as part of the hospital. The chapel [688, 689] is of a barn-like simplicity, relieved by a great retable set with paintings. The cloister [687] is equally simple; its rather dumpy proportions have a rustic charm. Some of their buildings at Saint-Germain-Laval remain in a dilapidated state[2] [691]; there is a simple cloister, with square pilasters with heavy cornice and groin vaults. The whole, simple as it is, has a faintly Italianate air.

At Vitry-le-François[3] their chapel still shows a classical 'frontispiece' between two plainer wings [690] in the manner of J. H. Mansart. Their cloister at Saint-Jean-de-Luz[4] is of extreme simplicity; it is only remarkable for a very simple four-sided fountain framed in Doric columns in the middle. At Bourg-Saint-Andéol their chapel and cloister occupy a square almost fortress-like building;[5] I was unable to visit the interior. At Chaumont-en-Vexin their buildings[6] occupy three sides of a square, and are of the utmost simplicity [696].

Their most interesting church is that of the English Recollets at Douai, dating from 1706. The exterior has a good classical façade [692, 693]. The interior is notably elegant with its colonnade of lofty Ionic pillars that is broken to form a false transept and continues again to frame the high altar. Behind it is a small semicircular Lady Chapel. Their chapel at La Rochelle[7] [694] dates from the same year; the façade offers a not dissimilar scheme in plainer style. Comparatively little survives of their house at Darney in the Vosges, rebuilt in 1735.[8] The gateway is modest; the monastic buildings unremarkable; only one or two rooms recall the original use of the building [695].

[1] Hautecœur, I, 545.
[2] In 1957 part seemed to be a factory and part a hostel. I could not get into the cloister, but saw it through a keyhole.   [3] Formerly Hôtel de Ville, but badly damaged in the last war.
[4] In private hands and now very dilapidated.   [5] Now the hospice.
[6] Now Hôtel de Ville.   [7] Now a Protestant church.   [8] Now a cheese factory.

3. THE CAPUCHINS

A reform of the Observants, close to primitive Franciscanism in its renunciation of the ownership of property, not only by the friars but also by the houses of the Order, was instituted in Italy about 1520 and received official recognition in 1538. Its members were called Capuchins from the hoods of their habits. Their discipline was rigid, and included two hours daily spent in private prayer. They came to France at a time when Catholicism was being reintroduced into Béarn, and one of their first tasks was its evangelization. By the middle of the eighteenth century they had four hundred and twenty houses in France. Curiously few of their buildings survive.

The prosperity of the Capuchins grew in some measure out of the Wars of Religion. Henri de Joyeuse, Comte de Bouchage and later Duc de Joyeuse, after serving in the Army left the world to enter the Capuchins as Père Ange. He was given seven years' dispensation to govern Languedoc to reduce the Huguenots to Catholicism. This done, he returned to the cloister, where he died in 1608.[1]

A movement of devotion began to centre round an image of the Virgin belonging to the family of Joyeuse, which had become known as Notre-Dame de la Paix by his household since they used to pray to it for peace during the Wars of Religion.[2] When peace came it was set up over the door of the chapel; and when war began again in 1648 great devotions were made to it. In 1653 the daughter of the Duc de Joyeuse, the Duchess of Guise, built a chapel for it in the Capuchin church at Paris: a handsome building of the Corinthian Order.

The Capuchins' first church in Paris was built in the Faubourg Saint-Honoré; it was finished in 1610. It is said[3] to have been rather simple; nothing remains.

The earliest surviving Capuchin church in France would seem to be that of Coulommiers, designed by Salomon de Brosses between 1617 and 1625. It is large and bare, with a barrel vault and round-headed windows.[4] The east end is on two floors, linked by a spiral staircase of wood on either side. The lower part is arranged as a kind of grotto to hold the altar; the upper forms a choir, behind a simple wooden balustrade. The general effect is curiously Protestant. Their church of 1627 at Saint Amand Montrond is no more than a plain room.

The Chapelle Saint-Louis at Saint-Servan[5] was erected in 1640. It is as bare as a ship's cabin, but for the retable, representing the sainted king, and statues on either side of it in wooden niches. The Capuchins of Fontenay-le-Château rebuilt their quarters in 1626; they survive [698] in a rather derelict state, as do their rather later quarters at Arbois [699]. The Capuchin convent of Notre-Dame-du-

---

[1] The Capuchin Père Hyacinthe founded the Communauté des Nouveaux Convertis in the rue Cuvier at Paris in 1632. Nothing remains. [2] Guillet de Saint Georges, I, 322.

[3] Hautecœur, I, 548. Their cloister at Évreux, built in 1612, seems to have disappeared. Their seventeenth-century house at Saint-Sever-sur-l'Adour has been remodelled out of all knowledge; it is now the hospice.

[4] Now in a park, it serves as a rather rudimentary museum. [5] Now the Collège.

Bon-Secours at Compiègne, founded in 1637 and restored by Anne of Austria in 1653, is a simple Gothic chapel with plain round-headed windows and an elaborate rib vault. There is a curious choir arch of cherubs on caryatid columns executed in a highly provincial style. The late seventeenth-century convent at Roscoff is of the ordinary town-house type. The remains of the convent at Avallon have been transformed past recognition to serve as a theatre; those at La Châtre are featureless.

The vitality which the Cordeliers lost towards the end of the seventeenth century passed to the Capuchins, who had no want of recruits. The cloister and much of the monastic buildings of the Paris house were rebuilt on a grand scale in 1686; it was one of the first classical cloisters to be glazed for warmth.[1] The church was rebuilt in 1715 and survives as the parish church of Saint-Jean-Saint-François [700]. It is as simple as the monastic buildings that adjoin it, with galleries under a triglyph frieze and many side chapels.

The portal of the house of Capuchin nuns near the Place Louis-le-Grand was rebuilt very handsomely in 1731[2] [701], and in 1735 the choir of their church was beautified.

The Capuchins, indeed, unlike the Cordeliers, continued to build in the eighteenth century. The chapel of their great Paris Novitiate was rebuilt in 1762; it survives in some sort as a lecture-room of the Hôpital Cochin,[3] as does their gateway [702]. The Capuchins of Lons-le-Saunier rebuilt their house between 1733 and 1742; it too survives, greatly modified. The Capuchins of Strasbourg engaged Kléber to design their chapel in 1774, as a rotunda on Ionic columns with a dome above a heavy frieze, rather in the style of Chalgrin.[4] It was never executed. Their house at Arnay-le-Duc was rebuilt in 1777; nothing remains; but their contemporary chapel at Tarare [703], of a severe and classical simplicity, survives as the Tribunal de Commerce. The Capuchin convent at Châteauroux [697] remains as a type of their late eighteenth-century buildings, with a classically pedimented central chapel framed by two projecting wings. The monastic buildings and chapel of their lesser Novitiate in the rue Caumartin[5] was rebuilt on the designs of Brongniart as late as 1780–2, with a massive and monumental façade with Doric columns à la Paestum, without bases [704, 705]. It was built by the government in exchange for the Novitiate house which had been compulsorily acquired. Each walk of the cloister has nine columns, with a plain storey above. The approach to the street is masked by a massive building, with pedimented pavilions on either side. A gateway in one gives access to the monastic buildings; one on the other side is, rather unexpectedly, the entrance to the church.[6] The

---

[1] Hautecœur, II, 856. [2] Piganiol de la Force, III, 10.

[3] 111 Boulevard de Port-Royal. A baldaquin of much the same date survives in the rebuilt church of Saint-Louis, Rochefort-sur-Mer. [4] Hautecœur, IV, 341 and fig. 191.

[5] Now the church of Saint-Louis-d'Antin and the Lycée Condorcet.

[6] The church follows an old Franciscan plan in having only one aisle, but this seems the result less of tradition than of an asymmetrical site.

design seems to reflect a wish to draw as little attention as possible to the fact that in 1780 the government had built an edifice devoted to the practices of religion. The church itself [706] was designed to be of a Tuscan simplicity; the Goddess of Reason could have been worshipped in it without giving anyone offence.

The women Capucines,[1] founded by the Duchesse de Mercœur in 1604–6, had a house near the rue Saint-Honoré. They were expropriated when Louis XIV built the Place Vendôme in 1688, and their chapel and convent[2] were rebuilt in the rue de la Paix by Jules Hardouin-Mansart.[3] The buildings, made at the royal expense, were unusually handsome; all the cells were panelled and the cloisters glazed in.[4] The façade of the church in the style of François Mansart was carved with angels by Vassé; it was designed as a part of the general scheme of the new square.

4. THE MINIMES

The Minimes had been founded by St François de Paule in Italy, as the Hermits of St Francis of Assisi, as early as 1454, but they did not enter France until 1482, when the royal patronage of Charles VIII introduced them at Plessis-lès-Tours, Amboise and Nigeon near Paris. Their Rule, based on the Franciscan constitution, aimed at the *vita quadragesimalis* which included a perpetual abstinence from meat. By the eighteenth century the Order included a hundred and fifty houses of men and two of women in France.

At Beauregard-l'Evêque in Auvergne a fine late sixteenth-century doorway survives, surmounted by a pedimented panel with two niched recesses framing the arms of the prior who built it; the very plain living quarters have been modified for private occupation. At Decize their house[5] [707, 708] has a pleasant plain cloister, with a low arcade on square piers. The chapel, now a cinema, has a Renaissance façade with niches that seems to date from the end of the sixteenth century.

The Minimes' convent at Aubeterre[6] [709, 710] was built in 1617. The chapel contains a fine baroque retable, with a broken pediment, double columns, and doors on either side the altar, comparable with that of the Cordeliers at Laval. Externally it is of extreme simplicity, as is the battered but picturesque little cloister. Their house at Sillé-le-Guillaume is now the hospital; it has been plastered over and offers little to the visitor.

Marie de Médicis founded a Paris house of Minimes in the Marais near the Place-Royale in 1611. The chapel [711], begun in 1630 by d'Orbay and finished before 1679 by François Mansart, has been wholly destroyed. Its lower part was

---

[1] Sometimes called Filles de la Passion.   [2] Both were demolished in 1806.

[3] Brice ascribed them to François Dorbay, but M. Ciprut has recently published fresh documents. (See 'L'auteur de l'église des Capucines', p. 261.)

[4] Piganiol de la Force, III, 38. They were, however, badly built and had to be partly reconstructed in 1750.

[5] Now a school. A second cloister, a good deal modified, is of mid-eighteenth-century date; one staircase has a good wrought-iron balustrade.   [6] Now the gendarmerie.

severely Doric, with triglyphs and a plain pediment; only a closer grouping of the columns stressed the central feature. It was to have had a dome, and to have been framed by wings with domed pavilions like those at the Château de Blois. The whole scheme was very slow in building.[1] A few doors of the convent remain.[2] The refectory was nine bays long; there was a library of 26,000 volumes.[3] The cloister, finished in 1682, had two storeys of galleries.[4]

In 1619 Martellange drew the façade of the Minimes' church at Nevers, with a high façade and two spires. It was designed on a central plan with four piers and three polygonal apses.[5] The church of the Minimes at Tours[6] [713, 714] was begun in 1629, again thanks to the munificence of Marie de Médicis. Its portal [712] was carved by two monks, Antoine Andric and Cot Taboué. It is unusually planned with three pentagonal chapels on each side and simple flamboyant windows. The simple interior is beautified by good ironwork and *boiseries* and by a handsome retable. The conventual buildings, now a good deal modified, are of a notable simplicity.

The house of Saint-Pierre-des-Minimes at Clermont-Ferrand [715], begun in 1630, has an extremely plain classical façade on which four rather flat Ionic pilasters hardly break the austere expanse of dark Volvic stone. The interior is no less austere, with a plain arcade and pilasters to the side chapels. All the splendour is centred on the high altar at the crossing, where yellow marble columns support an ornate dome on a high drum.

Most of the church of the Minimes at Orléans[7] was destroyed in the last war, but its rusticated cloister survives [718]. At Arlay in the Jura[8] [716, 717] the Minimes rebuilt their house, rather handsomely and in secular style, in 1655. The house of the Minimes of Arbois, dating from about 1600, has been almost entirely rebuilt.[9] The latest church of the Order to survive in France is that of Saint-François-de-Paule, built in 1744 at Toulon [719], which dates from the eighteenth century. Its choir is domed; the nave has balustraded galleries on a classical arcade.[10]

5. THE THIRD ORDER

Besides the secular third Order of St Francis, which is believed to have dated from the saint's lifetime, a regular Third Order arose towards the end of the thirteenth century, and was established in France by the fifteenth, with the usual three vows of poverty, chastity and obedience. The Paris houses, which had become very

[1] See Ciprut, 'Documents inédits', p. 157. [2] 12 rue de Béarn.
[3] Hélyot, *Dictionnaire*, II, 996. [4] Piganiol de la Force, IV, 440.
[5] Bib. Nat. Est., Ub9, fol. 55. See Bouchot in *Bibliothèque de l'École des Chartes*, XLVII (1886), 59.
[6] Now the Lycée, rue de la Préfecture. [7] Then the Archives.
[8] Now the Château d'Arenburg.
[9] The house of Minimes at Doulevant-le-Château, Haute-Marne, of the early eighteenth century, was burned in the Second World War and now offers nothing of interest.
[10] The church of the Minimes in the suburb of Saint-Pierre at Nancy (not then French) was built in 1738 by Emmanuel Héré de Corny.

relaxed, were reformed about 1592 by Vincent Mussart[1] into a congregation which had its centre after 1598 at Franconville-sous-Bois in the diocese of Beauvais. They were established in Paris at Picpus in 1601, and two years later all the remaining Third Order houses in France were included in the new reform. There were some nine houses of men, mostly in Normandy, and five of women, but not all survived the Wars of Religion. More were then founded, chiefly under the patronage of Louis XIII and the Dukes of Lorraine, and when Hélyot (a member of the Order) wrote in the middle of the eighteenth century, there were fifty-nine convents of men and five of women. None of them have been recognized in existing buildings, except for the church of the women's house in Paris, founded by Marie de Médicis in 1628,[2] which survives as Sainte-Élisabeth.

The noble façade [720], with its two storeys, framed in eight Ionic pilasters, is given width by the inclusion of two pedimented side windows. The triglyph and metope frieze of the façade recurs in the interior, where the metopes are filled with emblem-like groups of ecclesiastical vessels and instruments, from bells to cruets.[3] The nave arcade is on heavy piers; the ambulatory, however, has simple Doric columns. The only surviving provincial house of *Tiercelines* that I know of is that at Arbois, built between 1650 and 1678. The chapel now serves as a theatre.

---

[1] Hélyot, *Dictionnaire*, III, 188.   [2] *Ibid.* III, 215.
[3] Cf. those at Le Val-de-Grâce.

CHAPTER VIII

THE JESUITS

The greatest Order of the Counter-Reformation was that of the Society of Jesus. Its founder, St Ignatius Loyola, was inspired not by the idea of establishing an Order of religious, but by the personal imitation of Christ; yet the needs of his time forced him to canalize his work into an institution of 'a mendicant Order of clerks regular'.

Loyola was a Spaniard; much of the administrative inspiration of the Company of Jesus (as he first called it) came from Rome; yet most of the early development of the Order was worked out in France. Loyola came to Paris[1] early in 1528 as a student of theology. He and six of his friends took a vow at Montmartre in 1534 to go on pilgrimage to Jerusalem and to renounce the world. If they failed to get to Jerusalem they were to go to the Pope at Rome and to submit themselves to his orders.

In 1537 the company of friends, now swollen to ten, reached Rome as pilgrims; only Loyola himself, from motives of political discretion, remained at Venice. The Pope advised that they should form themselves into a society under a fixed Rule, and three years later he approved their Constitutions.

The first Jesuits, *avant la lettre*, who were almost all Spaniards, made their vows in France. Only in 1539 did they openly declare themselves and make the Paris palace of the Bishop of Clermont, the Hôtel de Clermont, their centre. A year later the king permitted the establishment of a College there, but even then the Parlement objected, and its resistance was not overthrown until 1554. The Bishop of Paris remained in opposition and a final settlement was not reached until 1561.[2]

For two hundred years after 1575 the kings of France had Jesuit confessors, and the prestige of the Order was assured. In 1594, however, the Parlement took the opportunity of an attempt on the king's life (in which the Jesuits took no part whatsoever) to expel the Society from France. The writ of the Parlement of Paris did not run everywhere and the Parlements of Bordeaux and Toulouse refused to agree to the expulsion. Jesuit activities continued, concentrated in the Spanish provinces of Franche-Comté, Flanders and Artois,[3] in the papal territory of Avignon and in the county of Nice.

In 1603 Henri IV readmitted the Society to his territories, allowing them to maintain their existing houses and to found fresh colleges at Lyons, Dijon and

[1] Hélyot, *Dictionnaire*, II, 637.

[2] The Collège de Clermont was rechristened Collège Louis le Grand in 1682 in honour of its royal benefactor. It was rebuilt in 1814–20. The Collège at Billom in the Puy de Dôme was one of the earliest to be founded; its buildings have been greatly modified.

[3] See Hautecœur, I, 558 for buildings in these districts.

La Flèche. By 1610 the Order had thirty-nine colleges in France.[1] Its authority gradually increased as in the congenial air of France its approach became more logical, and its preachers came to strive to appeal to the intelligence as well as to the heart. Bourdaloue, who entered the Order and came to Paris in 1647, was for more than thirty years one of the greatest and most logical of the French preachers. At the same time the work of the Jesuit Fathers in evangelizing the Indians of North America made their apostolate a part of French colonial expansion, and their missions to China a part of French foreign policy. They played a real part, too, in the city life of France by their fostering of sodalities of laymen devoted to the Virgin.[2]

From the first the aims of the Society were complex. On the one hand its members followed St Ignatius Loyola in the pursuit of the imitation of Christ; on the other they served the world as preachers, teachers and evangelists. The France of Louis XIII and Louis XIV was extremely conscious of the need for an intense, organized and classical education, and in that atmosphere this function of the Jesuits tended to become of major importance. Yet it entirely depended on the quality of the recruits that the Society could attract, and of the training it could offer them. France is a country where the idea of an *élite* is always congenial; and it may fairly be said that, after the Benedictines of the earliest Middle Ages and the chivalry of the time of St Louis, the Society of Jesus was the third *corps d'élite* of which it could boast.

The eventual organization of the Society of Jesus was based on no less than six kinds of houses. The first were *Maisons professes*, designed as centres of spiritual direction. The second were colleges, large day-schools for boys.[3] The third, *Pensionnats* or *Séminaires*, were boarding-schools for boys. The fourth were *Noviciats*, for training aspirants to the Society. The fifth were *Résidences*, smaller establishments in remoter parts that might combine more than one activity; and the sixth were missions in heathen lands. By 1749 there were a hundred and fifty Jesuit Houses in France.[4]

The first church of the Society, the Gesù of Rome, was built by the munificence of Alessandro Farnese in 1568. Through its influence a Vignolesque flavour is apparent in many Jesuit churches:[5] yet the Gesù is more showy and less functional than the Jesuit churches of France. The official plan[6] of the Jesuits for teaching

---

[1] Most significantly in 1607 Ligugé, a cradle of Benedictinism in France, was attached to the Jesuit college of Poitiers to serve as a country house for the community.

[2] See Moisy, *Les églises Jésuites*, I, 7; E. Villaret, *Les congrégations mariales*, Paris, n.d. (1947).

[3] These were divided into three categories according to size; (*a*) up to twenty regents and forty fathers; (*b*) up to thirty regents and fifty fathers, and (*c*) larger colleges. [4] Moisy, *Les églises Jésuites*, I, 7.

[5] Serbat, in *Bull. Mon.* LXVI (1902), 352 and LXVII (1903), 96, has pointed out how far the Jesuits of the Walloon provinces showed a preference for Gothic style in the seventeenth century; e.g. Tournai, 1599–1607, Valenciennes, 1601–13, Lille, 1605–11 and Saint-Omer 1615–36. In the last the apse has Gothic windows and buttresses but these are surmounted by classical volutes and a frieze of a heavy Flemish kind. At the same time Serbat seems to underestimate the Gothic elements in vaults and fenestration even in the work of Martellange (see below, p. 127). Aire-sur-le-Lys has an interesting Jesuit chapel built before the town was French, in Flemish classical style. [6] See Charvet, p. 13.

establishments—and in effect all of their six sorts of houses were educational centres—was of two, or in large houses three, parallel quadrangles. The first was for classes; the church usually formed one side of it. The second was for the lodgings of the fathers, and the third, if it existed, for the boarders.[1] In the seventeenth century the Jesuit colleges were usually paid for by the towns they served, and civic economy helped to keep their architecture very simple.[2] What splendour there was, was all in the church. This usually followed the Gesù in being aisleless, with side chapels, and in having a rather shallow transept.[3] They did not share the Benedictine duty of much choir chanting, and the choir became less important. In France, however, Jesuit churches early developed the feature of galleries over the side chapels to provide separate accommodation for the school-children of the colleges and their teachers. An early example, dating from 1608 to 1613, survives at Poitiers [721, 722]. This was built not by the city but through the generosity of Charlotte Flandrette of Nassau, abbess of Sainte-Croix. Its high-crowned lierne vault in five bays rests on a cluster of columns half-classical and half-Gothic in feeling. The two last bays have a heavy triglyph frieze and gallery, with figures of Virtues in the spandrels. The façade has two towers;[4] between them it offers a gable with a rose and four windows in a setting of Doric columns. M. Pierre Moisy[5] considers that it may have been designed by the Jesuit Frère Louis Mercier and the layman François Mignon.

The other Jesuit particularity was the introduction of an oratory[6] with a view of the Blessed Sacrament above the altar, where the fathers could meditate un-seen. Such rooms—for they were little more—were planned for Langres, Béziers, Dijon and many other houses; they were often set on the first floor above the sacristy. This was commonly set in the line of the aisle beyond the transept, and was often surmounted by a bell-turret. Their other very natural characteristic was a multiplicity of confessional boxes; these are indicated on many plans[7] but have in most instances been reduced in number.

The earliest surviving Jesuit building in France appears to be the college at Tournon [723], founded by the Cardinal of that name in 1536 and included in the Order almost as soon as it was organized. Its buildings[8] on the bank of the Rhône offer two courts, of which the first has arcades of a simple kind at either end. The façade to the street is dominated by a narrow central pavilion, with a pedimented feature above the rusticated arch. It holds two niches, with the arms and device of

---

[1] Sometimes the boarders shared the second quadrangle with the fathers; exceptionally, small houses, such as Pontoise and Embrun, had only one court. (Hautecœur, I, 562.)

[2] On the Jesuit preoccupation with economy see Moisy, *Les églises Jésuites*, I, 309, and on subsidiary uses of their chapels, I, 313.

[3] The plan was followed in France as early as 1604, when the Feuillants built their church at Bordeaux with side chapels and a false transept. It is now destroyed (Hautecœur, I, 634). Moisy ably analyses the relation of Jesuit churches to their quadrangles (*Les églises Jésuites*, I, 318).

[4] One is dated 1656, the other is modern. On the Jesuit use of towers see Moisy, *Les églises Jésuites*, I, 428.

[5] *Ibid.* I, 259.   [6] On these see *ibid.* p. 323.   [7] *Ibid.* p. 327.   [8] Now the Lycée.

the Cardinal.[1] This 'frontispiece' theme, destined to become a typical Jesuit motif,[2] recurs in 1602 on the Jesuit chapel at Valenciennes: a town not yet French but under French influences,[3] and at Poitiers, in the entrance pavilion of 1619 [721], where an elaborate niche frames a bust of Henri IV under a cartouche with the head of Louis XIII. This M. Pierre Moisy[4] considers to have been designed by the Jesuit Frère Pérandeau.

The Jesuit architecture of France in the early seventeenth century is dominated by a single figure, the Jesuit Father Etienne Martellange.[5] He was born at Lyons in 1568, the son of a successful painter. He entered the Jesuit house at Avignon in 1590 as 'Coadjuteur temporal'. After visiting Rome he returned to Lyons, where he worked as Architect-General to the Society, under the orders of the Provincial and the direction of the General of the Society at Rome, in the provinces of Paris, Lyons and Toulouse. He retired to the Novitiate at Paris about 1637, and died there in 1641. As Architect-General he made or revised the plans of all the Jesuit buildings in France before they were submitted to the General in Rome as ordered by the General Congregation of 1565. A hundred and seventy-five of his drawings survive in the Cabinet des Estampes.[6] In many cases confirmatory evidence goes to prove that he designed them himself; in others he is known to have modified them; and in a few instances he may have been only the channel through which the designs of others were forwarded to Rome.

His earliest dated plan, that for the Jesuit college at Le Puy,[7] made in February 1605, shows a close adherence to the official plan of a double quadrangle. A drawing of it, half built, is dated 1617 [725]. The chapel[8] was planned as a wide single nave with three chapels on either side, communicating by passages, a transept a little narrower than the nave, and a square-ended choir.[9] The scheme of the interior is based on a system of Tuscan pilasters. There are wooden galleries in the arcades over the chapels in the nave and over the ends of the transepts. It is, indeed, the simplest possible version of the current monastic usage, with the addition of galleries to meet the needs of a teaching Order that was also an Order of preachers. Because of the hardness of Vélay granite, the decoration is painted, not carved; but it follows the Jesuit formula of figures in the spandrels. The carved façade is adorned with a coat of arms and a round window; the later bell tower is small and insignificant.

---

[1] The church was planned by Martellange, but was built only in 1673 after his death. (Hautecœur, 1, 631.)   [2] See Moisy, Les églises Jésuites, 1, 424 ff.

[3] The interior is fundamentally Gothic, with Flemish Renaissance ornament. There are no galleries.

[4] 1, 259.   [5] See Charvet, Martellange, pp. 1 ff. and Moisy, Les églises Jésuites, passim.

[6] See Bouchot, pp. 17 and 20: Bib. Nat. Est., Hd 4a–d, and Ub 9. A new catalogue of them by the Institutum Historicum S.J. at Rome has been published as this book is in the press. It contains (p. 31*) some valuable information about the authors of proposed plans, and about the variations on the conventional scheme by M. Vallery-Radot. They are carefully studied by Moisy, Les églises Jésuites, pp. 28 ff.

[7] Charvet, op. cit. p. 13. Bib. Nat. Est., Hd 4b fol. 226.

[8] Charvet, op. cit. p. 25. Now the parish church of St Georges.

[9] Cabinet des Estampes, Ub 9a, p. 139.

Martellange's plan for the Jesuit college at Moulins also dates from 1605.[1] The existing buildings [724] conform to it,[2] and show a simple and almost secular style of brick relieved with groins and string courses of stone. In this year he also designed the college at Sisteron.[3]

Martellange's college at Vienne was planned between 1607 and 1610.[4] He first designed it with a chapel to the north of a very simple kind, but the design was not approved at the headquarters of the Society at Rome, to which all plans had to be submitted. He then made a second plan with the usual two quadrangles and a chapel on the plan of that at Le Puy, with two octagonal staircases at the angles of the façade. The final plan, made in 1610, showed some modifications in the living and working quarters and a three-sided choir.[5] In 1607 he designed the Jesuit house of the Trinité at Lyons with a chapel on the same lines[6] and began a great project for La Flèche,[7] which was finished in 1621.[8]

La Flèche[9] remains the most typical surviving Jesuit college of the seventeenth century. It was built by the King on the site of one of his castles, and here for the first time a French Jesuit establishment was built regardless of expense. The three splendid courts [726–8] continue the Jesuit tradition of simplicity, but are approached through a royal gateway. The chapel, which alone came directly under Martellange's care, was built between 1607 and 1621. It is still curiously and traditionally Gothic in its exterior [729, 730]. The interior shows the usual Jesuit galleried plan with side chapels, transept, a three-sided apse and a Gothic rib vault greatly enriched with sculptures and ornament.[10] The spandrels of the arcade have figures in relief; the transept has statues of the four cardinal virtues; and the marble retable, made by Pierre Corbereau in 1633, rivals the Benedictine retables of the same kind.[11]

Meanwhile, Martellange continued to turn out Jesuit colleges to the standard pattern, always under the censorship of the authorities in Rome. He began the design of their house at Vesoul[12] in 1610, at first with a single court and a second building behind, that could later be joined to it. The church formed part of the court, and was of the usual galleried type. This plan was not approved, and in 1613

---

[1] Charvet, *Martellange*, p. 53.

[2] Now the Tribunal. The church was built in 1661–4. See Moisy, *Les églises Jésuites*, I, 235.

[3] Bouchot, 'La vie de Martellange', p. 27; Bib. Nat. Est., Hd 4b, fol. 202. Here, as in many Jesuit colleges, the chapel was built last.

[4] Charvet, p. 44; the first plan, Bib. Nat. Est., Hd 4b, fol. 251, is dated 1605.

[5] The building of the chapel, now Saint-André-lé-Haut, was only begun in 1659 and was not finished until 1725.   [6] Bouchot, *op. cit.* p. 28; Bib. Nat. Est., Hd 4b, fol. 149.

[7] Charvet, *op. cit.* p. 87; Bouchot, p. 38; Bib. Nat. Est., Hd 4b, fols. 170, 171, 186, 194, 195 and Ub 9, fol. 28, 29, 32, 33. Ub 9, p. 32 shows it being built in 1612.

[8] In 1642 Mathurin Jousse published his *Secret d'Architecture* at La Flèche. It is mainly a practical discourse on construction, and it is possible that he was the builder of the college, in the practical sense of the word.

[9] Now a military school. (See Moisy, *Les églises Jésuites*, I, 210.)

[10] Martellange was interested in Gothic architecture; his notebooks in the Bibliothèque Nationale (Ub 9) show him drawing Gothic churches in every town he visited.

[11] Moisy, *Les églises Jésuites*, I, 322, points out that Jesuit churches rarely had more than three chapels.

[12] Charvet, *op. cit.* p. 71; Bouchot, *op. cit.* p. 33; Bib. Nat. Est., Hdb, fol. 196.

he made a second, by which the courts were completed and the construction of the church was postponed. The central court, of very simple design, survives as the Lycée; the church was never built. About 1610, again, he modified the elevation of the Jesuit chapel at Dôle[1] and redesigned their college at Dijon.[2] The buildings [731] are simple but for a few sculptured details. The chapel follows closely the formula of side chapels, galleries and polygonal apse. It retains Gothic vaults, but the arcades have their keystones sculptured with classical heads. In 1611 he planned, or modified the plans for, the college at Bourges [733];[3] the plans had to be altered several times before the building was finished in 1615.

In 1611 also he was responsible for the plans of the college of Saint-Pierre at Nevers.[4] The school buildings[5] were simple. The chapel, begun in 1612 and finished about 1635, is rather more complex than usual in plan; the transept has a half-octagon apsidal end to either arm, echoed in that of the apse, and there is a shallow dome over the crossing. Four little chapels with galleries over are fitted into the angles. The two-storeyed quality of the galleried arcade is stressed by a heavy triglyph frieze above the arch, that serves as a balustrade to the gallery. The horizontals are everywhere stressed except in the long windows of the transept and apse; the result has breadth rather than nobility. The simple vaults are enriched with *trompe-l'œil* perspectives of architecture. The handsome high-shouldered façade [734] is a screen that has little structural relation with the interior. Clearly Martellange had the Gesù at Rome in mind, though he fitted a part only of it into his narrow front.

He next directed the building of the Novitiate at Lyons in 1617 and supervised the Jesuit Colleges at Roanne[6] [732] and Orléans[7] and the Novitiate and College at Avignon.[8]

---

[1] Bouchot, 'La vie de Martellange', p. 31; Bib. Nat. Est., Ub9, fols. 79, 81, 82. It had been begun in 1591. Dôle was not French until 1636. The buildings remain as the Collège d'Art and Museum. They are said to have been begun by the Jesuit Père Antoine Dufour. (See Tournier, p. 277.)

[2] Bouchot, *op. cit.* p. 33; Bib. Nat. Est. Ub9, fols. 56, 61, 63, 67 and Hd4, fol. 191. They had been planned as early as 1585 but the drawings show them being built between 1610 and 1611. They survive as the municipal library and a school. (See Moisy, *Les églises Jésuites*, I, 198.)

[3] Bouchot, *op. cit.* p. 37; Bib. Nat. Est., Hd4b, fols. 135 and 137. Some buildings remain as the Petit Lycée and the Lycée Alain Fournier.

[4] It had been founded in 1572 by Louis Gonzaga, Duc de Nevers, but had been shut in 1595. (For the plans see Bib. Nat. Est., Hd4b, fol. 126 and Ub9, fols. 51–3. Moisy, *Les églises Jésuites*, I, 239.)

[5] Later the Lycée; they were destroyed in the bombardment of 16 July 1944. The chapel survives.

[6] Now the Lycée. It was founded in 1607 by Pierre Coton and his brother. The chapel was finished in 1626. The other buildings were rebuilt 1679–87 by the great-nephew of the founder, François Lachaise.

[7] Bouchot, *op. cit.* p. 41. Bib. Nat. Est. Hd4b, fols. 119, 120. It occupied the site of a former Benedictine monastery. Martellange's drawings date it to 1620 and show the chapel as long and narrow with a rounded apse. The school buildings were designed by Derand in 1632. (Moisy, *Les églises Jésuites*, I, 159.)

[8] Bouchot, *op. cit.* p. 30; Bib. Nat. Est. Ub9a, fols. 172 and 173. The church of the Novitiate has a short nave and a lantern on pendentives, with little tribunes with balustrades over the arcade. It survives as the Musée Lapidaire. Martellange's drawings show it being built between 1618 and 1619. (Bib. Nat. Est. Ub9a, fol. 103.) The very plain, and much dilapidated, chapel at Meaux (now part of the Collège de Jeunes Filles) is one of these simple Jesuit churches.

The repertory of his drawings in the Cabinet des Estampes includes plans for a plain rectangular chapel at Auch; a church with a three-sided apse and side chapels in the southern style at Béziers; one with a long nave of six bays and a small polygonal apse at Arras; a Benedictine plan, with sacristies built in behind the apse, at Aurillac;[1] and a very plain design for Besançon.[2]

Martellange's activities continued in the 1620's. In 1624 he designed the church of St Louis at Blois,[3] finished under Turmel with money given by the King's brother Gaston, duc d'Orléans, who lived at the Château.[4] The interior [736] is Doric, without galleries except in the choir, with a triglyph frieze of which the metopes contain the initials of St Louis in leafy crowns and the three nails of the Passion within a crown of thorns. The vault is still Gothic in system; a small lantern surmounts the crossing. There are the usual three bays of side chapels, and the apse is as usual three-sided. One arm of the transept has statues of the Theological Virtues, of which Charity once held the heart of Gaston d'Orléans; they are balanced in the other arm by Prayer, with book and censer, Love with a flame on an altar and Religion.[5]

The exterior is extremely plain; the walls are broken only by a cornice and window mouldings. The façade [735] is much richer, but has the curious flatness of something drawn on paper and not thought out in the round.[6] The three storeys of the three orders are linked by reversed volutes with vase buttresses. The school buildings[7] are very simple, and much like those of the contemporary buildings at the Benedictine abbey of Saint-Lomer de Blois.

The most esteemed work of Martellange's maturity was the Jesuit Novitiate at Paris, which was designed in 1628 and begun in 1631.[8] Marot's engravings (see Fig. 5) show the short nave[9] of two bays usual in the Novitiate houses, very much in the style of the Blois church, but with galleries in the arcades [737]. The façade [738] is simpler than that at Blois, but much better designed, with some reminiscences of the Gesù and a more considerable debt to the church of S. Maria del Monte at Rome, built by Giacomo della Porta in 1580.[10] It was doubtless its happy blend of austerity and richness that caught the fancy of Martellange's

---

[1] Bouchot considers that this was designed by Père Christophe Gruenberger.

[2] Hardly less plain Jesuit churches in eastern France are Gray, 1680, and Salins, 1701, both without aisles. (See Tournier, p. 294.)

[3] Now Saint-Vincent-de-Paul.

[4] Bouchot, 'La vie de Martellange', p. 44; Bib. Nat. Est. Hd 4c, fol. 21. The plans were made in 1624, approved at Rome 1625 and amended later. (See Moisy, Les églises Jésuites, I, 175.)

[5] These and the subsidiary figures of the Cardinal Virtues and of children carrying coats of arms, are all by the sculptor Gaspard Imbert.

[6] It is sometimes attributed to François Derand.   [7] Now the Bureau de Bienfaisance.

[8] Bouchot, op. cit. p. 47; Bib. Nat. Est. Hd 4b, fol. 172, Ub 9, fols. 2, 4, 5. Charvet, Martellange, p. 93, sets it a little earlier, but the evidence is against him. The Fathers' quarters were rebuilt in 1679. On the whole question of the Paris houses see Moisy, Les églises Jésuites, I, 247.

[9] The whole church was only 96 feet long and 42 feet wide.

[10] See Ciprut, 'Les Modèles de Martellange'. On the relation between Martellange and Derand here see Moisy in Bull. Mon. cx (1952), 237.

contemporaries. The residential quarters that accompanied it [739] were, too, a little less bleak than usual.

A second Jesuit church was being constructed at Paris at almost the same time, through the munificence of Louis XIII [740]. The gift was made in 1627, for the *Maison Professe*; the church was consecrated in 1641. As usual, Martellange supervised the design; with him was associated another Jesuit architect, Père François Derand.[1] According to Piganiol de la Force,[2] Martellange wished to imitate the Gesù at Rome, but Derand made his own design and this was preferred. The

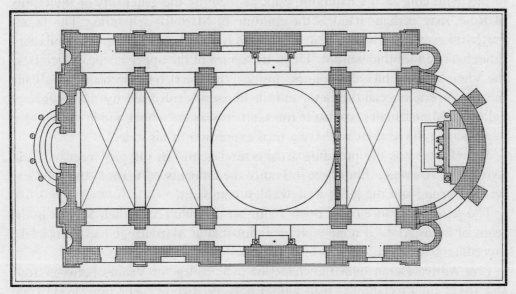

Fig. 5. Jesuit Novitiate, Paris.
Plan of church, by Martellange, 1628.

church survives as Saint-Paul-Saint-Louis. The very rich façade, given by Richelieu [742], has none of the flatness of the Jesuit church at Blois, though something of its scheme; it is worked out very successfully in the round. It owes little to Vignola and the Gesù. The interior [741], with its great Corinthian pilasters and its notably rich heavy frieze, is inspired by the Gesù, though not to the extent of plagiary. The characteristic development of the galleries in itself suffices to give it another flavour. The crossing and dome are the parts nearest to the prototype. There is a short choir of one bay, with semicircular absidioles before the galleried apse; the transept is very shallow. Contemporary criticism[3] found that the church was rather dark, and that the altar was too low for the celebrant to be easily seen; otherwise it was justly admired, and formed a fitting auditorium for the sermons of Bourdaloue. Some remains of the habitations of the Maison Professe may still be found in the Lycée Charlemagne: a good ironwork balustrade to a staircase

[1] See Moisy, *Les églises Jésuites*, I, 77, 438. Frère Turmel seems later to have been associated with the work (Hautecœur, I, 629).

[2] v, 4.   [3] Piganiol de la Force, v, 4.

[743], the richly decorated door of the Jesuits' library [744], a staircase with a painted ceiling and one wall at least of the courtyard.

The Paris houses were almost the last work of Martellange. Only the Jesuit college at Carpentras[1] is later, and that rather in execution than in design. The two courtyards of the college buildings were designed and the church begun in 1628, but it was long in building.[2] The church was planned as a lesser version of the Novitiate at Paris; its choir is square.[3]

Yet, though there is no documentary evidence to prove it his work, the church of the Jesuit college at Chaumont, built in 1629[4] by the generosity of the family of Rose, may perhaps stand as the epitome of Martellange's style.[5] The façade [745] still recalls Vignola's Gesù in its orders and the grouping of its pilasters, though a quasi-Gothic window forms the centre of the upper storey, which lacks the Vignolesque gables and volutes. Inside [746] the rich Corinthian capitals and the rinceau frieze recall the Gesù, and the likeness is enhanced by the absence of galleries. Martellange's familiar lierne vault crowns the whole, and in the baroque explosion of the retables we have a final expression of his style.[6]

Martellange was the presiding architectural genius in the provinces of Paris, Lyons and Toulouse. Elsewhere in France the influence of Vignola and the Gesù was less strong and the Jesuit style was less consistent.

The Jesuits of France could boast a number of architects in their Society in the reign of Louis XIV,[7] if none were so influential as Martellange had been in the preceding generation.

Père Adrien Deran built the chapel of their college at Vannes between 1661 and 1682,[8] on a rectangular plan with a polygonal choir.[9] The fine façade [747] still has reminiscences of the Gesù, though the pediment of the door is set lower and pyramids take the place of volutes to weight it at the sides. A drawing for Cahors, with a chapel on a central plan and an immense apse, is dated 1663.[10] Père Paul Clausse planned the college at Chalons-sur-Marne[11] in 1678; Père Chesneau that at Clermont-Ferrand between 1677 and 1679;[12] and Père Nicolas André that at Caen, Notre-Dame-de-la-Gloriette, between 1684 and 1687. Its façade [748], if not highly original, is at least wholly independent of the Gesù.

[1] Charvet, *Martellange*, p. 65; Bouchot, 'La vie de Martellange', p. 28; Bib. Nat. Est., Hd 4c, fol. 129. Now the Lycée Henri Fabre.

[2] It stopped soon after 1628, and continued, thanks to a legacy, in 1669. The dome was only finished in 1687.

[3] It should be recorded that Martellange also designed in Gothic style; it was he who planned the Gothic transept of the cathedral at Orléans when it was rebuilt. (Lanson, p. 9.)

[4] Now the chapel of the Lycée. (Hautecœur, I, 546.)

[5] M. Pierre Moisy does not consider the design to be his (*Les églises Jésuites*, I, 192).

[6] An octagonal dome was added in 1740, but replaced by a lantern in 1817 (*ibid.* I, 192).

[7] See Hautecœur, II, 716.   [8] See *Cong. Arch.* (1914), p. 419; Moisy, *Les églises Jésuites*, I, 296.

[9] The monumental retable is by Jean Boffrand of Nantes, 1685.

[10] Bib. Nat. Est., Hd 4b.   [11] Now destroyed. See Bib. Nat. Est., Hd IV, p. 146.

[12] A drawing for it, apparently by Martellange, will be found in the Cabinet des Estampes, Hd 4b, with a trefoil apse, a small nave and galleries.

The graceful Ionic interior gets in the necessary galleries with less interruption of line than usual by giving them wrought-iron balustrades to the nave. The choir is splendid with gilt bronzes and fine iron grilles.

The hand of Martellange's colleague, Père François Derand,[1] has been recognized in the buildings of the Jesuit college of Rouen,[2] of which the foundation stone was laid by Marie de Médicis in 1614. It was consecrated in 1631 but finished only in 1656. The portal of the chapel as designed by Derand was never executed; the existing one, with statues of Charlemagne and St Louis, dates from 1703. The interior of the chapel [749, 750] still has Martellange's Gothic vaults and windows, and his familiar gallery appears in each arm of the transept, though not in the nave. The transept and choir have polygonal apses. The spandrels are filled with figures of angels; in place of keystones figures of Joseph, of the Man of Sorrows, of the Virgin and Child, appear over the arches. The high altar and the altars of the transept have elaborate retables. The school buildings [751, 752] are more carefully planned than in many Jesuit colleges, but would not be remarkable in a Benedictine monastery. The only direct Benedictine influence, however, is in the later gateway to the college.

The Jesuit College at Rennes[3] was built in 1624; the three-storeyed classical façade [754] incorporates two towers, each with a cupola; the church is without galleries but has a heavy triglyph frieze. Its design was almost certainly due to Derand,[4] though Martellange had made plans for it, which he handed over to another Jesuit, Charles Turmel,[5] who seems to have learned his skill as a coadjutor of Martellange, notably at Blois and Orleans. Turmel planned[6] a chapel for the college at Quimper [753] in the style of those at Rouen and Nevers, and designed others, never executed, for Amiens, Caen and Alençon.[7]

The Jesuit college at Eu was founded about 1582 by Catherine of Cleves, wife of Henri de Guise.[8] The collegiate buildings [755] are simple, with their ornament

[1] See Moisy, Les églises Jésuites, I, 77. His L'architecture des voûtes (Paris, 1643), is a practical work for masons.

[2] Now part of the Lycée Corneille. (See Bouchot, 'La vie de Martellange', p. 49; Charvet, Martellange, p. 186; E. Chartier-Alain; Moisy, 'Derand', p. 153, and Les églises Jésuites, I, 272, where he gives a detailed account of the work.)

[3] Bouchot, 'La vie de Martellange', p. 43; Moisy, Les églises Jésuites, I, 268. It was drawn by Martellange for submission to Rome in 1624 (Bib. Nat. Est., Hd 4b, fol. 81) but does not seem to have been designed by him; the plans (ibid. fol. 180) are by another hand.

[4] Moisy, 'Derand', p. 155.

[5] See H. Bourde de la Rogerie; P. Delattre 'Frère Charles Turmel'; and Moisy in Bull. de la Soc. de l'hist, de l'art français (1950), p. 70 and Les églises Jésuites, I, 209. A volume in the library at Quimper contains plans by him collected at his death. His father was probably the architect of Quimper Hospital (Delattre, ibid. p. 30).

[6] Moisy, Les églises Jésuites, I, 79.

[7] We know that the scholastic buildings at Besançon were designed about 1664 by Père Antoine Dufour (Bouchot, p. 32) and the chapel (now church of Saint-François-Xavier) which completed them in 1660, a few years before Besançon became French, has enough reminiscences of the Gesù about it to indicate that its architect was completely familiar with the church.

[8] Moisy, op. cit. I, 204.

concentrated in the heraldic decoration of the doorways [758]. The first stone of the chapel was laid in 1613; it was finished in 1628. The exterior in brick and stone [756, 757] is still essentially Gothic in feeling; the interior in its galleries and Gothic vaults betrays the influence of Martellange [759].[1]

The great building of the Jesuit college at Brest[2] [762] initiated at the end of the seventeenth century a new scheme with a pilastered central feature rising to a dome, that forms the centre of a long range of austere building. The idea owes something to the older 'frontispiece', but congruous though it was with the Jesuit style, it seems not to have set a fashion. The later buildings at Angers have only a bell-cote to break their long front [763].[3]

At Maubeuge the seventeenth-century chapel[4] is still more Gothic in style, even to string course and hood mould; it may well date from before the Treaty of Nimegen gave Maubeuge to France.[5] The college at Soissons is notable for its two gateways, one with delightful figures of Pallas and Ceres [760]; and a main entrance much like that at Rouen. Cassel became French in 1678; the Jesuit chapel there was built in 1687 on the familiar 'frontispiece' formula. Apart from the façade the exterior is of a barrack-like plainness. The English Jesuits at Saint Omer rebuilt their house in 1726 in Flemish style, with brick pilasters; no building could be less English, or, indeed, less French. The Jesuit church at Cambrai [761], built after the town became French, is still very Flemish in style; but the little house of English Jesuits at Watten, also of the late eighteenth century, seems to have been inspired by the architecture of the Norman Benedictine monasteries.[6]

Further east the Jesuits of Besançon rebuilt their church between 1686 and 1688, and their buildings between 1718 and 1737.[7] The church [764], dedicated to St François Xavier, was designed by Père Louis Hoste.[8] Its interior is most impressive, with a wide vault, splendid piers on Corinthian pilasters, and a frieze with classical foliage centred on the device of the man under whose bequest it was built. There is a false transept, and an octagonal cupola at the crossing. The façade has reminiscences of the Gesù. The school buildings[9] [765, 770, 771, 772] are linked to the chapel by a screen wall. The courtyard has an impressive cloister, and the buildings a no less impressive staircase. The Salle du Conseil survives as the Chapel of the Lycée.

[1] See Moisy, 'Le recueil des plans jésuites de Quimper'.
[2] It served as a training school for naval chaplains. [3] Moisy, Les églises Jésuites, I, 275.
[4] Now a public hall, the Salle Sthrau.
[5] A gateway to the college, dated 1765, is extremely arriéré in style.
[6] The Fathers owned a Reliquary of the Holy Thorn made in London c. 1600, which was conveyed to them in 1666. In 1773 it came into the possession of the Bishop of Ghent who gave it to the church of St Michael in that city. (See Fr John Morris in The Month, XLIV (1882), 549 and C. C. Oman, English Church Plate, 1957, p. 285.)
[7] See Moisy, Les églises Jésuites, I, 172. He attributes the work to Père Louis Hoste. The chapel of the sodality survives as that of the Lycée des garçons.
[8] So Moisy, ibid.; Tournier, p. 311, ascribes it to Père de Hoye and Claude Coquart.
[9] Now Lycée Victor-Hugo.

The Jesuits at Verdun in 1731 erected a chapel that transmutes the Cambrai front into pure and elegant classicism [766, 767]. It seems to have been designed by the Jesuit Père Maugrain.[1] The interior is characteristically east French in its round columns and elaborate capitals.

Notre-Dame-de-Metz, built between 1735 and 1739, is wholly different from the general idea of a Jesuit church in its unadorned and extremely sophisticated severity [768].

The Jesuit house at Langres[2] [769], which dates from 1746, follows the Chaumont tradition in integrating the entrance to the school into the scheme dominated by the handsome façade of the chapel. This forms one side of a quadrangle, of which two are occupied by school buildings and one by the screen wall to the street. The college chapel of Saint-Pierre-de-Colmar had its chapel[3] rebuilt about 1760. A very plain exterior with a high-pitched roof masks a lofty interior of unexpected splendour, with nave galleries fitted into the coved ceiling, splendidly domed aisles, and a richly decorated apse [773, 774, 775, 776].

South of the Loire we know much less of the Jesuit architects, apart from Martellange.[4] In the Massif Central one can guess at the work of an architect with a passion for doorways framed in twin Corinthian columns; they appear, for example, at Mauriac [777] and at Cahors.[5] The scheme is enriched at Rodez to form a 'frontispiece' [778] to buildings that could hardly be plainer. The excellent buildings of the college at Limoges[6] [779, 780], dating from 1685, differ little but in their attics from a contemporary Benedictine house. The chapel is earlier and recalls Martellange.

The chapel[7] at Alençon, built between 1686 and 1706 [781, 782], is a most elegant little edifice in which the eighteenth-century sense of modulation of surface is already beautifully expressed. The curves of the complex ground plan are echoed in the cornice and finally resolved in the roof. The door is richly, if not quite so fashionably, carved. The college at Autun, founded in 1709, was never more than half built, but is none the less extremely impressive [783, 784] in its severe regularity. Its great glory is the magnificent grille to the street, set up in 1772, decorated with trophies of the arts, with globes and orreries for finials. The seminary at Auxerre,[8] built in 1714, has a chapel with a plain classical façade,

---

[1] Moisy, *Les églises Jésuites*, I, 297. It was damaged in 1944, but has been repaired.

[2] Now the Collège Diderot. I was not permitted to enter the chapel. (See Moisy, *Les églises Jésuites*, I, 212.)

[3] Now the chapel of the Lycée. (See *ibid.* 194.)

[4] On Père Moreau, who worked chiefly in the Lyonnais, see *ibid.* I, 127 ff. and on Louis Mercier, who worked mainly in Aquitaine, *ibid.* pp. 148 ff.

[5] Now the Lycée Gambetta. The tower shows the medieval tradition of the south-west transmuted into classical style.

[6] Now the Lycée Gay-Lussac (Moisy, *op. cit.* I, p. 218). The chapel of 1633 is still mainly Gothic in style. The College at Avallon is equally modest and local in style. That at Mâcon (now the Lycée Lamartine) is masked in plaster; it was built in 1675.

[7] Now the Library (*ibid.* p. 160).   [8] Now the Lycée Paul Bert.

crowned by a pediment with the Society's badge; the other buildings, round a three-sided court, are without pretension in the local style.[1]

The fine Jesuit church of Saint-Paul at Bordeaux[2] [785, 786], built between 1663 and 1676, is another Louis XIV church with a plain cornice and rich key-stones to the arches. It has galleries only in the choir. The contemporary pulpit dominates the nave. The façade, with hanging garlands between Corinthian pilasters, is notably rich; the residential quarters[3] are handsomer than usual.

The Jesuit college at Auch,[4] traditionally said to have been built by Pierre II Souffron between 1624 and 1627,[5] is on a simpler scale; its central range, between two projecting wings, is centred by a rounded pediment. At Rodez the chapel [787, 788] is chiefly remarkable for its retable; it is in a Jesuit style with fewer Gothic influences than that of northern France. The collegiate quarters are digni-fied but very plain.

The chapel at Cahors, built before 1644, recalls that at Dijon and is in the Martellange style; the collegiate buildings seem to be some seventy years later. At Pau the buildings[6] are on a loftier plan; the chapel,[7] however, is extremely plain, with a façade adorned with simple Doric pilasters. At Carcassonne a com-plex of Jesuit buildings exist, considerably modified, as the College. Its façade to the street is very well designed in an extremely austere style [791]. The courtyard within has a very simple cloister along the side nearest to the chapel.[8] This has a hexagonal tower, that carries on the medieval tradition of the south into classical style. The fine brick college at Pamiers,[9] built between 1702 and 1719, still has ogival windows to its chapel and many reminiscences of the local late medieval style.

The Jesuit buildings of southern France have a tradition of splendid entrance doorways; it is well exemplified at Albi[10] [789, 790] and Toulouse[11] [792]. Their chapels are no less splendid.

The plan survives[12] of the chapel built at Albi in 1658. It is based on a cross inscribed within a quadrangle, with barrel-vaulted arms, a cupola at the crossing, and cross-vaulted chapels fitted into the angles. At Arles the Jesuit chapel, begun, soon after 1652,[13] follows the plan and style of that at Avignon ,not yet French, and has a three-sided apse, and a typically heavy Provençal cornice over the arcade. It is chiefly remarkable for the extremely delicate and varied carving of

---

[1] One side is of 1589. [2] See Moisy, *Les églises Jésuites*, I, 177.

[3] Now a lycée. [4] Now the Lycée. [5] Hautecœur, I, 510.

[6] Now a lycée; about half the old buildings have recently been demolished.

[7] I was not able to enter. Moisy (*Les églises Jésuites*, I, 254), dates its beginning to 1687.

[8] It was not possible to visit the interior; it was said to be modern.

[9] Moisy, *op. cit.* I, 245. It now serves as a cinema.

[10] Now the Lycée. [11] Now Petit Lycée.

[12] Bib. Nat. Est., Hd 4, fol. 154; Hautecœur, I, 635; Moisy, *op. cit.* p. 159. A chapel completed later survives as the chapel of the Lycée.

[13] Now the Musée d'Art Chrétien. The roof dates from after 1737; the retable, 1679, probably gives the date of the original completion.

its rich frieze [793, 794]. The only gallery is at the west end. At Nîmes both chapel and college survive.[1] The college is plain in style, but designed with unusual nobility with a rather Benedictine cloister built between 1673 and 1678 [796]. The chapel [795, 797, 798] has a baroque façade with a few reminiscences of the Paris Novitiate, and a southern abundance of arrises. Inside it has a lofty apse, now bereft of its retable, with balustraded galleries on either side. They continue round the church, but in the false transept become balconies with wrought-iron railings projecting on heavy consoles.

The southern tradition is continued in the Jesuit college at Aix-en-Provence, rebuilt under royal patronage in the years after 1681. The church, of which the façade was never completed, is dedicated to St Louis. It owes something to the Maison Professe at Paris in its galleries, high-set and heavily balustraded, its Corinthian pilasters and its rich decoration[2] [799]. Its several courtyards are plain [801], but for a few fine doorways [800] and a delightful grotto [802]. The same tradition continues at Grenoble,[3] where the chapel, though a little less Provençal, has a façade in the Nîmes manner [803, 804] designed by Père Louis Hoste in 1705. The courtyard rivals Aix in severity. At Montpellier the Jesuit chapel survives as the parish church of Notre-Dame-des-Tables [805, 806].[4] Its façade is in the familiar tradition, but the interior is more original. The unusually wide nave has a dome at the crossing of the false transept; there are side chapels; the east end is flat, and filled with an elaborate retable. There are no galleries, except for those simulated by balustrades and pictures in the east wall of the transept and in the choir. The Corinthian pilasters and the wall spaces are veneered with coloured marbles. It is essentially a preaching church, simple in plan and rich in decoration.

The college at Tournon rebuilt its chapel in the local grey stone between 1673 and 1721. The façade is from the former building of 1606,[5] and not very well designed; the interior still perpetuates the style of Martellange in its balustraded galleries and its triglyph frieze, and the Spanish tradition of the house in its splendid high altar, which clearly comes from an earlier church.

In 1753[6] the Jesuit father Pierre Laugier, a 'petit abbé' at the court of King Stanislas at Nancy, published his *Essai sur l'Architecture*. His idea of a perfect church[7] shows how far the ideas of Martellange had become a part of Jesuit doctrine. He considers that it should be planned as a Latin cross, with square

---

[1] Now the library, museum and lecture hall. (Moisy, *Les églises Jésuites*, I, 241.)

[2] Some of the inlaid marble altars from the church are now in that of Saint-Nicolas, Pertuis. It retains the chapel of its sodality.

[3] Now the Lycée de jeunes filles (see Moisy, *op. cit.* I, 208). The chapel is a gymnasium and I was unable to see the interior.

[4] *Ibid.* I, 233. The college survives as the Lycée but its two courtyards are now rather featureless. Moisy (*loc. cit.*), is inclined to attribute them to the architect Frère Pierre Chesneau.

[5] Moisy, *op. cit.* I, 291.

[6] I have had to use the second edition of 1755, as the first is not in the British Museum. He was much criticized at the time: see Hautecœur, IV, 50.

[7] 1755 ed. p. 178.

chapels in the arcade. The interior should be in two orders, with coupled columns, and a vault above. The apse should be square. He deprecates a dome, however, but favours two towers decorated with the classical orders[1] as the basis of structure, and declares against twisted columns, niches and pedestals; even the architrave separating two orders should be plain.[2] He greatly favours the use of detached columns, especially of the Corinthian order,[3] in place of engaged columns or piers.[4] He is so much shocked by the idea of a flying buttress that he advises the raising of the walls of side chapels as a screen to hide them, with a balustrade above and sham windows.[5]

He is a man of his time—even a precursor of the Romantics—in basing the general principles of architecture on 'la simple Nature'.[6] Fifty years before Chateaubriand he finds the origin of columns in tree-trunks, of capitals in their leafage, of pediments in the construction of huts; and finds in those three things the essentials of architectural composition.

His *Observations sur l'Architecture*, published in 1765, shows a distinct swing towards classical taste. He writes of the 'mauvais effet' of Romanesque and Gothic churches, and on the difficulty of decorating a building in the Gothic style. They have noble vistas, and must be respected; but if anything classical and modern is brought into them, it must be on a big scale and with an over-all plan. A Greek altar in a Gothic church will not do. His final section envisages the creation of a new order.

Most of his instances are drawn from cathedrals, but at one point[7] he discusses the problem of the stalls of a monastic church masking the bases of the columns of the ambulatory, that should be visible . Either the choir must not be columniated (which would be a pity); or the columns must stand on a high plinth (a better solution), or, as at Sainte-Geneviève, the aisles must be higher than the nave. Stalls are a Gothic invention, and very difficult to reconcile with a modern classical church. The best plan is to have the high altar at the crossing and a choir behind it. Organs are another unclassical necessity; he finds no easy solution of where to place them, but dismisses 'tribunes' and galleries as unclassical.

Three great schemes of Jesuit building were undertaken in 1757, at Clermont-Ferrand, Strasbourg and Autun.[8] They show a remarkable variation of style, and completely ignore Laugier's recommendations. Their college at Clermont-Ferrand,[9] with austere granite buildings curved to form a courtyard [*807*] is composed in another idiom. The great building by Massol at Strasbourg [*809*],[10]

---

[1] Laugier, p. xvi.   [2] *Ibid*. p. xx.   [3] *Ibid*. p. 20.

[4] In the preface to the second edition (1755) he says that he has been severely criticized for his want of respect for the tradition of Palladio and Vignola, and for his attacks on pilasters and arcades. He unfavourably criticized (p. 16) the triple order of Saint-Paul-Saint-Louis as 'an architecture in bas-relief'.

[5] *Ibid*. p. xxix.   [6] *Ibid*. p. 8.

[7] Laugier, *Observations sur l'Architecture* (1755), p. 119.

[8] Their collegiate buildings at Alençon seem also to date from this year.

[9] Now Lycée Blaise-Pascal. On its history see Moisy, *Les églises Jésuites*, I, 193.

[10] Now Lycée Fustel de Coulanges.

with its rusticated corner pavilions and its pedimented centre, owes something to the grandeurs of Benedictine Saint-Denis.

The chapel at Autun, designed by Jean Baptiste Caristie,[1] also in 1757, externally recalls Père André's work at Caen. The aisled interior [810] is severe in effect, in spite of the dropping garlands of its pilasters. The arcade stops to form a false transept. There are galleries on either side of the altar and at the west end. It is, indeed, a final expression of a tradition inherited from the Paris Novitiate by way of Saint-Paul de Bordeaux.

These three buildings are the last of any importance erected by the French Jesuits.[2] The fortunes of the Society of Jesus in France began to ebb about 1750. The superior of the Jesuit Mission in the French settlement of Martinique went bankrupt for a large sum in 1753, and a case against the procurator of the Paris province went to the Courts. In May 1761 the Society's ancient enemy, the Parlement of Paris, found against the Order, and in August 1762 issued an *arrêt* condemning it to extinction. The King's intervention brought eight months' delay, and a final hope was offered if the Society in France would sever itself from the international Order, under a French Vicar. This was refused, and on 1 April 1762 the *arrêt* against them was put into execution and the Jesuits were ordered to renounce their vows or go into banishment. At the end of November 1764 the King unwillingly signed an edict dissolving the Society in his dominions. The province of Paris had nine hundred and eighteen members, of whom four hundred and ninety-five were priests; in France as a whole there were nearly four thousand Jesuits, of whom over seventeen hundred were priests.[3] Some provincial Parlements, notably in Franche-Comté, Alsace and Artois, still protected them; but none the less the doom of the French Jesuits was accomplished. They did not return to France until 1815.

[1] See *ibid.* 167.

[2] It has already been noted that the grille of their college at Autun was put up in 1772, and the façade of the chapel at Moulins dates from 1765. The College at La Rochelle is so late in style as to suggest that it was never Jesuit.

[3] The province of Bordeaux had 437 (240 priests), Lyons 773 (405), Toulouse 655 (344), Champagne 594 (292). (Hélyot, *Dictionnaire*, II, 670.)

CHAPTER IX

LESSER ORDERS

I. MEN

A number of minor medieval religious Orders continued to exist in the centuries of the Renaissance, though their life was a question of survival rather than of development; and a number were founded which, in their turn, failed to multiply. In so far as I have encountered their recognizable memorials in art and architecture they will be considered in this chapter, but I am well aware that the tally is far from complete.

The two rival Orders devoted to the ransom of prisoners, the Mathurins (or Trinitarians)[1] and the Pères de la Merci, or Mercedarians, continued to survive, though the crusades which had brought them into being were at an end and the chivalric conception of ransom was obsolete. The Pères de la Merci were the more important. Their house at Paris was rebuilt in 1613 by the munificence of Marie de Médicis on the designs of Cottar.[2] Its high altar[3] was adorned with statues of the saints of the Order, St Pierre Nolasque and St Raymond de Pennafort, which were considered to be the masterpieces of Michel Anguier. The later portal, by Boffrand, was notably elaborate and large, to harmonize with the neighbouring Hôtel de Soubise. Their church at Metz[4] [811] was rebuilt with some elegance in 1720. They had a house at Montpellier, rebuilt between 1740 and 1748, but it does not appear to survive. Both Orders were suppressed in 1768.

The Order of Antonins, with a mother-house at Saint-Antoine in the Dauphiné, founded in 1070, has left a few visible remains. Their house at Saint-Marc-la-Lande, near Mazières-en-Gâtinais, has a church built in 1509, with an elegant façade [812]; the royal arms that figure upon it suggest that it may have been a princely gift. The simple monastic buildings are of the same date. The mother-house at Saint-Antoine[5] was rebuilt in 1620, after it had been ruined by the Huguenots; the earlier church and much of the buildings remain. A monumental flight of steps and a fine gateway lead up to the abbey precinct. The buildings, now for the most part private houses of a modest kind, have been considerably modified, but their *ensemble* still dominates the town [813, 814]. The Curé's house, with a good ironwork balcony, seems to be what remains of an eighteenth-century abbot's lodging. The church contains a fine set of stalls carved by François

---

[1] Their Paris house was a medieval structure.
[2] Plans of the church made in 1646 will be found in Arch. Nat., Plans N III, Seine 876 (1–9).
[3] Piganiol de la Force, IV, 329.   [4] Now a Protestant chapel.
[5] Near Saint-Marcellin, Isère. I am indebted to Mademoiselle Chalufour for information and photographs.

Hamard of Lyons in 1630. The Antonins' chapel at Besançon, designed by Galetot in 1739, is now cut by a floor; it has a square choir with a low-pitched cupola.[1] In 1776 the Antonins were united to the Order of Malta, and so endured to the Revolution.

The Camaldules of France, founded at Lyons in 1626, never spread very far. One of their churches remains at Val-Jésus, near Saint-Rambert-sur-Loire. It was built in 1626, in the form of a Greek cross, with a low wooden ceiling with small painted cofferings.

The Order of St John of Jerusalem (of Malta) has left a few buildings in France:[2] a sixteenth-century farm at Chalon-Moulineux, Seine-et-Oise; a Commandery of 1632 at Les Echelles, Savoie; and the chapel of St John Baptist at Questembert in the Morbihan. At Poitiers the hotel remains[3] which was the residence of the prior of the Order of Malta for the province of Aquitaine. Their finest remaining building is that at Toulouse [815, 816] built by J. P. Rivals between 1668 and 1685. They left a priory at Aix-en-Provence.[4] A description of the sculptures of the Paris house is given by Guillet de Saint Georges.[5]

The church of the Barnabites at Paris is known from an engraving in Blondel.[6] Part of their buildings remains at Lescar[7] [817] with a good gateway and a chapel door; two wings were destroyed in 1958.

The College of the Pères Doctrinaires at Brive has an unusually elegant screen to the street [818], dating from 1665. Early eighteenth-century plans of the house of the Pères de Nazareth in the rue du Temple at Paris survive.[8]

The Italian Order of Theatines was brought to Paris from Rome by Mazarin in 1642. He left 100,000 crowns to build them a church, and Brother Camillo Guarini came from Rome to design it. It was designed on an immense scale, and begun in 1662, but was never completed. In 1714 a lottery was authorized for it, and the architect Liévain tried to complete it cheaply as far as the transept. It was designed with a dome (never executed) on heavy piers, a transept of two semi-domes, and a monks' choir behind the altar. Germain Brice wrote[9] criticizing 'la bizarrerie du dessin', and declaring the foolishness of bringing an Italian to France to display 'la forfanterie de sa nation'.[10] Some monastic buildings were erected by Desmaisons between 1747 and 1770. A façade on the rue de Lille and a small courtyard survives.

2. WOMEN

A number of small Orders of women, were founded in France in the seventeenth and eighteenth centuries, but few have left architectural remains which have

---

[1] See Tournier, p. 316. [2] Its Paris church in the rue Thénard was destroyed in 1854.
[3] 157 Grande Rue.
[4] Now the Museum. The Grand Prieuré d'Auvergne at Bourganeuf, Creuse, has been restored out of recognition. [5] I, 364. [6] Hoffbauer, p. 22. [7] Now a school.
[8] Arch. Nat., Plans N III, Seine 400 (1–15). [9] 1698 ed., II, 302. [10] Gillet, p. 93.

been recognized. The Filles de la Compagnie de Notre-Dame,[1] for example, founded in 1607 by a Feuillantine under Jesuit influence, had no less than twenty-nine houses, but none of them appear to survive, unless it be the convent of 1624 (now a prison) at Laon [*819, 820*]. The Congrégation des Sœurs de Saint Joseph, founded at Le Puy in 1650 by a Jesuit to be like the Visitandines before they were enclosed, had branches all over France; some remains of their house in the rue Saint-Dominique are incorporated in the Ministère de la Défence Nationale, but much was rebuilt about 1810. No other surviving building has been identified as theirs, unless it be a chapel at Chalons-sur-Marne. The buildings of the Filles Saint Michel at Paris survive only in plans.[2] The house of the Filles de la Société de la Vierge, founded in 1660 at 4 rue Palatine, Paris, was destroyed in 1903.

The Couvent de la Charité at Bayeux,[3] a house of an Order founded by Père Eudes in 1641 [*821*], has a simple but noble façade, depending for effect on the arch of the cornice over the central oculus. The curve is effectively echoed in the arch of the entrance to the conventual buildings.

In 1678 a Breton lady founded under Jesuit influence the Institution de la Retraite at Quimper, intended to serve as a convent where ladies could retire from the world and follow the spiritual exercises of St Ignatius. The Order still survives, as does its mother-house [*822*], though this now serves as offices for the Gendarmerie of Quimper.

The Sœurs de la Providence at Ribeauvillé showed an extraordinary conservatism in the building of their chapel in the middle of the eighteenth century. The arcade of the nave and the chancel arch are in late fifteenth-century Gothic style, though each arch has rocaille shellwork at the top; the flattened vault is similarly decorated, with a good painting framed into the middle of the nave. It is a rare instance of 'Gothick' in a French nunnery; but one feels that it is due less to taste than to the innate conservatism of religious women.

[1] Hélyot, *Dictionnaire*, I, 1065.
[2] Arch. Nat., Plans N III, Seine 127 (1–7).   [3] Now the gendarmerie.

CONCLUSION

The fortunes of the religious Orders in France in the middle of the eighteenth century were strangely varied. The great abbeys—Cluny, Cîteaux, Clairvaux, Saint-Ouen, Saint-Riquier, Saint-Vaast, and the rest—were rich, and were spending their riches on great ranges of monastic buildings. Yet not all could afford such expenditure. At Chaalis the buildings begun in 1737 were never finished; they cost so much that in 1785 the King closed the abbey as bankrupt. Saint-Cyprien de Poitiers,[1] that in the fifteenth century had had between two and three hundred monks, had in 1790 barely finished rebuilding its monastery after the devastations of the Wars of Religion two hundred years before, and the Madeleine of Châteaudun was not in much better case. The ancient Benedictine house at Menat was by 1789 reduced to an abbot and a prior, who did not reside, and three monks to worship in the great dilapidated Romanesque church. Most of the dormitory had fallen down and only one walk of the fifteenth-century cloister remained upright.

The Augustinians new and old were still building; the Carthusians, who still had a hundred and twenty-two houses in France, were building at Gaillon between 1764 and 1776; the brethren of the Charterhouse at Moulins ordered a new retable as late as July 1781. The Carmelites were still building, even if at the royal expense, at Saint-Denis in 1767. The Franciscans were in decline, though the Capuchins were still building in Paris in 1780 to 1782, if, in one case, because their old house had been demolished to make a new road; the Dominicans were still building, if modestly, at Lisieux between 1775 and 1777. The Jesuits had been exiled from France in August 1763, leaving an immense number of fine churches and colleges as memorials of their Company.

The centralization of life in Paris, that had begun under Richelieu, still continued, even in monastic circles (apart from the rich Benedictine houses) and it was in the Metropolis that building was concentrated. Brice, writing in 1752, could say:

Since 1716 or thereabouts the monastic communities [of Paris] have erected buildings to a cost of several million [*livres*]. The Premonstratensians may be named first, then the Benedictines of Saint-Germain-des-Prés and the Abbaye-aux-Bois; the Carmelites of the rue de Grenelle, the Jesuits at the Novitiate in the rue du Pot-de-Fer, the Theatines, the Lazarists, the Blancs Manteaux, the monks of Saint-Martin-des-Champs; the Capuchins of the rue Saint-Honoré who have had a great new block erected; the Capuchins of the Marais, who have built an entire new church; the monks of Sainte-Geneviève, who have built fine new houses for private individuals on their land; the

---

[1] Migne, *Dictionnaire des Abbayes*, col. 236. The chapel was Doric and 46 metres long.

Discalced Carmelites of the rue du Regard, not forgetting the Filles Saint-Thomas of the rue Saint-Augustin, who in 1715 had a whole new church built, and several other Orders so numerous that people would be surprised if a complete list were drawn up.[1]

Yet already the passing bell had begun to toll. In 1749 Machault d'Arnouville promulgated an edict against mortmain. In 1764 the Society of Jesus was expelled from France; ten years later their much-admired Novitiate in the rue Bonaparte had become the seat of the Freemasons' Lodge of the Grand Orient of France. In 1765 the feeling that the monastic houses were anachronisms in the Age of Reason found official expression.[2] A General Assembly of the clergy of France was convened to consider the reform of the regular clergy. In May 1766 a royal edict set up a commission to inquire into the moral and financial state of all the monasteries of the realm. It consisted of five prelates and five Conseillers d'État, mostly known to hold anti-clerical views. Its appointment and its discussions naturally raised high feelings; and its recommendations did nothing to allay them. The Commission recommended the suppression of the Congregations, the modification of the Rule in certain Orders, and the liquidation of some houses where few monks were left.

A royal edict issued in March 1768 implemented some of the more important of the recommendations of the commission. It fixed the minimum age for taking vows at 21 for men and 18 for women. It further set about reducing the number of houses with only a few professed members. All monasteries (and there were still six hundred abbeys in France) were to enter one of the Congregations, except for those which were administered directly under an archbishop or bishop. These were only to be permitted to survive if they had at least fifteen choir monks or nuns, not counting the abbot or prior. Houses that were in a Congregation might survive if they had at least eight choir monks and an abbot or prior. All these houses were forbidden to admit their novices to vows. Each Order or Congregation was to have only two houses in Paris and only one in other towns. The edict[3] ordered the Benedictines, Cistercians, Minimes, Cordeliers, Recollets, Capuchins, Third Order of St Francis, Carmelites, Dominicans, Augustinians, Antonins, Premonstratensians, and regular canons to elect deputies to form a general chapter for the codification and reform of statutes, the amalgamation of monasteries, and other acts required by the recent edicts. All constitutional reforms were to be approved by the King before they became valid.

The Pope, rivalling the commission in his zeal, reformed the Celestines, who depended directly upon him, in the same fatal year of 1768,[4] and suppressed some fourteen houses. By 1779 the Order was practically extinct in France; a few monks from all over the country were allowed to live together in the monastery of Marcoussis. In 1768 the two Orders devoted to the ransoming of prisoners, the

---

[1] III, 468. I translate. [2] See Prat, p. 148.
[3] Prat, p. 206. The Carthusians were the only ancient Order exempted.
[4] *Ibid.* p. 214.

Mercedarians and the Trinitarians, were suppressed; the Antonins followed in 1771.[1]

In 1770 the houses of the Exempt Benedictines (that is, those outside the Great Congregations) were suppressed, whatever their size. The foundations of French monasticism had been shaken at their base. 'More than a thousand distinguished communities suppressed, entire Orders abolished, dissension introduced in others, Rules and customs weakened and upset, vocations ended, the religious life shaken to its foundations; all this the Commission was able to do in less than six years.'[2]

The story was not yet told. The richer and stronger Orders were still striving to face facts. The endless controversy between the Cistercians of the Strict and of the Common Observance dragged on, and the new statutes approved by the Commission were not adopted until 1788. In August 1788 the Order of Cluny was discussing the question of closing forty-two houses[3] of the Order at which few monks were left, and of granting a pension to such of their monks as preferred to return to the world.

Already the work of the commission and the edicts it dictated had greatly diminished the population of the monastic houses. By 1774 this had already been reduced to 26,674; by 1790 only 17,500 remained.[4] The great house of Clairvaux had only twenty-six professed religious (including the abbot), ten lay brethren and ten pensioners. Only forty-seven Benedictines remained at Saint-Germain-des-Prés; only seven professed nuns, five lay sisters and two novices at Le Val-de-Grâce;[5] yet there were still forty-nine monastic houses of men and seventy-three of women in Paris.

In May 1789 the States-General were opened. There had been an enormous (and deliberate) over-representation of the parochial clergy at the meetings of the *bailliages* which elected the clerical representatives, and the religious Orders were seriously under-represented. Every parish priest had the right to attend. The Chapters were allowed to send one delegate for every ten canons, but each monastic house could only send one delegate to represent the community. The representatives elected included forty-four prelates, two hundred and eight parish priests, fifty canons and commendatory abbots, and only a few monks—five Benedictines, a Carthusian and two Premonstratensians.[6] The mob hostility towards organized Congregations was expressed at the moment of the opening of the States-General by the invasion of the house of the Lazarists at Paris by revolutionaries, who broke and profaned everything but the vessels of the altar.[7]

On 4 August 1789 the States-General abolished all feudal rights and tithes, and on such rights and tithes much of the economic life of the great Benedictine,

---

[1] By 1768 they had been replaced at their mother-house of Saint-Antoine in the Viennois by the Knights of Malta.

[2] Prat, p. 216. I translate. [3] They had secularized their house at Auch in 1739.

[4] Hautecœur, IV, 182. [5] Ruppricht-Robert, p. 28.

[6] Prat, p. 237. There were also an Oratorian and a priest of a mission to represent the Congregations.

[7] *Ibid.* p. 245.

Cistercian and Augustinian abbeys depended, for they represented the greater part of their medieval endowments. Talleyrand then proposed that no one should henceforward be allowed to take monastic vows, and the motion was passed in November. On 12 October Mirabeau proposed that the ownership of all church property should be transferred to the nation; his motion was passed on 2 November. Teaching and nursing Orders were at first exempted but their suppression quickly followed.

The Benedictines, and more especially the Cluniacs, were perfectly aware what this measure portended and pursued a policy to meet it. On 28 September 1789, the Cluniac monks of Saint-Martin-des-Champs at Paris offered their property to the nation if they might be allowed to continue their work.[1] The Cluniacs, too, had their tenants and neighbours behind them; when in 1789 bands of insurgents came to Cluny to incite the townsfolk to revolution, the people, led by the monks, received them with gunfire and stones flung from the windows of the narrow streets.[2]

On 17 December Treilhard moved that useless convents should be closed, and their religious be free to release themselves from their vows. His motion provoked long and heated discussions, and it was not until 13 February 1790 that the States-General decreed that the law no longer recognized monastic vows and suppressed the Orders and Congregations.[3] It was decreed that whose who wished might remain in the cloister. When the first reduction of houses in Paris was effected at the beginning of March,[4] Saint-Martin-des-Champs was left as an asylum for the exempt Benedictines; Saint-Germain-des-Prés for the Congregation of Saint-Maur; their house in the rue du Bac for the Dominicans; the Petits Pères for the Augustinians; the Carmes Déchaux for the Carmelites; their house in the Chaussée d'Antin for the Capuchins, and similarly for the lesser Orders. It was directed that all other monastic houses were to be sold by the local assemblies of the Revolution.

The old structure of artistic patronage tumbled into ruin. The sculptor Houdon, passing through a time when it was difficult even for an artist to concentrate on his work, retouched an old St Scholastica; he was denounced to the Convention and saved himself only by turning her into a statue of Philosophy.

The decrees of the Assembly were an acid test for the sincerity of the monks of France. All the Jacobins of Paris retired into secular life; most of the Cordeliers, Petits Pères, Capuchins and Génofévains followed them; but the great majority of the Benedictines,[5] Carthusians, Discalced Carmelites and Minimes chose the cloistered life.

The vacuum caused by the cowards was quickly filled. When the Assembly

---

[1] It was their abbot, Benoît le Duc (then dispossessed) who after the execution of Louis XVI had the courage to try to gain possession of the royal corpse in order to save it from material destruction and to give it Christian burial. (A. De Beauchesne, *Louis XVII*, 1873, I, 486.)   [2] De Vasière, p. 256.

[3] Prat, p. 309. The last meeting of the French Carthusians before the Revolution was held at Champmol on 12 April 1790.   [4] *Ibid.* p. 345.

[5] When the cloistered life ceased to be possible, they served as parish priests. Dom Louis, a monk of Cluny before the Revolution, lived until 1837 as a priest at Trévoux in the Belley.

moved from Versailles to Paris the deputies who had used to meet at the Café Amaury at Versailles hired the empty refectory of the Jacobins for 200 francs a year, and for another 200 francs its chairs and tables.[1] The Club des Jacobins, thus formed, had few members at first, and the relapsed monks in their habits used to attend the sessions, sitting in a group at the back of the hall. When in the spring of 1790 the club became better attended, the former monks invited its members into the library over the church.[2] Thus it was that from a church of Friars Preachers the doctrine of the Revolution was preached and propagated.

Most of the larger monasteries of Paris were turned into prisons, and are remembered in history only for the massacres of their prisoners. Saint-Germain-des-Prés was transformed into a parish church in 1791, and turned into a saltpetre manufactory in 1794. Le Val-de-Grâce became a Maternity Hospital, and after 1793 a central depot for military hospital supplies. Sainte-Geneviève was in 1791 transmuted into a national Pantheon, which it still is. Quatremère de Quincy, the Commissioner of Works, wrote: 'L'édifice entier sera le catéchisme figuré des devoirs de l'Homme en Société.' The saints and angels of Coustou were removed, and instead of the figure of St Peter receiving the keys, statues were set up to symbolize 'les bienfaits de l'Instruction Publique'.

The provincial authorities were faced with the problem of an infinity of disused monastic buildings, at the moment when a new constitution faced them with the problem of housing any number of new institutions. Education had been taken over by the State; any number of Jesuit or Benedictine houses lay empty, and could be taken over as schools without adaptation. The empty monastic houses in cities and towns were ready to become Hôtels de Ville, Mairies, Préfectures and Sous-Préfectures; and when these needs were met there were many others to which they could be adapted. A cloister might become a fish-market; the house of an enclosed Order, a prison (as Clairvaux and Fontevrault are to this day). With little change houses on the outskirts of the cities could become hospitals and asylums. The great abbeys of Cluny and Le Bec-Hellouin became stud-farms. Other abbeys lent themselves to manufacture; several, with good water-supply, became paper-mills. Some lesser monastic houses were sold for private occupation; many were pulled down for what the stone of their buildings and the lead of their roofs were worth. A surprising number of monastic chapels are still in use as cinemas, theatres, garages and barns. Much of what happened in England at the Reformation can be paralleled in France at the Revolution; only the possibility of immediate use saved a building.

Very few Orders had realized that their doom was imminent. The Dames de la Providence, who lived in the old Hôtel Chamond at Paris, as late as 1781 built themselves a fine new convent and a chapel with a Doric portico.[3] In 1782 the abbot of Clairvaux signed a contract for a great new mausoleum for the body of

---

[1] Lenôtre, p. 292.   [2] *Ibid.* p. 297.

[3] It was destroyed in 1906; there is a drawing in the Carnavalet. (Hautecœur, IV, fig. 199.)

10-2

St Bernard, to cost 60,000 *livres*. Only one statue had been roughed out when the Revolution came.[1] At the Benedictine abbey of Saint-Ouen de Rouen the thirteenth-century refectory, guest-house and other buildings were pulled down in 1789 for rebuilding in the modern style.

None the less, before the suppression of 1790 the abbot and monks of La Trappe had voluntarily gone into exile and so preserved the continuity of their Order until their return in 1815. The international Orders, too, could receive fugitive monks from France and so maintain the links of the chain. Yet in the main it was a total break; and by 1792 the long web of the history of monasticism in France had been severed from the loom.[2]

In 1793 Mercier could write of the monastic churches in his *Nouveau Paris*: 'They fall on every side; in a few more years no one will know where the churches of the Cordeliers, the Jacobins, the Augustinians, the Carmelites or the Bernardine nuns, lie buried.'[3]

It was in England, which had destroyed its own monasteries more than two hundred years before, that the *Oraison Funèbre* of the French monastic Orders was preached by the Protestant Edmund Burke in 1790:

The confiscation of the goods of monks and nuns, and abolition of their order...does not affect England as a precedent... (yet) it sets justice, the common concern of mankind, at defiance....The monks are lazy. Be it so. Suppose them no otherwise employed than by singing in the choir. They are as usefully employed as those who neither sing nor say. As usefully even as those who sing upon the stage. Why should the expenditure of a great landed property...appear intolerable to you and me, when it takes its course through the accumulation of vast libraries, which are the history of the force and weakness of the human mind; through great collections of ancient records, medals and coins, which attest and explain ancient laws and customs; that by imitating nature seem to extend the limits of creation...?

To realize the tragic shock of the Revolution that broke up that monastic world in France, it is not enough for the traveller to see the noble buildings of the past turned to the usually secular and often sordid uses of today; he must also remember the monks, and above all the nuns, evicted from their conventual lodgings and astray in the hard and sometimes cruel world of the Directorate and the Empire. He must recall that the break was ennobled by the courage of some of the French religious, especially the nuns, who brought to the guillotine the devotion of martyrs. Madame de Soulanges, the abbess of the Fontevrist house of Royal-Lieu, and her nuns went to their death together,[4] singing the *Veni Creator* in the tumbril and even upon the scaffold. The abbess passed the last under the guillotine, and chanted until its blade fell.

---

[1] King, p. 317.

[2] Yet even in 1796 a fresh house of a teaching Order for poor girls, the Sœurs de la Présentation de Marie, or Dames Blanches, was founded at Montpezat.

[3] Chapter CCXIX: 'Démolition des Églises.' I translate.

[4] Campan, 1823 ed., I, 9. Thirteen Dominicans of Bollène were guillotined in 1794.

CONCLUSION

In our own time Bernanos and Poulenc have celebrated the devotion of the Carmelites of Compiègne, who defied the order of secularization, dedicated their lives upon the scaffold to the ending of the Terror, and went to their death singing the *Salve Regina*. It is for the present generation of Frenchmen to see that the later churches and monastic buildings of the abbeys and convents of France are not allowed to perish. They are memorials of devotion, learning, and courage and of the obstinate continuity of religion and learning in their country; as a foreigner I salute them.

PLATES

1 The 'Refuge' of the Benedictine Abbey of   2 Abbey of Cluny. Palace of Jacques d'Amboise, 1485–1510.
Saint-Vincent, Laon. 1529.

3 Benedictine Abbey of Saint-Ouen, Rouen. Abbot's lodging, c. 1500 (demolished 1817).

4 Benedictine Abbey of Brantôme. Gazebo.

5 Benedictine Abbey of Brantôme. Summer house, built by abbot Pierre Mareuil, c. 1530.

6 Benedictine (Cluniac) Priory of Souvigny. Prior's house, c. 1550.

7 Benedictine (Cluniac) Priory of Souvigny. Prior's house, c. 1550.

8   Benedictine Abbey of Bernay. Abbot's lodging, *c.* 1550.

9   Benedictine Abbey of Vendôme. Abbot's lodging, *c.* 1550.

10   Benedictine (Cluniac) Priory of Monstierneuf. Dovecote, *c.* 1550.

11   Benedictine Abbey of Beaulieu-lès-Loches. Abbot's lodging, *c.* 1570.

12   Benedictine Abbey of Saint-Germain-des-Prés, Paris. Abbot's lodging, 1586.

13   Benedictine Abbey of Saint-Germain-des-Prés, Paris. Cloister, 1555.

14 Benedictine Nunnery, Pont-l'Évêque. Living quarters, *c.* 1540.

15 Benedictine Nunnery of Sainte-Austreberthe, Montreuil-sur-Mer.
Living quarters, mid sixteenth century.

16 Benedictine Abbey of Saint-Martin, Tours. Lesser cloister, by Bastien François, 1508–19.

17 Benedictine Abbey of Saint-Martin, Tours. Lesser cloister, by Bastien François, 1508–19.

18 Benedictine Abbey of Marmande. Cloister, *c*. 1550.

19 Benedictine Abbey of La Trinité, Fécamp. Tabernacle of the Precious Blood, by Pace Gaggini (?), *c*. 1507.

20 Benedictine Abbey of La Trinité, Fécamp. Sacristy door, *c*. 1511.

21   Benedictine Abbey of La Trinité, Fécamp. Screen in choir, *c.* 1515.

22   Benedictine Abbey of Saint-Michel, Dijon. Façade, between 1530 and 1661.

23 Benedictine Abbey of Mozac. Door with the arms of Duprat, 1542.

24 Benedictine Abbey of Decize. Portal, *c.* 1540.

25 Benedictine Abbey of Valmont. Ruins of the choir, *c.* 1525.

26 Benedictine Abbey of Valmont. Vault of the Lady Chapel, begun 1517.

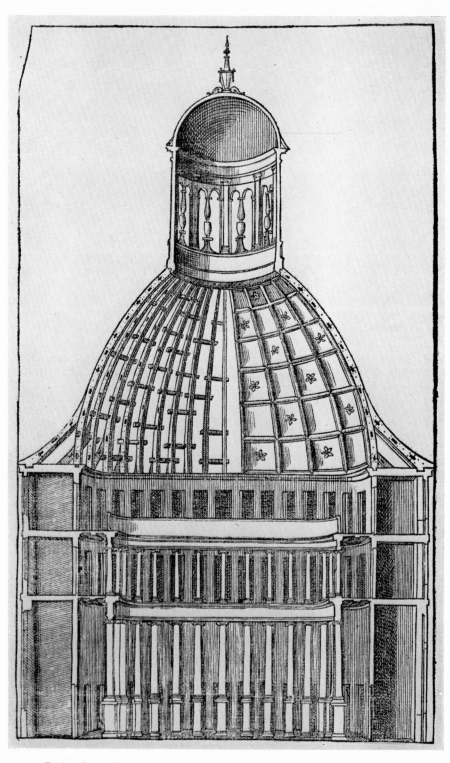

27 Design for the Benedictine Nunnery of Montmartre, by Philibert de l'Orme, 1555.

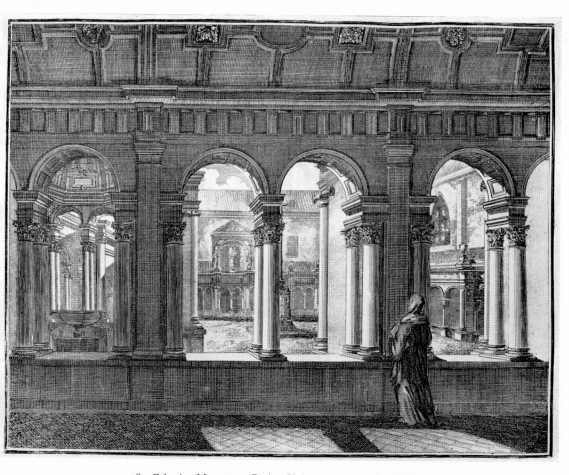

28 Celestine Monastery, Paris. Cloister, 1539–50, after Millin.

29 Celestine Abbey of Marcoussis. Stalls, now in the parish church, *c.* 1600.

30   Benedictine Abbey of Saint-Riquier. Choir screen, mid seventeenth century.

31 Benedictine Abbey of Saint-Riquier. Monastic quarters, *c.* 1660.

32 Benedictine Priory of Val-au-Grès, near Bolbec. Mid seventeenth century.

33   Benedictine Abbey of La Trinité, Fécamp. Monastic buildings, *c.* 1650.

34   Benedictine Abbey of Toussaint, Angers. Monastic buildings, *c.* 1650.

35   Benedictine Abbey of Saint-Wandrille. Monastic quarters.

36   Benedictine Abbey of Saint-Wandrille. Doorway, *c.* 1636.

37   Benedictine Abbey of Saint-Wandrille. Staircase, *c.* 1631.

38   Benedictine Abbey of Bernay. Monastic buildings, 1628.

39   Benedictine Abbey of Saint-Georges-sur-Loire. A wing of the monastic buildings, *c.* 1625.

40 Benedictine Abbey of Pontlevoy. One of the cloisters, *c.* 1635.

41 Benedictine Abbey of Pontlevoy. One of the cloisters, *c.* 1635.

42   Benedictine Abbey of Pontlevoy. A façade, *c.* 1635.

43   Benedictine Abbey of Pontlevoy. A façade, *c.* 1635.

44   Benedictine Abbey of Josaphat.   Monastic building, *c.* 1640.

45   Benedictine Abbey of Saint-Savin-sur-Gartrempe.   Monastic buildings, begun 1640.

46   Benedictine Abbey of Solignac. Monastic buildings, *c.* 1640.

47   Benedictine Abbey of Corme-Royal. Monastic buildings, *c.* 1630.

48   Benedictine Abbey of Ébreuil. Chapter-house and monastic buildings, *c.* 1640.

49   Benedictine Abbey of Ébreuil. Chapter-house and monastic buildings, *c.* 1640.

50 Benedictine Abbey of Saint-Jean-d'Angely. Monastic buildings, *c.* 1640.

51 Benedictine Abbey of Saint-Jean-d'Angely. Entrance, *c.* 1700.

52   Benedictine Abbey of Brantôme. Façade.

53   Benedictine Abbey of Brantôme. Terminal pavilion, *c.* 1640.

54 Benedictine Abbey of La Chaise-Dieu. Monastic buildings, *c.* 1650.

55 Benedictine Abbey of Ferrières-en-Gâtinais. Monastic buildings, *c.* 1650.

56 Benedictine Abbey of Flavigny. Exterior, *c.* 1650.

57 Benedictine Abbey of Flavigny. Exterior, *c.* 1670.

58   The Arcades of the Place des Vosges, Paris, 1605–10.

59   Benedictine Abbey of Redon. Cloister, *c*. 1630.

60   Benedictine Abbey of La Réole. Lesser cloister, *c*. 1640.

61   Benedictine Abbey of Souillac. Cloister, *c*. 1640.

62 Benedictine (Cluniac) Priory of Paray-le-Monial. Cloister, *c.* 1640.

63 Benedictine Abbey of Sainte-Croix, Quimperlé. Cloister, *c.* 1650.

64 Benedictine Abbey of Redon. Cloister door, *c.* 1630.

65   Benedictine Abbey of Le Bec-Hellouin. Cloister, 1644–6.

66   Benedictine Abbey of Le Bec-Hellouin. Cloister, 1644–6.

67 Benedictine Abbey of Le Bec-Hellouin. Cloister niche and door, 1644–6.

68 Benedictine Abbey of Saint-Wandrille. Garden entrance, *c.* 1610.

69 Benedictine (Cluniac) Priory of Souvigny. Entrance pavilion, *c.* 1610.

70   Benedictine Abbey of Saint-Germain-des-Prés,
Paris. Portal, *c.* 1620.

71   Benedictine Priory of Saint-Gildas-d'Auray.
Church, 1623–4.

72   Benedictine Abbey of Saint-André, Le Cateau. Façade, begun 1625.

73 Benedictine Abbey of Saint-André, Le Cateau. Interior.

74   Benedictine Abbey of Saint-Sépulchre, Cambrai. Nave, mid seventeenth century.

75　Benedictine Abbey of Saint-Jouin-de-Marnes.　Stalls, *c.* 1650.

76　Benedictine Abbey of Saint-Riquier.　Stalls, *c.* 1650.

77   Benedictine Abbey of Pontlevoy. Retable of High Altar, by Antoine Charpentier, 1651.

78   Benedictine Abbey of Saint-Remi, Rheims. Choir screen, 1658.

79 Benedictine Nunnery of Notre-Dame-de-Bon-
Secours, Paris. *C.* 1648.

80 Benedictine Nunnery of the Filles du Calvaire, Paris.
Monastic buildings, 1622–31.

81 Benedictine Nunnery, Valognes. Façade of the church.

82 Benedictine Nunnery, Valognes. Living quarters, *c.* 1631.

83 Benedictine Nunnery, Châtillon-sur-Seine. 1629.

84 Benedictine Nunnery of the Abbaye-aux-Dames, Saintes. Living quarters, c. 1630.

85 Benedictine Nunnery of the Abbaye-aux-Dames, Saintes. Monastic buildings, *c.* 1630.

86 Benedictine Nunnery of the Abbaye-aux-Dames, Saintes. Door, *c.* 1630.

87   Benedictine Nunnery of Puyberland. Door (now in the Hospice, Melle), *c.* 1644.

88   Abbaye-aux-Dames, Saintes. Door to the cells, *c.* 1630.

89   Benedictine Nunnery of Le Val-de-Grâce, Paris. Façade of the refectory.

90   Benedictine Nunnery of Le Val-de-Grâce, Paris. Main building, 1645.

91 Benedictine Nunnery of Le Val-de-Grâce, Paris. Cloister, 1645.

92 Benedictine Nunnery of Le Val-de-Grâce, Paris. Cloister, 1645.

93   Benedictine Nunnery of Le Val-de-Grâce, Paris. Dome, 1645.

94   Benedictine Nunnery of Le Val-de-Grâce, Paris. Nave and choir, 1645.

95   Benedictine Nunnery of Le Val-de-Grâce, Paris. Vault of the nave, 1645.

96   Benedictine Nunnery of Saint-Pierre, Lyons, by François des Noyers de la Valfenière. Outer façade, 1659.

97   Benedictine Nunnery of Saint-Pierre, Lyons, by François des Noyers de la Valfenière. Church, 1676–1748.

98   Benedictine (Cluniac) Priory of Lons-le-Saunier. By Dom Vincent Duchesne, 1680. Cloister.

99   Benedictine (Cluniac) Priory of Lons-le-Saunier. By Dom Vincent Duchesne, 1680.
Abbot's lodging.

100 Benedictine Nunnery of La Ronceray, Angers. Monastic buildings, *c.* 1650.

101 Benedictine Nunnery of La Ronceray, Angers. Monastic buildings, *c.* 1650.

102   Benedictine Nunnery of Bonne-Nouvelle, Orléans. Monastic buildings, 1653. (Before 1939.)

103   Benedictine Nunnery of Notre-Dame-de-Liesse, Paris. Cloister, 1644.

104   Benedictine Abbey Church of Saint-Maixent. Nave, by François Leduc de Toscane, 1670–82.

105   Benedictine Abbey of Corbie. West front, by Nicolas Léveillé,
begun 1701, finished 1719.

106   Benedictine Abbey of Corbie. West fro
by Nicolas Léveillé, begun 1701, finished 171

107 Benedictine Abbey of Saint-Georges-de-Boscherville. Living quarters over the
chapter-house, probably by Dom Marc Rivard, *c.* 1670.

108   Abbaye-aux-Hommes, Caen. Cloister, by Dom Guillaume de la Tremblaye, 1704.

109   Benedictine Abbey of Saint-Maixent. Cloister, by Dom François Leduc de Toscane, 1670–82.

110 Abbaye-aux-Dames, Caen. Screen probably by
Dom Guillaume de la Tremblaye, 1704.

111 Benedictine Abbey of Saint-Maixent, by Dom François
Leduc de Toscane, 1660–c. 1670. Monastic buildings.

112 Benedictine Abbey of Saint-Maixent, by Dom François
Leduc de Toscane, 1660–c. 1670. Cloister.

113 Benedictine Abbey of Saint-Maur. Monastic buildings.

114 Benedictine Abbey of Saint-Maur. Cloister, 1664–87.

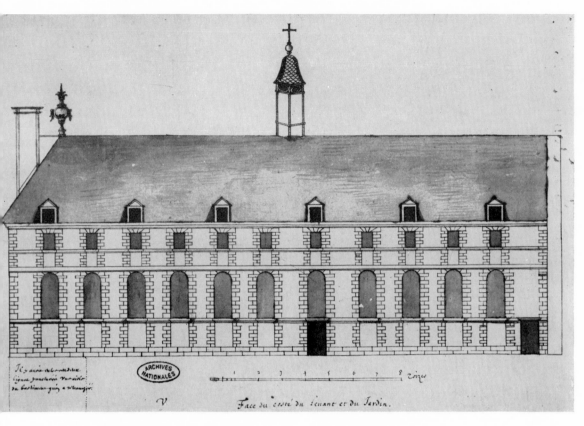

115 Benedictine Abbey of Saint-Fuscien-aux-Bois, Amiens. Design for garden front, *c*. 1680.

116 Benedictine (Cluniac) Priory of Morteau. Design for garden front, *c*. 1680.

117   Benedictine (Cluniac) Abbey of Saint-Martin-des-Champs, Paris.
Monastic buildings, by Antoine, *c.* 1710–22.

118   Benedictine (Cluniac) Abbey of Saint-Martin-des-Champs, Paris.
Monastic buildings, by Antoine, *c.* 1710–22.

119   Benedictine Abbey of Le Bec-Hellouin. Guest house, *c.* 1680.

120   Benedictine Priory of Framecourt. Monastic buildings, 1713.

121   Benedictine Abbey of Saint-Lomer, Blois. Monastic buildings, begun by Paul and
Jacques Hubert, 1663, finished by Dom Guillaume de la Tremblaye, 1703.

122   Benedictine Abbey of Saint-Remi, Rheims. Monastic buildings, c. 1705.

123   Benedictine Abbey of Le Bec-Hellouin. Refectory, by Dom Guillaume de la Tremblaye, *c.* 1678.

124   Abbaye-aux-Dames, Caen. Screen, inner face. Probably by Dom Guillaume de la Tremblaye, 1704.

125　Abbaye-aux-Dames, Caen.　First cloister.

126　Abbaye-aux-Dames, Caen.　Screen, outer face,
probably by Dom Guillaume de la Tremblaye, 1704.

127   Abbaye-aux-Dames, Caen. Second Cloister.

128   Abbaye-aux-Dames, Caen. Staircase pavilion, probably by Dom Guillaume de la Tremblaye, 1704.

129   Abbaye-aux-Dames, Caen. Hall and staircase, probably by Dom Guillaume de la Tremblaye, 1704.

130   Abbaye-aux-Hommes, Caen. Main block.

131   Abbaye-aux-Hommes, Caen. Entrance block, by Dom Guillaume de la Tremblaye, 1704.

132   Benedictine Abbey of Sainte-Croix, Bernay. Monastic buildings, *c.* 1690.

133   Benedictine Abbey of Beaulieu-lès-Loches. Monastic buildings, *c.* 1700.

134 Benedictine Abbey of Saint-Georges-de-Boscherville. Monastic buildings, probably by Dom Marc Rivard, *c.* 1680.

135 Benedictine Abbey of Saint-Georges-de-Boscherville. Monastic buildings, probably by Dom Marc Rivard, *c.* 1680.

136 Benedictine Nunnery of Saint-Georges, Rennes. Monastic buildings, begun 1670.

137 Benedictine Abbey of Saint-Riquier. Monastic buildings, *c.* 1690.

138 Benedictine Abbey of Saint-Serge, Angers. Monastic buildings, *c.* 1700.

139 Benedictine Abbey of Saint-Serge, Angers. Monastic buildings, *c.* 1700.

140 Benedictine Abbey of Saint-Serge, Angers. Staircase, *c.* 1700.

141   Benedictine Abbey of Sainte-Croix, Bordeaux. Main building.

142   Benedictine Abbey of Sainte-Croix, Bordeaux. Entrance door, finished 1672.

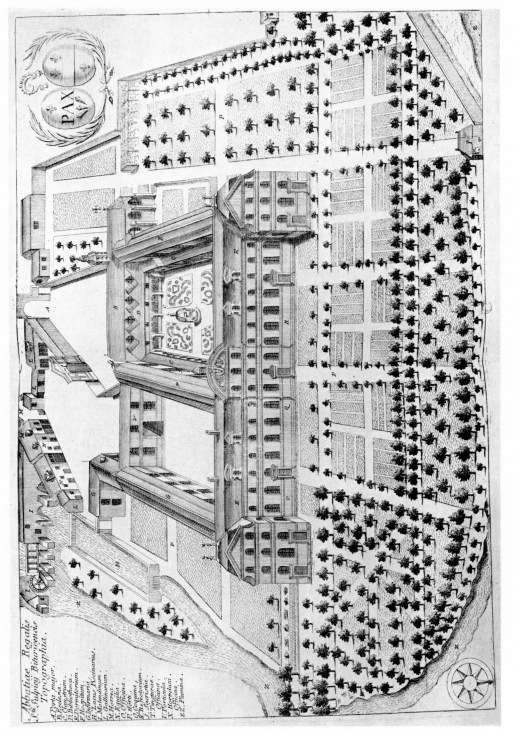

143 Benedictine Abbey of Saint-Sulpice, Bourges, from an engraving c. 1680.

144   Benedictine Abbey of Toussaint, Angers. *C.* 1680.

145   Benedictine Abbey of Montivilliers. *C.* 1680.

146 Benedictine Abbey of Bourgeuil. Monastic buildings, 1735.

147 Benedictine Abbey of Bourgeuil. Monastic buildings, 1735.

148　Benedictine Abbey of the Madeleine, Châteaudun. Monastic buildings, *c.* 1680.

149　Benedictine Abbey of the Madeleine, Châteaudun. Monastic buildings, *c.* 1680.

150 Benedictine Abbey of Moutiers-Saint-Jean. Monastic buildings, *c.* 1680.

151 Benedictine Priory of Le Paraclet-des-Champs, Ailly-sur-Noye. *C.* 1680.

152   Benedictine Abbey of Moutiers-Saint-Jean. Cloister, *c.* 1680.

153   Benedictine Abbey of Moutiers-Saint-Jean. Cloister, *c.* 1680.

154   Benedictine Abbey of Sorèze. Exterior.

155   Benedictine Abbey of Sorèze. Main cloister, *c.* 1680.

156   Benedictine Abbey of La Réole.   Monastic buildings.

157   Benedictine Abbey of La Réole.   Cloister, *c.* 1690.

158   Benedictine Abbey of Montmajour. Monastic buildings, 1703–37.

159 Benedictine Nunnery of Faverney. By Dom Vincent Duchesne, 1711–14. Nuns' quarters.

160 Benedictine Nunnery of Faverney. By Dom Vincent Duchesne, 1711–14. Cloister.

161 Benedictine Abbey of Saint-Sever-sur-Odon. Abbot's lodging, *c.* 1690.

162 Benedictine Abbey of Saint-Vincent, Besançon. By Dom Vincent Duchesne, *c.* 1720.

163 Benedictine Abbey of Notre-Dame de Lyre. Design for cloister, 1704.

164 Benedictine Abbey of Marmoutier. Elevation of façade, 1675, by Dom Pierre Ledo.

165 Benedictine Abbey of Saint-Sulpice-lès-Bourges. Mill. Seventeenth century.

166 Benedictine Abbey of Méry-ès-Bois. *C.* 1680?

167 Benedictine Abbey of Sainte Melaine, Rennes. Abbot's lodging, 1672.

168 Benedictine Abbey of Nouaillé. Abbot's lodging, *c*. 1665.

169 Benedictine Abbey of Jumièges. Abbot's lodging, 1666.

170 Benedictine Abbey of Saint-Gildas de Rhuis. Cloister, 1700–5.

171   Monastery of English Benedictines, Paris. Hall and staircase, 1661–91.

172   Monastery of English Benedictines, Paris. Exterior, 1661–91.

173 Monastery of English Benedictines, Paris. The Chapel of St Edmund, 1661–91.

174 Benedictine Abbey of Sainte Melaine, Rennes. Cloister, *c.* 1672.

175 Benedictine Abbey of Sainte Melaine, Rennes. Cloister, *c.* 1672.

176   Benedictine Abbey of Saint-Michel-en-Thiérache. East front.

177   Benedictine Abbey of Saint-Michel-en-Thiérache. Cloister, c. 1680.

178   Benedictine Abbey of Saint-Michel-en-Thiérache. Church, *c.* 1680.

179   Benedictine Abbey of Saint-Michel-en-Thiérache. Church, *c.* 1680.

180   Benedictine Abbey of Saint-Jean-de-l'Osne. *C. 1696.* Baldaquin.

181   Benedictine Abbey of Saint-Jean-de-l'Osne. *C. 1696.* Sacristy door.

182   Benedictine Abbey of Saint-Clément, Metz. Interior. By Spinga, 1680–93.

183   Benedictine Abbey of Saint-Mihiel. Nave, *c.* 1700.

184 Benedictine Abbey of Saint-Pierre, Chalon-sur-Saône. By Dom Vincent Duchesne, 1697–1713. West front.

185 Benedictine Abbey of Saint-Pierre, Chalon-sur-Saône. By Dom Vincent Duchesne, 1697–1713. Apse.

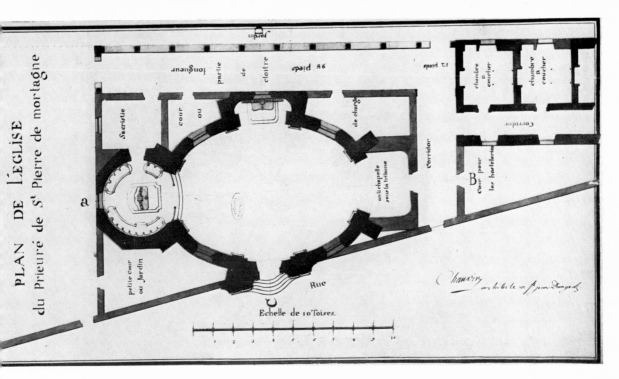

186 Benedictine Priory of Mortagne-sur-Sèvre. Plans by Chauvin of Saint-Jean-d'Angely,
c. 1712. Plan of church.

187 Benedictine Priory of Mortagne-sur-Sèvre. Plans by Chauvin of Saint-Jean-d'Angely,
c. 1712. Section.

188   Benedictine Abbey of Aniane. Façade, 1714.

189   Benedictine Abbey of Aniane. Nave.

190 Benedictine Abbey of Saint-Mihiel. Church, *c*. 1700. Exterior.

191 Benedictine Abbey of Saint-Mihiel. Monastic buildings, *c*. 1700.

192 Benedictine Abbey of Notre Dame, Vitré. Doors, 1689.

193   Benedictine Abbey of Saint-Sernin, Toulouse. Stalls, 1670.

194   Benedictine Abbey of Le-Moûtier-d'Ahun. Stalls, by Simon Bauer of Menat, 1673–81.

195 Benedictine Abbey of Saint-Clément, Metz. Façade, 1715–37.

196 Benedictine Nunnery of Sainte-Austreberthe, Montreuil-sur-Mer. Façade, c. 1740.

197 Benedictine Abbey of Saint-Vincent, Metz. By Barlet, Louis and Lhuillier. Façade, 1768–86.

COUPE SUR LA LONGUEUR, DE L'ÉGLISE DE L'ABBAYE ROYALE DE S^T. LOUIS A METZ.

198 Design by J. F. Blondel for the noble Benedictine Abbey of Saint-Louis, Metz, 1760–7.

199   Benedictine Abbey of Notre Dame, Guebwiller, 1706. Façade.

200   Benedictine Abbey of Notre Dame, Guebwiller, 1706. Interior.

201 Benedictine Abbey of Saint-Vaast, Arras. Façade.

202 Benedictine Abbey of Saint-Vaast, Arras. Nave and choir, 1754.

MAISON D'ARRÊT DE St J. D'ANGÉLY.

D'après le dessin original de l'Architecte même chargé de la Construction de cet Edifice, qui en principe, devait être la façade d'une
Eglise paroissiale, élevée sur l'emplacement de celle qui fut détruite par les Calvinistes en 1568. La 1re pierre fut posée par les Bénédictins,
le 11 7bre 1741.

Nota. Cet edifice n'ayant point été achevé les Sculptures seulement qui se voient ici n'ont point été exécutées.

203 Benedictine (Cluniac) Abbey of Saint-Jean-d'Angely. Design for the façade, 1740.

204   Benedictine (Cluniac) Abbey of Saint-Jean-d'Angely.   Designed 1740, begun 1755.

205   Benedictine (Cluniac) Abbey of Saint-Jean-d'Angely.   Designed 1740, begun 1755.

206 Benedictine Abbey Church of Notre-Dame-de-la-Daurade, Toulouse. By Hardy, 1764.

207 Benedictine Abbey Church of Notre-Dame-de-la-Daurade, Toulouse. By Hardy, 1764.

208   Design for the façade of a conventual church.   J. F. Blondel, *Cours d'Architecture, c.* 1750.

209   Design for the interior of a conventual church.   J. F. Blondel, *Cours d'Architecture, c.* 1750.

210   Benedictine Abbey of Saint-Georges-sur-Loire. Façade of the church, *c.* 1770.

211   Benedictine Nunnery of Saint-Pierre-de-Montmartre, Paris. Façade of the church, *c.* 1770.

212 Benedictine (Cluniac) Priory of Saint-Pierre, Abbeville. Design by Franque, 1772. Façade.

213 Benedictine (Cluniac) Priory of Saint-Pierre, Abbeville. Design by Franque, 1772.
Section of church.

214 Benedictine Nunnery of Saint-Désir, Lisieux. Façade, *c.* 1770. (Before 1939.)

215 Benedictine Nunnery of Saint-Désir, Lisieux. Interior, *c.* 1770 (before 1939).

216   Benedictine Abbey of Saint-Étienne, Uzès. West end of church, 1775.

217   Benedictine Abbey of Saint-Étienne, Uzès. Interior of church, 1775.

218 Benedictine Priory of Saint-Martin-des-Champs, Morlaix. 1773–88. Façade.

219 Benedictine Priory of Saint-Martin-des-Champs, Morlaix. 1773–88. Interior.

220 Benedictine Abbey of La Trinité, Fécamp. Façade by Gallot, 1744.

221 Benedictine Abbey of La Trinité, Fécamp. Statue on façade, 1744.

222   Benedictine Abbey of La Trinité, Fécamp. Baldaquin over High Altar, 1751.

223 Benedictine (Cluniac) Abbey of Saint-Pons-de-Thomières. Screen.

224 Benedictine (Cluniac) Abbey of Saint-Pons-de-Thomières. High Altar, *c.* 1780.

225   Benedictine Abbey of Saint-Bénigne, Dijon.
Abbot's throne, c. 1750.

226   Benedictine Abbey of La Trinité, Fécamp.
Abbot's throne, 1748.

227   From the Benedictine Abbey of Saint-Martin, Autun.
Panelling, c. 1760.

228   Benedictine Abbey of Saint-Étienne, Caen.
Paschal candlestick, c. 1780.

229 Benedictine Abbey of Saint-Wandrille. Chapter-house, *c.* 1740.

230 Benedictine Abbey of Saint-Étienne, Caen. Refectory, 1747.

231   Benedictine Abbey of Saint-Serge, Angers. Chapter-house, *c.* 1745.

232   Benedictine Abbey of Saint-Denis. Cloister, by Robert de Cotte, 1718–52.

233   Benedictine Abbey of Corbie.   Entrance gate, by Franque, 1740.

234   Benedictine Abbey of Notre-Dame-de-la-Couture, Le Mans.   Cloister, 1720–39.

235   Benedictine Abbey of Saint-Denis.   Niche in cloister, by Robert de Cotte, 1718–52.

236   Benedictine Abbey of Saint-Denis.   One of four staircases from cloister
by Robert de Cotte, 1718–52.

237 Benedictine Abbey of Saint-Denis. By Robert de Cotte.
West façade, 1718–52; the bay later.

238 Benedictine Abbey of Saint-Denis. By Robert de Cotte. South façade.

239   Benedictine Abbey of Saint-Denis. Staircase.

240   Benedictine Abbey of Saint-Denis. Refectory, by Robert de Cotte. 1718–52.

241 Benedictine Abbey of Saint-Denis. Grille between cloister and staircase, *c.* 1750.

242 Benedictine Abbey of Saint-Martin, Séez. Monastic buildings, 1720–39.

243 Benedictine Abbey of Notre Dame, Évron. Corridor to the cells, 1726.

244 Benedictine Abbey of Le Bec-Hellouin. Monastic buildings.

245 Benedictine Abbey of Le Bec-Hellouin. Corridor to the cells, 1743–7.

246 Benedictine Abbey of Notre Dame, Évron. Garden façade, 1726.

247 Benedictine Abbey of Notre-Dame, Évron.
Great staircase, 1726.

248 Benedictine Abbey of Saint-Maixent.
Staircase, c. 1750.

249 Benedictine Abbey of Saint-Étienne, Caen.
Grille to cells, c. 1730.

250 Benedictine Abbey of Saint-Étienne, Caen.
Staircase, c. 1750.

251 Benedictine Abbey of La Trinité, Fécamp.
Staircase, c. 1730.

252 Benedictine Abbey of Notre-Dame-de-la-Couture, Le Man
Great staircase, 1770.

253   Benedictine Abbey of Le Bec-Hellouin. Staircase to the cells, 1742.

254   Benedictine Abbey of Le Bec-Hellouin.   North court, *c.* 1750.

255   Benedictine Abbey of Le Bec-Hellouin.   North court, *c.* 1750.

256 Benedictine Abbey of Saint-Vaast, Arras. Monastic buildings by Contant d'Ivry, 1746.
West façade.

257 Benedictine Abbey of Saint-Vaast, Arras. Monastic buildings by Contant d'Ivry, 1746.
South court.

258 Benedictine Abbey of Saint-Vaast, Arras. Gateway, by Contant d'Ivry, 1746.

259 Benedictine Abbey of Saint-Ouen, Rouen. Monastic buildings by J. P. Defrance and Le Brument, 1753. East front.

260 Benedictine Abbey of Saint-Ouen, Rouen. Monas buildings, by J. P. Defrance and Le Brument, 1753- Cloister passage.

261 Benedictine Abbey of Saint-Ouen, Rouen. Entrance hall, by J. P. Defrance and Le Brument, 1753–9.

262 Benedictine Abbey of Saint-Ouen, Rouen. Entrance hall, by J. P. Defrance and Le Brument, 1753–9.

263 Benedictine Abbey of Saint-Ouen, Rouen. Entrance Hall, by J. P. Defrance and Le Brument, 1753–9.

264 Benedictine Abbey of Saint-Riquier. Monastic buildings, c. 1755.

265 Benedictine Abbey of Lessay. Monastic buildings, 1752–7.

266 Benedictine Nunnery of Jouarre. Buildings, c. 1750.

267   Benedictine Abbey of Saint-Léonard, Corbigny. North front, begun 1754.

268   Benedictine Abbey of Saint-André, Villeneuve-lès-Avignon. Monastic buildings, 1755.

269   Benedictine Abbey of Lure. Monastic buildings, 1770–89.

270 Benedictine Priory of Fontaine-lès-Luxeuil. Monastic buildings, 1731.

271 Benedictine Priory of Commercy. Monastic buildings, 1737.

272　Benedictine Priory of Commercy.　Staircase, 1737.

273　Benedictine Abbey of Cluny.　Staircase, 1750.

274 Benedictine Abbey of Saint-Germain, Auxerre.
Cloister, begun 1720.

275 Benedictine Abbey of Cluny. Cloister, 1750.

276 Benedictine Abbey of Cluny. Monastic buildings, 1750.

277 Benedictine Abbey of Saint-Pierre, Lagny. Monastic buildings, *c.* 1750.

278 Benedictine Abbey of Saint-Wandrille.
Porte de Jarente, 1754.

279 Benedictine Abbey of Saint-Wandrille.
Monastic buildings, *c.* 1750.

K-2

280   Benedictine Abbey of Le Monastier-Saint-Chaffre. Cloister, 1754.

281   Benedictine Abbey of Le Monastier-Saint-Chaffre. Monastic buildings, 1754.

282   Benedictine Abbey of Valmont. Monastic buildings, 1760.

283   Benedictine Abbey of Saint-Pierre, Chartres. Monastic buildings, *c.* 1760.

284   Benedictine Abbey of Lagrasse.   Central block, 1760.

285   Benedictine Abbey of Lagrasse.   Cloister, 1760.

286 Benedictine Abbey of Lagrasse. Staircase, 1760.

287 Benedictine Nunnery of Saint-Désir, Lisieux. Central block and one side pavilion,
c. 1760. (Before 1939.)

288 Benedictine Priory of Fontaine-lès-Luxeuil. Prior's house, 1731.

289   Benedictine (Cluniac) Abbey of Lavoulte-Chilhac. Monastic buildings, *c.* 1760.

290 Benedictine Nunnery of Baume-les-Dames. Church by Jean Pierre Galezot.
Begun 1738. Interior of dome.

291 Benedictine Nunnery of Baume-les-Dames. Church by Jean Pierre Galezot.
Begun 1738. Exterior of church.

292   Benedictine Abbey of Saint-Martin, Séez.   Abbot's lodging, 1720–39.

293   Benedictine Abbey of Saint-Seine.   Abbot's lodging, *c.* 1740.

294 Benedictine Abbey of Saint-Germain, Auxerre. Abbot's lodging, *c.* 1750.

295 Benedictine Abbey of La Trinité, Fécamp. Abbot's lodging, *c.* 1750.

296 Benedictine Abbey of Saint-Valéry-sur-Somme. Abbot's lodging, *c.* 1750.

297 Benedictine Abbey of Saint-Remi, Rheims. Abbot's lodging, by Durocher, 1774.

298   Benedictine (Cluniac) Priory of Paray-le-Monial. Prior's lodging, *c.* 1760.

299   Benedictine (Cluniac) Priory of Souvigny. Prior's lodging and entrance, *c.* 1775.

300 Benedictine Abbey of Sorèze. Abbot's lodging, *c*. 1775.

301 Benedictine Abbey of Sorèze. Abbot's lodging, *c*. 1775.

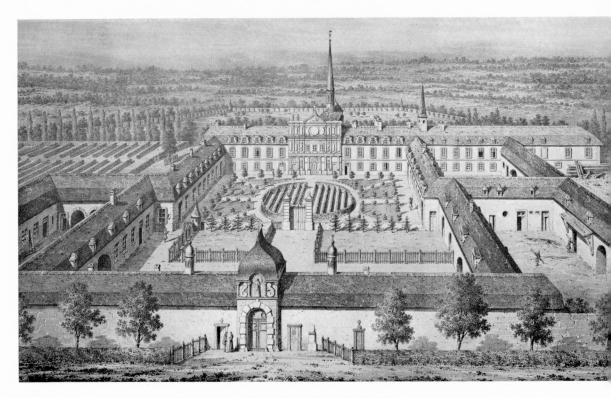

302　Cistercian Abbey of Sept-Fons.　*C.* 1663.　From an engraving.

303　Cistercian Abbey of Barbeaux.　High Altar, *c.* 1570.　(Destroyed.)

304 Cistercian Abbey of Vaux-de-Cernay. Remains of cloister, *c.* 1540.

305 Cistercian Nunnery of La Joie-Notre-Dame, Hennebont. Buildings, *c.* 1550.

306   Cistercian Abbey of Melleray.   Abbot's lodging, *c.* 1550.

307   Cistercian Nunnery of La Joie-Notre-Dame, Hennebont.   Abbess's lodging, *c.* 1660.

308 Cistercian Abbey of Breuil-Benoît, near Marcilly-sur-Eure, *c*. 1550.

309 Cistercian Abbey of Breuil-Benoît, near Marcilly-sur-Eure, *c*. 1550.

310   Cistercian Abbey of Beaubec. Pigeon house, *c.* 1600.

311   Cistercian Abbey of La Garde-Dieu. Pigeon house, *c.* 1600.

313 Cistercian Priory of Fontaine-lès-Dijon. Chapel: interior, 1611–19.

312 Cistercian Priory of Fontaine-lès-Dijon. Chapel: interior, 1611–19.

ELEVATION DU PORTAIL
de l'Eglise des Religieuses Feuillantines

Situé rue du Faubourg S.t Jacques

Plan

Echelle de   1   2   3   4   6   6 toises

JOMBERT . excudit .

200

314   Nunnery of the Feuillantines, Paris. Begun 1622.

Elevation du Portail de l'Eglise des Feuillans, rue S. Honoré à Paris, bâti en 1624 sur les deßeins de François Mansard.

382

315   Monastery of the Feuillants, Paris. Façade, by François Mansart, 1624–9.

E-SLEVATION DV PORTAILLE DE L·ESGLISE DV POT - ROYAL
VEVE EN PERSPECTIVE DV COSTE DE L·ENTREE

Par ANTHOINE LE PAVTRE Ar-chitecte du Rey
Aux Feuillans

326 Cistercian Nunnery of Port-Royal, Paris. Entrance to the church, by Antoine Lepautre, 1646-8

317 Cistercian Nunnery of Port-Royal, Paris. Section of the church, by Antoine Lepautre, 1646–8.

318 Cistercian Nunnery of Port-Royal, Paris. Cloister, by Antoine Lepautre, 1646–8.

319 Cistercian Nunnery of Port-Royal, Paris. Cloister, by Antoine Lepautre, 1646–8.

320   Cistercian Nunnery of La Bénisson-Dieu.   Retable in the Lady Chapel, *c.* 1637.

321   Cistercian Abbey of Bonport. Stalls, *c.* 1650. Now in the church of Pont-de-l'Arche.

322   Cistercian Abbey of Bonport. Stalls, *c.* 1650. Now in the church of Pont-de-l'Arche.

323 Cistercian Abbey of Pontigny. Stalls, c. 1676.

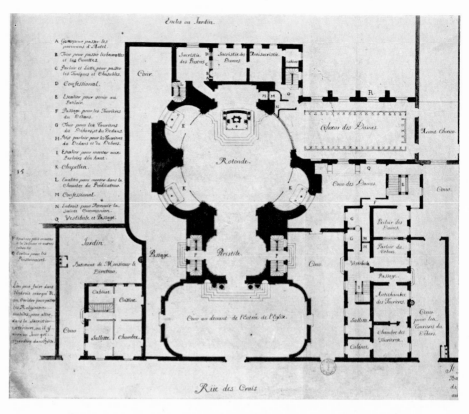

324   Plan (not executed) by Pierre Lambert for the Bernardines of Dijon. 1709.

325   Design (not executed) for the façade of the Chapel of the Bernardines of Dijon, *c.* 1707.

326 Chapel of the Bernardines, Dijon. Façade, by Pierre Lambert, 1707.

327   Chapel of the Bernardines, Dijon. Interior, by Pierre Lambert, 1707.

328 Cistercian Nunnery of Panthemont, Paris. Interior of chapel, by Contant d'Ivry, 1747.

329 Cistercian Nunnery of Panthemont, Paris. Interior of chapel, by Contant d'Ivry, 1747.

330 Cistercian Abbey of Valloires. Church, by Raoul Coignart, 1750–6.

331 Cistercian Abbey of Valloires. Church, by Raoul Coignart, 1750–6.

332 Cistercian Abbey of Valloires. Choir of the church, by Raoul Coignart, 1750–6.

333   Cistercian Abbey of Valloires. High Altar, 1756.

334 Cistercian Abbey of Valloires. Angels above the High Altar, 1756.

335 Cistercian Abbey of Pontigny. Shrine of St Edmund Rich, 1749.

336 Cistercian Abbey of Fontmorigny. Church façade and buildings, *c*. 1640.

337 Cistercian Abbey of Fontmorigny. Cloister, *c*. 1640.

338   Cistercian Abbey of Mortemer.   Monastic buildings, *c.* 1640.

339   Cistercian Abbey of Mortemer.   Cloister, *c.* 1640.

340 Cistercian Abbey (Strict Observance) of Notre-Dame-de-Boisgroland.
Monastic buildings, *c.* 1650.

341 Cistercian Abbey of Le Pin. Monastic buildings, *c.* 1700.

Echelle de six toises.

1   2   3   4   5   6 toises.

Plan.

342   Monastery of the Feuillants, Paris.   Entrance, by François Mansart, 1667.

343   Cistercian Abbey of Boulbonne. Cloister, *c.* 1670.

344   Cistercian Abbey of Boulbonne. Cloister, *c.* 1670.

345   Cistercian Abbey of Boulbonne.   Exterior, *c.* 1670.

346   Cistercian Abbey of Boulbonne.   Gateway, 1738.

347 Cistercian Abbey of Boulbonne. Refectory, *c.* 1740.

348 Cistercian Abbey of Boulbonne. Refectory, *c.* 1740.

349   Cistercian Abbey of La Ferté-sur-Grosne.   Monastic buildings, 1682; the central block, 1777.

350   Cistercian Abbey of Pontigny.   Cloister, *c.* 1675.

351   Cistercian Abbey of Pontigny.   Cloister, *c.* 1675.

352   Cistercian Abbey of Pontigny.   Entrance gate, *c.* 1680.

353   Convent of Bernardines, Dijon.   Monastic buildings, *c.* 1630.

354 Cistercian Nunnery, Orgelet. By Dom Vincent Duchesne, 1708–18. Exterior.

355 Cistercian Nunnery, Orgelet. By Dom Vincent Duchesne, 1708–18. Cloister.

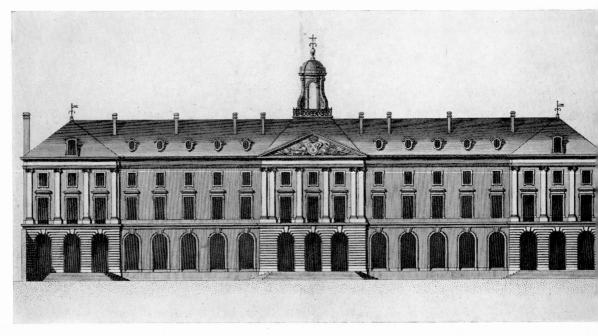

356   Cistercian Nunnery of Panthemont, Paris, by Contant d'Ivry, 1747. From an engraving by Le Canu.

357   Cistercian Nunnery of Panthemont, Paris, by Contant d'Ivry, 1747. From an engraving by Le Canu.

358 Cistercian Nunnery of Panthemont, Paris, by Contant d'Ivry, 1747. Main front.

359 Cistercian Nunnery of Panthemont, Paris, by Contant d'Ivry, 1747.
One of the entrances.

360   Cistercian Nunnery of Saint-Antoine-des-Champs, Paris. Monastic buildings by Lenoir
'Le Romain', 1767.

361   Cistercian Nunnery of Mercoire. Monastic buildings, 1766.

362   Cistercian Priory of Val-des-Choux. Quadrangle, *c.* 1670?

363   Cistercian Priory of Val-des-Choux. Quadrangle, *c.* 1670?

364   Cistercian Abbey of Morimond. Gateway.

365   Cistercian Abbey of Morimond. Monastic buildings, *c.* 1690.

366 Cistercian Abbey of Cherlieu. Monastic buildings, 1708.

367 Cistercian Abbey of Cherlieu. Monastic buildings, 1708.

368 Cistercian Abbey of Coët-Malouen. Façade of church.

369 Cistercian Abbey of Coët-Malouen. Ruins of monastic buildings, 1709.

370 Cistercian Abbey of La Grâce-Dieu. Passage to the cells, 1720–6.

371 Cistercian Abbey of Acey. Monastic buildings, 1720–46.

372   Cistercian Abbey of Langonnet.   Cloister, *c.* 1724.

373 Cistercian Abbey of Chaalis. Monastic buildings.

374 Cistercian Abbey of Chaalis. Unfinished cloister, by Jean Aubert, 1737.

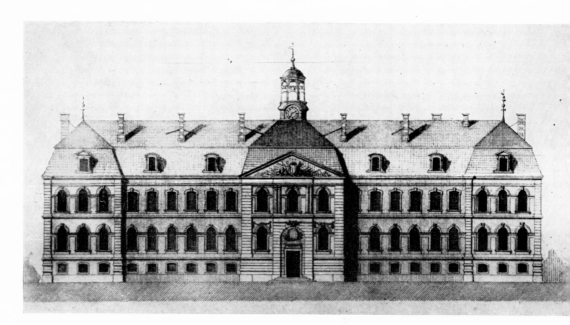

375 Cistercian Abbey of Signy-l'Abbaye. Drawings of monastic buildings, *c.* 1740.

376 Cistercian Abbey of Ourscamp. One half of the monastic buildings, *c.* 1740.

377 Cistercian Abbey of Valloires. Monastic buildings, begun 1738.

378 Cistercian Abbey of Valloires. Monastic buildings, begun 1738.

379 Cistercian Abbey of Cercamp. Main block, north, *c.* 1740.

380 Cistercian Abbey of Cercamp. Main block, south, *c.* 1740.

381 Cistercian Abbey of Cercamp. Entrance and *communs*.

382 Cistercian Abbey of Cercamp. Abbot's *salon*, c. 1740.

383   Cistercian Abbey of Trois-Fontaines. 1734–41. Main gateway.

384   Cistercian Abbey of Trois-Fontaines. 1737–41. Staircase in monastic quarters.

385 Cistercian Abbey of Trois-Fontaines. 1737–41. Screen and pavilions.

386 Cistercian Abbey of Trois-Fontaines. 1737–41. Screen and pavilions.

387   Cistercian Abbey of Auberive, *c.* 1750. Cloister.

388   Cistercian Abbey of Auberive. *C.* 1750. Monastic quarters.

389   Cistercian Abbey of Auberive. *C.* 1750. Main gateway.

390   Cistercian Abbey of Auberive. *C.* 1750. Staircase.

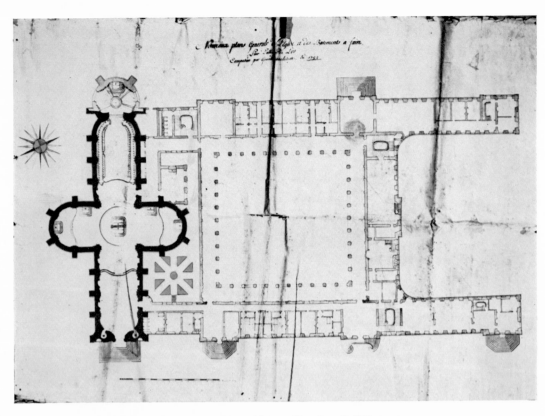

391 Cistercian Abbey of Loos. Plan for rebuilding, 1752.

392 Cistercian Abbey of Loos. Entrance gate (destroyed 1918).

393　Cistercian Abbey of Loos.　Centre of main block, 1752.

394　Cistercian Abbey of Loos.　Part of a wing, 1752.

395 Cistercian Abbey of Cîteaux. Half the design of the main front, by Lenoir, 1760.

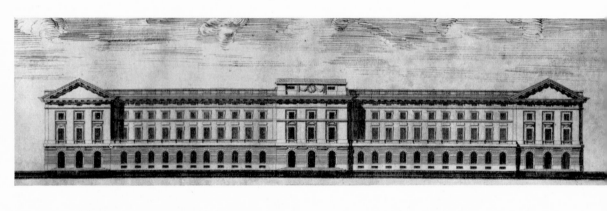

396 Cistercian Abbey of Cîteaux. Designs for the side façades, by Lenoir, 1760.

397 Cistercian Abbey of Cîteaux. Cloister.

398 Cistercian Abbey of Cîteaux. Staircase, 1760.

399 Cistercian Abbey of Bégard. Monastic buildings, *c.* 1765.

400 Cistercian Abbey of Bégard. Monastic buildings, *c.* 1765.

401 Cistercian Abbey of Bégard. Monastic buildings, *c.* 1765.

402 Cistercian Abbey of Clairvaux. Entrance door, 1765.

403　Cistercian Abbey of Clairvaux.　Outer façade, 1765.

404　Cistercian Abbey of Melleray.　Monastic buildings, 1761.

405   Cistercian Abbey of La Valasse. Centre of main block.

406   Cistercian Abbey of La Valasse. General view, *c.* 1760.

407 Cistercian Priory of Sainte-Colombe, Blendecques. Main building,
c. 1760.

408 Cistercian Priory of Sainte-Colombe, Blendecques. Entrance, *c.* 1760.

409 Cistercian Abbey of Clairvaux. Cloister, *c.* 1765.

410 Cistercian Abbey of Clairvaux. Staircase to abbot's lodging, *c.* 1765.

411 Cistercian Abbey of Le Relec. Remains of the abbot's garden, c. 1760.

412 Cistercian Abbey of Bonpas. C. 1760.

413 Cistercian Abbey of Royaumont. Guest-house? C. 1750.

414 'Refuge de l'Abbaye de Loos', Lille. C. 1720?

415 Cistercian Abbey of La Ferté-sur-Grosne. Abbot's staircase, 1777.

416 Cistercian Abbey of La Ferté-sur-Grosne. Abbot's hall, 1777.

417   Cistercian Abbey of La Ferté-sur-Grosne. Abbot's *petit salon*, 1777.

418   Cistercian Abbey of La Ferté-sur-Grosne. Trophy in the abbot's *salon*, 1777.

419 Cistercian Abbey of Royaumont. Abbot's lodging, by Louis le Masson, 1785. After Millin.

420 Génofévain Priory of Saint-Jean-de-Côle. Cloister, *c.* 1540.

421   Génofévain Priory of Saint-Jean-de-Côle. Monastic buildings, *c.* 1600.

422   Génofévain Abbey of Évaux. Entrances to church and
monastery, *c.* 1640.

423   Convent of Augustinian nuns, Lannion.
Mid seventeenth century.

424 Génofévain Abbey of Notre-Dame de Livry-en-l'Aulnoy, near Gonesse.

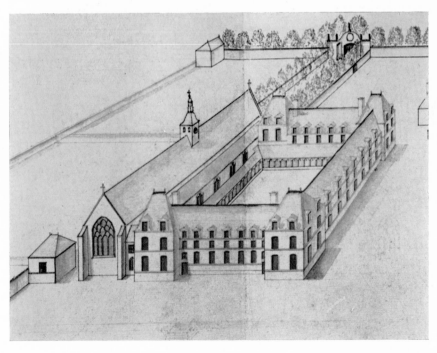

425 Génofévain Priory of Mont-aux-Malades, Mont-Saint-Aignan.

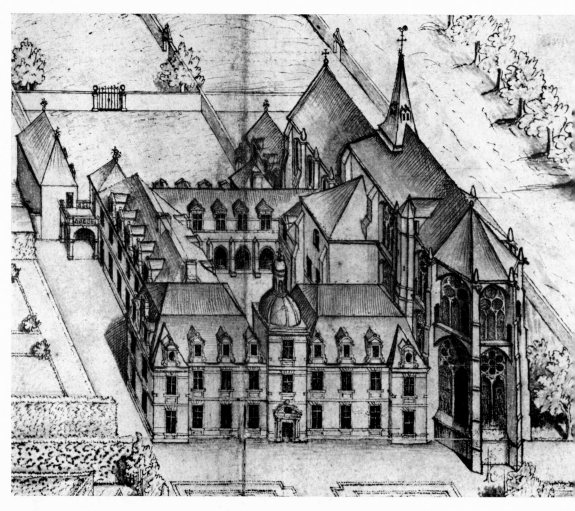

426 Génofévain Abbey of Saint-Acheul, Amiens. *C.* 1630.

427 Augustinian Abbey of Saint-Ambroix, Bourges.
Monastic buildings, *c.* 1625.

428 Augustinian Abbey, rue Mirabeau, Bourges.
Remains of cloister, *c.* 1640.

429 Augustinian Priory of Château-l'Hermitage, near Pontvallain.

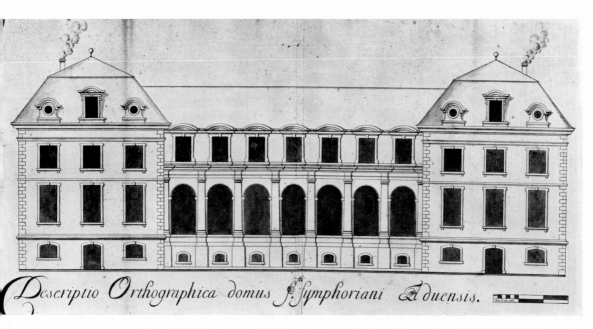

Descriptio Orthographica domus S. Symphoriani Æduensis.

430 Augustinian Abbey of Saint-Symphorien, Autun. Mid seventeenth century.

431 Augustinian Abbey of Crémieu. Cloister, mid
seventeenth century.

432 Augustinian Abbey of La Rochelle. Cloister, 166(

433 Augustinian Abbey of Saint-Martin-ès-Aires, Troyes.
Cloister, c. 1640.

434 Augustinian Abbey of Saint-Martin-ès-Aires, Tro
Entrance gateway, c. 1640.

435 Génofévain Abbey of Châtillon-sur-Sèvre. Wing of monastic buildings, *c.* 1660.

436 Augustinian Nunnery of Beaurepaire. Abbess's lodging, *c.* 1700.

437 Saint-Cyr. By J. H. Mansart, 1685-6.

438   Saint-Cyr. By J. H. Mansart, 1685–6. Chapel.

439   Saint-Cyr. By J. H. Mansart, 1685–6. *Pavillon des Archives*.

440   Saint-Cyr. By J. H. Mansart, 1685–6. Western entrance.

441   Saint-Cyr. By J. H. Mansart, 1685–6. *Pavillon Louis XIV.*

442 Augustinian Abbey of Beaugency. Monastic buildings, *c.* 1655.

443 Génofévain Abbey of Celles-sur-Belle. Monastic buildings, by François Leduc de Toscane, 1670–80.

444   Augustinian Abbey of Saint-Acheul. Living quarters, *c.* 1690.

445   Augustinian Abbey of Saint-Acheul. Living quarters, *c.* 1690.

446 Augustinian Abbey of Saint-Laon, Thouars. Living quarters, *c.* 1700.

447 Augustinian Nunnery of Notre-Dame-de-Saint-Augustin, Châteauroux. Cloister, 1741.

448 Augustinian Abbey of Saint-Quentin-lès-Beauvais. Monastic buildings, *c.* 1670.

449 Augustinian Nunnery of Hazebrouck. Monastic buildings, left wing, 1718.

450 Augustinian Abbey of Saint-Pierre, Châtillon-sur-Seine. Church door, *c.* 1750.

451 Augustinian Abbey of Saint-Loup, Troyes. Monastic buildings, *c.* 1750.

452 Augustinian Abbey of Saint-Pierre, Châtillon-sur-Seine. Entrance, *c.* 1750.

453 Augustinian Abbey of La Couronne. Entrance, *c.* 1730.

454 Augustinian Abbey of Sainte-Geneviève, Paris. Cloister.

455 Augustinian Abbey of Sainte-Geneviève, Paris. Monastic buildings, *c.* 1720.

456 Augustinian Abbey of Sablonceaux. Abbot's lodging, *c.* 1730?

457 Augustinian Abbey of Sablonceaux. Gateway, finished 1788.

458 Augustinian Abbey of La Couronne. *C.* 1750.

459 Génofévain Abbey of Saint-Irénée, Lyons. Monastic buildings, by Soufflot, 1749.

460 Augustinian Abbey of Saint-Vincent, Senlis. Main block, 1759.

461 Augustinian Abbey of Saint-Vincent, Senlis. Secondary block, 1759.

462 Augustinian Abbey of Saint-Vincent, Senlis.
Central cloister, 1759.

463 Augustinian Abbey of Saint-Vincent, Senlis.
Central cloister, 1759.

464 Augustinian Abbey of Wissembourg. Conventual buildings, 1784.

465 Augustinian Abbey of Saint-Père-en-Vallée, Auxerre. Interior, *c.* 1575.

466 Augustinian Abbey of Saint-Père-en-Vallée, Auxerre. Façade, by Blaise Chéreau and
F. Laligne, 1630–58.

467   Discalced Augustinians, Notre-Dame-des-Victoires, Paris. Begun 1629.

468 Discalced Augustinians, Notre-Dame-des-Victoires, Paris. Façade, by Cartaud, 1739.

469 Discalced Augustinians, Notre-Dame-des-Victoires, Paris. Woodwork, c. 1720.

470 Génofévain Abbey of Saint-Léger, Soissons. Façade, c. 1640.

471 Génofévain Church of Châtillon-sur-Sèvre. Interior, c. 1720.

472 Augustinian Abbey of Saint-Ruf, Valence. Interior of the church, c. 1720.

473 Augustinian Abbey of Sainte-Geneviève, Paris. By Soufflot, 1757. Nave.

474 Augustinian Abbey of Sainte-Geneviève, Paris. By Soufflot, 1757. Dome.

475   Augustinian Abbey of Sainte-Geneviève, Paris. By Soufflot, 1757. Exterior.

476   Augustinian Abbey of Saint-Amable, Riom, 1747.

ELEVATION PERSPECTIVE DU

Dédié à Monsieur

CHAPITRE NOBLE DE L'ARGENTIERE

Frère du Roy

477   Noble Canonesses of l'Argentière.   Project by Desarnod, c. 1777.

478   Abbey of Fontevrault. Chapter-house door, *c.* 1545.

479   Abbey of Fontevrault. Air view.

480   Abbey of Fontevrault. Cloister, 1548–60.

481   Abbey of Fontevrault. Buildings for lay servants.

482   Abbey of Fontevrault. Main gateway, *c.* 1760.

483   Abbey of Fontevrault. Nuns' building, *c.* 1580.

484   Abbey of Fontevrault. Nuns' building, *c.* 1580.

485   Abbey of Fontevrault. Monastic buildings, *c.* 1760.

486   Abbey of Fontevrault. Abbess's lodging, *c.* 1775.

487 Premonstratensian Abbey of Saint-Martin, Laon. Panelling in the church, *c.* 1680.

488 Premonstratensian Abbey of Laval-Dieu. Stalls, *c.* 1690.

498 Premonstratensian Abbey of Verdun. By Thomas Mordillac, 1686.
Monastic quarters, *c.* 1700.

499 Premonstratensian Abbey of Verdun. By Thomas Mordillac, 1686.
Monastic quarters, *c.* 1700.

500 Premonstratensian Abbey of Verdun. By Thomas Mordillac, 1686.
Cloister.

501 Premonstratensian Abbey of Verdun. By Thomas Mordillac, 1686. Refectory.

502 Premonstratensian Abbey of Jean d'Heurs. By Père Nicholas Pierson, 1731–42. Main block.

503 Premonstratensian Abbey of Jean d'Heurs. By Père Nicholas Pierson, 1731–42. Entrance Hall.

504 Premonstratensian Abbey of Jean d'Heurs. By Père Nicholas Pierson, 1731–42. Cloister.

505 Premonstratensian Abbey of Jean d'Heurs. By Père Nicholas Pierson, 1731–42. Passage between abbot's lodging and sacristy.

506 Premonstratensian Abbey of Jean d'Heurs. By Père Nicholas Pierson, 1731–42. Staircase.

507 Premonstratensian Abbey of Mondaye. By Père Eustache Restout, c. 1720.

508 Premonstratensian Abbey of Mondaye. By Père
Eustache Restout, c. 1720. Façade.

509 Premonstratensian Abbey of Mondaye. By Père
Eustache Restout, c. 1720. Nave.

510   Premonstratensian Abbey of Mondaye. By Père Eustache Restout, *c.* 1720. Cloister.

511   Premonstratensian Abbey of Mondaye. By Père Eustache Restout, *c.* 1720. Great staircase.

512 Premonstratensian Abbey of Mondaye. By Père Eustache Restout, *c.* 1720. Church exterior.

513 Premonstratensian Abbey of Mondaye. By Père Eustache Restout, *c.* 1720. Monastic buildings.

514 Premonstratensian Abbey of Mondaye. By Père Eustache Restout, *c.* 1720. Monastic buildings.

515 Abbey of Prémontré. Northern wing of west block, *c.* 1720.

516 Abbey of Prémontré. The central block, *c.* 1720.

517 Abbey of Premontré. Side blocks, *c.* 1720.

518 Abbey of Prémontré. Side blocks, *c.* 1720.

519 Convent of the Sœurs de Notre-Dame-de-Charité-de-la-Refuge, Besançon.
Chapel, by Nicole, 1739–45.

520 Convent of the Sœurs de Notre-Dame-de-Charité-de-la-Refuge, Besançon.
Chapel façade, by Nicole, 1739–45.

521 Ursuline Convent, Espalion. Entrance, before 1674.

522   Ursuline Convent, Vesoul. Courtyard.

523   Ursuline Convent, Vesoul. Entrance, *c.* 1620.

524 Ursuline Convent, Eu. Doorway, 1618.

525 Ursuline Convent, Montpezat. Cloister, 1631.

526 Ursuline Convent, Château-Gontier. *C.* 1630.

527 Ursuline Convent, Château-Gontier. *C.* 1630.
Detail of cloister.

528 Ursuline Convent, Château-Gontier.
Façade of Church of Trinité, *c.* 1630.

529 Ursuline Convent, Château-Gontier.
C. 1630. Cloister.

530 Ursuline Convent, Abbeville. Chapel. 1642.

531 Ursuline Convent, Bollène. Entrance door, mid seventeenth century.

532 Ursuline Convent, Bollène. Staircase, mid seventeenth century.

533 Ursuline Convent, Aix-en-Provence.
Gateway, c. 1650.

534 Ursuline Convent, Aix-en-Provence. Façade of
church, 1647.

535 Ursuline Church, Angers. Door,
mid seventeenth century.

536 Ursuline Chapel, Quimperlé. 1652.

537   Ursuline Convent, Luçon.   *C.* 1650.   Chapel.

538   Ursuline Convent, Poligny.   1673.

539 Ursuline Convent, Quimperlé. 1652.

540 Ursuline Convent, Quimperlé. 1652.

541   Ursuline Convent, Bayeux. *C.* 1680.

542   Ursuline Convent, Beaune. Cloister, 1697.

543   Ursuline Convent, Montferrand. *C.* 1700.

544   Ursuline Convent, Saint-Hippolyte. 1700.

545   Ursuline Convent, Saint-Hippolyte. 1700.

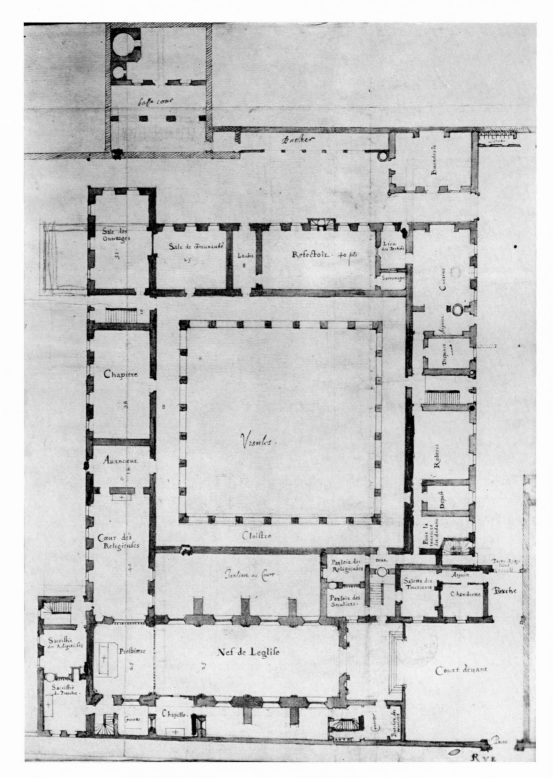

546   Ursuline Convent, Dijon. Plan by Guillaume Tabourot, 1643.

547 Ursuline Convent, Vannes.
     Chapel, 1688–90.

548 Ursuline Convent, Bourges. By François Mansart, 1695.

549 Ursuline Convent, Bourges. By François Mansart, 1695.

550 Ursuline Convent, Quimper. Second
     half of eighteenth century.

551 Ursuline Convent, Langres. Façade of Chapel.

552 Ursuline Convent, Langres. Nuns' quarters.

553 Ursuline Chapel, Arbois. By Attiret, 1764.

554 Ursuline Chapel, Seurre. 1776.

555 Ursuline Convent, Versailles. Entrance, by Richard Mique, 1766–72.

556 Ursuline Convent, Versailles. Chapel, by Richard
Mique, 1766–72.

557 Ursuline Convent, Versailles. Chapel, by
Richard Mique, 1766–72.

558 Ursuline Convent, Versailles. By Richard Mique,
1766–72.

559 Ursuline Convent, Versailles. By Richard Mique,
1766–72.

560   Dames de l'Assomption, Paris. Church, by Charles Errard, 1670–6.

561   Dames de l'Assomption, Paris. Church, by Charles Errard, 1670–6.

562 Institution de Saint-Aure, Paris. *C.* 1730.

563 Visitandines of Grenoble. Chapel door.

564   Visitandines of Saumur. Chapel door, *c.* 1630.

565   Visitandines of Tours. Courtyard (later additions, 1656).

566 Visitandines of Paris, Notre-Dame-des-Anges. By François Mansart, 1632–4.

567   Visitandine Chapel, Moulins. Side view of chapel, *c.* 1640.

568   Visitandine Chapel, Moulins. Cloister, *c.* 1645.

569 Visitandine Convent, Toulouse. Mid seventeenth century.

570 Visitandines of Avallon. *C.* 1650.

571 Visitandines of Nevers. Chapelle-Sainte-Marie, 1639–49.

572 Visitandines of Montbrison. Chapel, 1700–2.

573 Visitandines of Paray-le-Monial. C. 1650.

574 Visitandines of Le Mans. By Sœur Anne-Victoria
Pillon, 1730–7. Façade.

575 Visitandines of Le Mans. By Sœur Anne-Victoria
Pillon, 1730–7. Interior of Choir.

576 Visitandines of Auxerre. Chapel, c. 1740.

577 Visitandines of Limoges. Chapel, 1700.

578 'Refuge' of the Chartreuse of Val-Saint-Pierre, Laon.
Right-hand part, c. 1540; left dated 1613.

579 Chartreuse of Saint-Pierre, Toulouse.
Cloister, c. 1620.

580 Chartreuse of Saint-Pierre, Toulouse.
Entrance to church, c. 1630.

581 Chartreuse of Val-Bénite, Villeneuve-lès-
Avignon. Entrance gate, 1649.

582　Chartreuse of Val-Bénite, Villeneuve-lès-Avignon. Entrance gate, *c.* 1675.

583　Pulpit from the Chartreuse of Val-Saint-
　　Pierre, 1681. Cathedral of Laon.

584　Chartreuse of Val-Bénite, Villeneuve-lès-
Avignon. High Altar, now in the Collégiale of
Villeneuve-lès-Avignon, by Antoine Duparc,
c. 1740?

585 Saint-Bruno, Bordeaux. 1665. Entrance of the former convent.

586 Saint-Bruno, Bordeaux. 1665. Façade.

587 Saint-Bruno, Bordeaux. Decoration of north side of choir, 1672.

588 Chartreuse of Apponay. Living quarters, c. 1680.

589 Chartreuse of Vaucluse, Onoz. Courtyard, mid seventeenth century.

590   Chartreuse of Le Liget, *c.* 1690. Inner gateway.

591   Chartreuse of Le Liget, *c.* 1690. Monastery.

592   Chartreuse of Le Liget. Entrance gateway, *c.* 1690.

593   Chartreuse of Vaucluse, Onoz. Gateway, *c.* 1650.

594 Saint-Bruno-des-Chartreux, Lyons. Dome, *c.* 1740.

595 Saint-Bruno-des-Chartreux, Lyons. Nave, 1733–6.

596   Saint-Bruno-des-Chartreux, Lyons. Stalls, 1744–7.

597   Saint-Bruno-des-Chartreux, Lyons. Choir, 1733–6.

598   Saint-Bruno-des-Chartreux, Lyons. High Altar, by Soufflot, 1743–9.

599   Saint-Bruno-des-Chartreux, Lyons. Details of stalls, 1744–7.

600   Chartreuse of Auray. Cloister, 1730.

601   Chartreuse of Auray. Cloister, 1730.

602   Chartreuse of Auray. Entrance, *c.* 1740.

603   Chartreuse of Auray. Chapel, 1730.

604   Chartreuse of Saint-Pierre, Toulouse. Crossing, by L. Cammas, c. 1780.

605 Chartreuse of Saint-Pierre, Toulouse. *C.* 1680. Chapter-house.

606 Chartreuse of Saint-Pierre, Toulouse. *C.* 1680. Sacristy.

607 Chartreuse of Saint-Pierre, Toulouse. High Altar. Angels and urn by F. Lucas, 1785.

608 Chartreuse of Saint-Pierre, Toulouse.
Chapter-house, c. 1680.

609 Chartreuse of Saint-Pierre, Toulouse. Choir,
decorated 1683 and 1749.

610   Chartreuse of Gaillon. 1776.

611 Door of the Carmelite Monastery, Saint-Amand, Mont-rond. Mid sixteenth century.

612 Discalced Carmelites, Paris. Saint-Joseph-des-Carmes, 1628–30.

613 Discalced Carmelites, Paris, Saint-Joseph-des-Carmes. 1628–30. Façade. After Marot.

614   Discalced Carmelites, Paris, Saint-Joseph-des-Carmes. Door to choir, *c.* 1630.

615   Carmelite Nunnery of Les Billettes, Paris. Façade, 1756.

616   Carmelite Nunnery of Les Billettes, Paris. Nave, 1756.

617   Carmelite Nunnery of Ploërmel. Cloister, 1604.

618   Carmelite Nunnery of Ploërmel. Cloister, c. 1700.

619   Carmelites of Toulouse. Chapel, begun 1622.

620 Carmelites of Sainte-Anne-d'Auray. Cloister, *c.* 1630.

621 Carmelites of Sainte-Anne-d'Auray. Cloister, *c.* 1630.

622   Carmelites of Vannes. Cloister, 1632.

623   Carmelite Nunnery of the Incarnation, Paris. Remains of cloister, *c.* 1602.

624 Carmelites of Beaune. Chapel, *c.* 1630.

625 Carmelites of Notre-Dame-du-Mont-Carmel,
Marseilles. Entrance, *c.* 1640.

626 Carmelites of Poitiers. Chapel, 1660.

627 Carmelites of Auch. Chapel, *c.* 1650?

628 Carmelites of Chartres. Chapel, 1663.

629 Carmelites of Rouen. Church of Saint-Romain, 1676–1730.

630 Discalced Carmelites, Arles. Details of the chapel, begun 1673.

631 Discalced Carmelites, Arles. Details of the chapel, begun 1673.

632   Carmelites of La Rochelle. *C.* 1670? Doorway.

633   Carmelites of La Rochelle. *C.* 1670? Cloister.

634 Carmelites of Tulle. Chapel, *c.* 1690.

635 Carmelites of Besançon. Cloister, 1685–95.

636 Carmelites of Lille. Church of Saint-André. Pulpit, *c.* 1702.

637 Carmelites of Lille. Church of Saint-André. 1702. Façade.

638 Carmelites of Vannes. Church, 1747.

639 Carmelites of Vannes. Church, 1747.

640   Discalced Carmelites, Clermont-Ferrand. Church, 1720.

641   Carmelites of Saint Denis. Church, by Mique, 1767.

642   Dominican Nunnery of Pont-l'Évêque. Living quarters, sixteenth century.

643   Dominicans of Saint-Sever-sur-l'Adour. Cloister, 1660.

644 Dominicans of Rennes. Cloister, *c.* 1670.

645 Dominicans of Pamiers. Cloister, *c.* 1650.

646 Dominicans of Paris, Saint-Thomas-d'Aquin. Interior, 1682–1722.

647 Dominicans of Paris, Saint-Thomas-d'Aquin. Façade, 1770.

648   Dominicans of Paris, Cloister, *c.* 1700.

649   Dominicans of Aix-en-Provence. Church of Sainte-Marie-Madeleine. Nave, 1703.

650 Dominicans of Notre-Dame, Bordeaux. 1684–1707. Façade.

651 Dominicans of Nîmes. Church of Sainte-
Marie-Madeleine, c. 1770.

652 Dominicans of Auch. Portal, c. 1700.

653 Dominicans of Marseilles. Church of
Saint-Cannat, c. 1690.

654 Dominicans of Saint-Maximin. Stalls, 1692.

655 Dominicans of Saint-Maximin. Pulpit, 1756.

656 Dominican Nuns of Poissy. Design for window by Robert de Cotte, *c.* 1715.

657   Dominican Sisters of St Catharine of Siena, Dinan. By Poussin, 1661–4.

658   Dominicans of Poligny. Monastic buildings, by Amondry, 1715.

659   Dominicans of Poligny. By Amondry, 1715. Chimney piece.

660   Dominicans of Poligny. By Amondry, 1715. Staircase.

661   Dominicans of Bordeaux. Monastic buildings, *c.* 1700.

662   Dominicans of Saint-Maximin. Monastic buildings, *c.* 1750.

663 Cordeliers of Chartres. Monastic buildings, *c.* 1630.

664 Cordeliers of Chartres. Monastic buildings, *c.* 1630.

665 Cordeliers of Châlons-sur-Marne. Entrance, *c.* 1640.

666 Cordeliers of Autun. Entrance, *c.* 1690.

667 Cordeliers of Châtillon-sur-Seine. Monastic buildings, *c.* 1670.

668 Cordeliers of Châtillon-sur-Seine. Monastic buildings, *c.* 1670.

669   Cordeliers of Autun. *C.* 1690. General view.

670   Cordeliers of Autun. *C.* 1690. Cloister.

671   Cordeliers of Lons-le-Saunier.   Façade of chapel, 1714–31.

672   Cordeliers of Dôle.   1737–47.   Entrance.

673 Cordeliers of Dôle. Cloisters, by Père Nicole, 1731–60.

674 Cordeliers of Dôle. Room, perhaps Chapter-house, 1737–47.

675 Convent of Clarisses, Aubeterre. 1608. Entrance.

676 Convent of Clarisses, Aubeterre. 1608. Courtyard.

677   Convent of Clarisses, Sarlat. Cloister, *c.* 1650.

678   Convent of Clarisses, Poligny. 1680. Gateway.

679   Convent of Noble Clarisses, Montigny-lès-Vesoul. 1686. Chapel.

680   Convent of Noble Clarisses, Montigny-lès-Vesoul. 1686. Staircase in nun's quarters.

681   Convent of Clarisses, Aigueperse. Gateway.

682   Convent of Clarisses, Aigueperse. Conventual buildings, *c.* 1680.

683   Convent of Clarisses, Arras. Chapel, 1769.

684   Convent of Clarisses, Toulouse. Cloister, *c.* 1700.

685   Recollets of Paris. Monastic buildings, *c.* 1685.

686   Recollets of Saint-Céré. 1662.

687   Recollets of Sézanne. Main Cloister, *c.* 1650.

688　Recollets of Sézanne.　Chapel, mid seventeenth century.

689　Recollets of Sézanne.　Chapel, mid seventeenth century.

690 Recollets of Vitry-le-François. *C.* 1680?

691 Recollets of Saint-Germain-Laval. Seventeenth century.

692　English Recollets, Douai.　Chapel, 1706.

693　English Recollets, Douai.　Chapel, 1706.

694   Recollets of La Rochelle. Façade of chapel, 1706.

695   Recollets of Darney, 1735. A cell.

696   Recollets of Chaumont-en-Vexin. Seventeenth century.

697   Capuchins of Châteauroux. *C.* 1775.

698 Capuchins of Fontenay-le-Château. 1626.

699 Capuchins of Arbois. Late seventeenth century.

700   Capuchins of Paris, Saint-Jean-Saint-François, 1715.

Portail de l'Eglise des Capucines, Scitué en face de la Place de Louis le Grand.

Plan.

Echelle de   1   2   3   4 toises.

585

701   Capuchin Nuns of Paris. Portal, 1731.

702   Capuchins of Paris, Novitiate. Entrance, *c.* 1760.

703   Capuchins of Tarare. Church, 1780?

704   Capuchins of Paris, Novitiate, Saint-Louis-d'Antin. By Brongniart, 1780–2.

705   Capuchins of Paris, Novitiate, Saint-Louis-d'Antin. By Brongniart, 1780–2.

706 Capuchins of Paris, Novitiate, Saint-Louis-d'Antin. By Brongniart, 1780–2.
From a lithograph by F. Delpuech, 1821.

707 Minimes of Decize. Cloister, *c.* 1600.

708 Minimes of Decize. Portal, late sixteenth century.

709 Minimes of Aubeterre, 1617. Chapel.

710 Minimes of Aubeterre, 1617. Cloister.

Livre IV. N.° XIV. Pl. 2

711 Church of the Minimes, Paris. By François Mansart, 1611–79. After Marot.

712   Church of the Minimes, Tours. Portal, by Frère Antoine Andric and Frère Cot Taboué, 1629.

713   Church of the Minimes, Tours. Convent wall.

714   Church of the Minimes, Tours. 1629.

715   Saint-Pierre-des-Minimes, Clermont-Ferrand. 1630.

716 Minimes of Arlay. 1655.

717 Minimes of Arlay. 1655.

718   Minimes of Orléans. Cloister, *c.* 1650.

719   Minimes of Toulon. Interior, 1744.

720 Franciscan Third Order, Church of Sainte-Elizabeth, Paris. 1628–46.

721 Jesuit College, Poitiers. Entrance pavilion, 1619.

722 Jesuit College, Poitiers. Chapel, 1608–13.

723   Jesuits of Tournon. 1536.

724   Jesuits of Moulins, 1605.

The College of La Flèche, from a drawing by Martellange, 1617.

726 Jesuit College, La Flèche. A courtyard, by Martellange, 1607–21.

727 Jesuit College, La Flèche. A courtyard, by Martellange, 1607–21.

728 Jesuit College, La Flèche. Third courtyard, *c.* 1607–21.

729 Jesuit College, La Flèche. Chapel, by Martellange, 1607–21.

730 Jesuit College, La Flèche. Chapel, by Martellange, 1607–21.

731   Jesuit College, Dijon. Courtyard, by Martellange, 1610.

732   Jesuit College, Roanne. Drawing by Martellange, 1611.

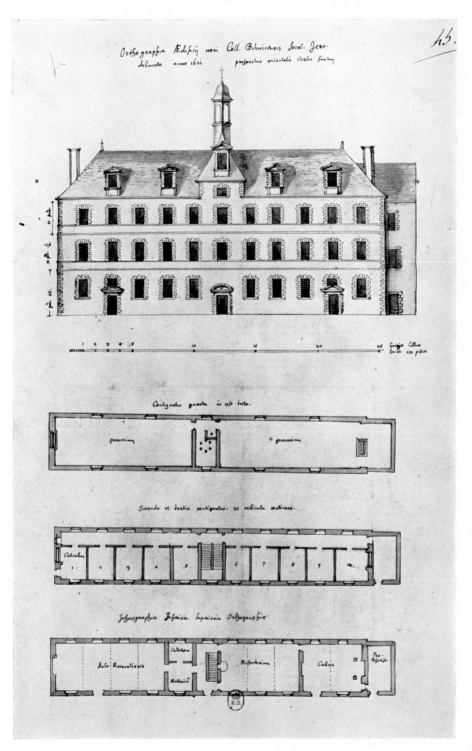

733   Jesuits of Bourges. Martellange's designs, 1611.

734 Jesuit College, Nevers. Chapel, 1612.

735 Jesuit College of Saint-Louis (now Saint-Vincent-de-Paul), Blois. Façade, by Martellange, 1625.

736   Jesuit College of Saint-Louis (now Saint-Vincent-de-Paul), Blois. Interior, by Martellange, 1625.

10 Toises

Portail de l'Eglise du Nouitial des Iesuistes de Paris

737   Jesuit Novitiate, Paris. By Martellange, 1631. Chapel interior. After Marot.

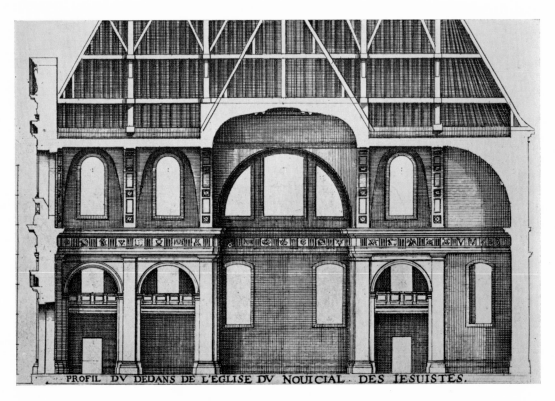

PROFIL DV DEDANS DE L'EGLISE DV NOUICIAL DES IESUISTES.

738 Jesuit Novitiate, Paris. By Martellange, 1631. Chapel façade. After Marot.

739 Jesuit Novitiate, Paris. Living quarters, drawing by Martellange, 1630.

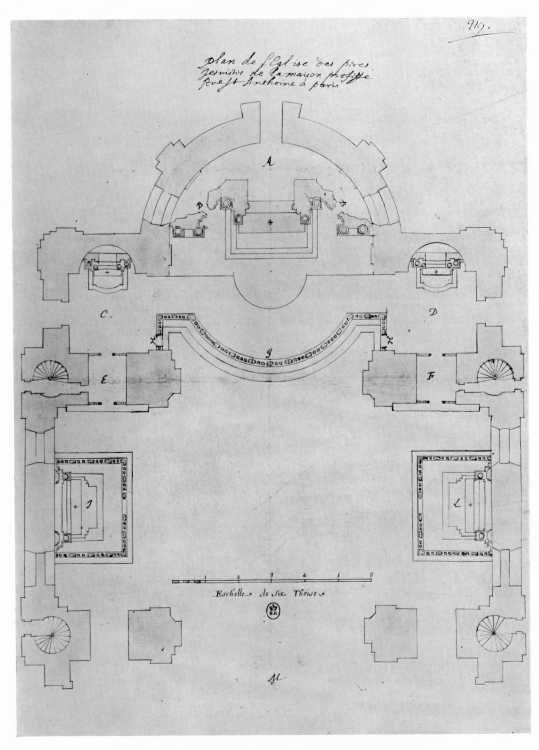

740 Plan of the chapel, Jesuit Maison Professe, Paris (Saint-Paul-Saint-Louis),
by Martellange and Derand, 1627.

741   Jesuit Maison Professe, Paris. Chapel (Saint-Paul-Saint-Louis). Interior,
by Martellange and Derand, 1627–41.

742   Jesuit Maison Professe, Paris. Chapel (Saint-Paul-Saint-Louis). Façade,
by Martellange and Derand, 1627–41.

743 Jesuit Maison Professe, Paris. By Martellange and Derand, 1627–41. Staircase.

744 Jesuit Maison Professe, Paris. By Martellange and Derand, 1627–41. Library door.

745 Jesuit College, Chaumont. Chapel exterior, 1629.

746   Jesuit College, Chaumont. Chapel interior, 1629.

747 Jesuit College, Vannes. Chapel, by Père Adrian Deran, 1660–4.

748 Jesuit College, Notre-Dame-de-la-Gloriette, Caen. By Père André, 1684-7.

749   Jesuit College, Rouen.   Chapel, 1616–56.

750   Jesuit College, Rouen.   Chapel, 1615–56.

751   Jesuit College, Rouen. 1614–56. Exterior.

752   Jesuit College, Rouen. 1614–56. Parlour.

753   Jesuit College, Quimper. Chapel façade, by Charles Turmel, 1640.

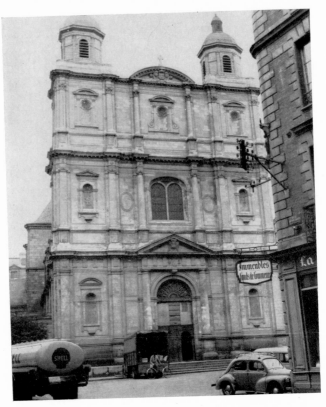

754   Jesuit College, Rennes. Chapel façade, by Derand and Turmel, 1624–57.

751   Jesuit College, Rouen. 1614–56. Exterior.

752   Jesuit College, Rouen. 1614–56. Parlour.

753   Jesuit College, Quimper. Chapel façade, by Charles Turmel, 1640.

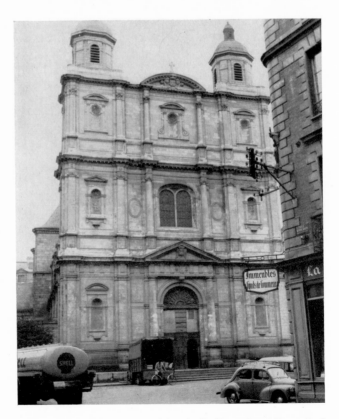

754   Jesuit College, Rennes. Chapel façade, by Derand and Turmel, 1624–57.

755 Jesuits of Eu. College, founded 1582.

756 Jesuits of Eu. Chapel, from the north, 1613–24.

757 Jesuits of Eu. Façade of chapel, 1613–24.

758 Jesuits of Eu. Doorway from the Place du Collège.

759   Jesuits of Eu. Interior of chapel, 1613–24.

760   Jesuit College, Soissons. Gateway, *c.* 1690.

761   Jesuits of Cambrai. Façade of chapel, 1692.

762   Jesuit Seminary, Brest. 1686.

763   Jesuit College, Angers. *C.* 1730.

764   Jesuits of Besançon. Church by Père Louis Hoste, 1686–8.

765   Jesuits of Besançon. 1718–37. Façade to street.

766 Jesuits of Verdun. Chapel by Père Maugrain, 1731.

767   Jesuits of Verdun.   Façade of chapel, by Père Maugrain, 1731.

768   Jesuits of Metz.   Chapel of Notre-Dame, 1735–9.

769 Jesuits of Langres. Chapel, by Père Maugrain, 1746.

770 Jesuits of Besançon. Scholastic buildings, 1718–37.

771　Jesuits of Besançon. 1718–37. Cloister.

772　Jesuits of Besançon. 1718–37. Staircase.

773   Jesuit Church of Saint-Pierre, Colmar. 1742–50. Nave.

774   Jesuit Church of Saint Pierre Colmar. 1742–50. Aisle.

775   Jesuit Church of Saint Pierre, Colmar. 1742–50. Apse.

776   Jesuit Church of Saint Pierre, Colmar. 1742–50. From the apse into the aisle.

777   Jesuit College, Mauriac. Entrance, *c.* 1605.

778   Jesuit College, Rodez. Entrance, *c.* 1640.

779   Jesuit College, Limoges. 1685.

780   Jesuit College, Limoges. 1685.

781   Jesuits of Alençon. Chapel, 1686–1706.

782   Jesuits of Alençon. College, *c.* 1759.

783   Jesuit College, Autun. 1709–31. Façade, 1757.

784   Jesuit College, Autun. 1709–31. Chapel façade, 1757.

785 Jesuits of Bordeaux. Church of Saint Paul, 1663–76. Interior.

786 Jesuits of Bordeaux. Church of Saint Paul, 1663–76. Façade.

787   Jesuits of Rodez. Chapel.

788   Jesuits of Rodez. Passage to the parlour, *c.* 1630.

789   Jesuit College, Albi. Doorway, *c.* 1630.

790   Jesuit College, Albi. Doorway, *c.* 1630.

791   Jesuit College, Carcassonne. Façade to street, 1663–6.

792   Jesuit College, Toulouse. Doorway, c. 1630.

793   Jesuits of Arles. Details of chapel, begun 1652.

794   Jesuits of Arles. Details of chapel, begun 1652.

795   Jesuit College, Nîmes.   Façade.

796   Jesuit College, Nîmes.   Cloister, *c.* 1680.

797   Jesuit College, Nîmes.   Interior, *c.* 1680.

798   Jesuit College, Nîmes.   Interior, *c.* 1680.

799   Jesuit College, Aix-en-Provence. Chapel, 1681.

800   Jesuit College, Aix-en-Provence. Doorway, c. 1680.

801   Jesuit College, Aix-en-Provence. *C.* 1680. Courtyard.

802   Jesuit College, Aix-en-Provence. *C.* 1680. Grotto-fountain.

803   Jesuit College, Grenoble, Chapel façade, by Père Louis Hoste, 1705.

804   Jesuit College, Grenoble. Doorway, 1664.

805 Jesuit College, Montpellier. Chapel, now Notre-Dame-des-Tables, by Jean Giral and Frère Monestier, 1707–48. Façade.

806 Jesuit College, Montpellier. Chapel, now Notre-Dame-des-Tables, by Jean Giral and Frère Monestier, 1707–48. Interior.

807 Jesuit College, Clermont-Ferrand. 1757.

808 Jesuit College, Vaugirard. Mid eighteenth century.

809   Jesuit College, Strasbourg. By Massol, 1757.

810   Jesuit College, Autun. Chapel, 1757.

811   Church of the Trinitarians, Metz. 1720.

812   Antonin Church, Saint-Marc-la-Lande. Begun 1509.

813   Antonin Monastery, Saint-Antoine-en-Viennois. Abbot's lodging, early eighteenth century.

814   Antonin Monastery, Saint-Antoine-en-Viennois. General view of buildings, 1620.

815   Hospitallers of St John, Toulouse. By J. P. Rivals, 1668–85.

816   Hospitallers of St John, Toulouse. By J. P. Rivals, 1668–85.

817   Barnabites of Lescar.   *C.* 1680.

818   College of Pères Doctrinaires, Brive.   Screen to the street, 1665.

819   Couvent de la Congrégation, Laon, 1694.

820   Couvent de la Congrégation, Laon, 1694.

821   Couvent de la Charité, Bayeux. *C.* 1690.

822   Institution de la Retraite, Quimper. *C.* 1690.

BIBLIOGRAPHY

When not otherwise stated, books written in French are published in Paris, and those in English in London

ANON. *Sainte-Jeanne-Françoise-Frémyot de Chantal. Sa Vie et ses Œuvres.* 8 vols. 1874–9.

ASSIER, A. *L'abbaye de Clairvaux en 1517 et en 1709.* 1876.

ASSOCIATION BOURGUIGNONNE DES SOCIÉTÉS SAVANTES, Congrès de 1927. *Saint Bernard et son temps.* Dijon, 1928.

AUGUIER, P. *Pierre Puget.* n.d. [1903].

AURIOL, A. *La construction de l'église des Chartreux à Toulouse.* Toulouse, 1897.

AVRIL, E. *Temples anciens et modernes.* 1774.

BAYET, J. *Les édifices religieux [de Paris], XVIIe, XVIIIe, XIXe siècles.* 1910.

BEAULIEU, M. 'Gabriel Le Duc, Michel Anguier et le maître-autel du Val de Grâce', *Bull. de la Soc. de l'hist. d'art français* (1945–6), p. 150.

BENARD, L. *Instructions monastiques sur la règle de Sainct Benoist.* 1618.

BLOMFIELD, R. *A History of French Architecture from the Reign of Charles VIII till the Death of Mazarin. 1494–1661.* 2 vols. 1911.

BLOMFIELD, R. *A History of French Architecture from the Death of Mazarin till the Death of Louis XV. 1661–1774.* 2 vols. 1921.

BLONDEL, J. F. *Cours d'architecture.* 9 vols. 1771–7.

BLONDEL, J. F. *L'architecture française.* Reprint, ed. Guadet et Pascal, 4 vols. n.d. (c. 1900).

BLUNT, A. *Art and Architecture in France, 1500–1700.* 1953.

BLUNT, A. *Philibert de l'Orme.* 1958.

BOSSEBŒUF, L. *Fontevrault: son histoire et ses monuments.* Tours, n.d. (c. 1890).

BOUCHOT, H. 'Notice sur la vie et les travaux d'Étienne Martellange, architecte de Jésuites, 1569–1641', *Bibliothèque de l'École des Chartes,* XLVII (1886), 17.

BOUCHOT, H. 'Catalogue des dessins d'Étienne Martellange', *ibid.* p. 207.

BOUILLART, J. *Histoire de l'abbaye royale de Saint-Germain-des-Prés.* 1724.

BOURDE DE LA ROGERIE, H. *Notice sur un Recueil de plans d'édifices construits par les architectes de la Compagnie de Jésus, 1607–72.* 1904.

BOUTEILLER, —. 'Notice sur les anciennes abbayes de Saint-Pierre et de Sainte-Marie de Metz', *Mem. de l'acad. impériale de Metz,* II (1862–3), 25.

BRAHAM, A. 'Mansart Studies, I: The Val-de-Grâce', *Burlington Magazine* (August 1963), p. 351. (This article appeared too late to be used in the text.)

BRICE, G. *Description de la Ville de Paris.* 4 vols. 1752.

BROGLIE, E. DE. *Mabillon et la société de l'abbaye de Saint-Germain-des-Prés. 1664–1707.* 1888.

BRUNE, P. *Histoire de l'Ordre hospitalier du Saint Esprit.* Lons-le-Saunier and Paris. 1892.

Bulletin Monastique.

CAMPAN, J. L. *Mémoires.*

CHABEUF, H. *Dijon: Paroisses et Couvents.*

CHAMPION, P. *Histoire poétique du XVe siècle.* Paris, 1923.

CHARTIER, ALAIN E. *Lycée Corneille de Rouen.* Rouen, n.d. [1954].

CHARVET, E. L. G. *Étienne Martellange, 1589–1641.* Lyons, 1874.

CHARVET, E. L. G. *Les des Noyers de la Valfenière et l'Abbaye royale des Bénédictines de Saint-Pierre, Lyon.* Lyons, 1870.

CHARVET, E. L. G. 'Le refectoire de l'Abbaye des Dames de Saint-Pierre à Lyon', *Revue du Lyonnais*, 3rd series XX (Lyons and Paris, 1876), 57.

CHARVET, E. L. G. 'Recherches sur…Thomas Blanchet, peintre et architecte', *Revue du Lyonnais*, XIX (Lyons, 1895), 57, 156, 269, 351 and 431.

CHAULIAT, A. *Histoire de l'Abbaye Sainte-Croix de Bordeaux (Archives de la France monastique*, vol. IX). Ligugé and Paris, 1910.

CHENESSEAU, G. *L'Abbaye de Fleury à Saint-Benoît-sur-Loire.* 1931.

CHENNEVIÈRES, P. DE and MONTAIGLON, A. DE. *Abecedario de P. J. Mariette.* 6 vols. 1851–3.

CIPRUT, E. J. 'Documents inédits sur l'Eglise des Minimes de la Place Royale', *Bull. de la Soc. de l'hist. de l'art français* (1954), p. 151.

CIPRUT, E. J. 'Les modèles de Martellange pour l'église du Noviciat de Paris', *XVIIe Siècle* (1954), no. 23.

CIPRUT, E. J. 'L'architecte du Palais abbatial de Saint-Germain-des-Prés', *Bull. de la Soc. de l'hist. de l'art français* (1956), p. 219.

CIPRUT, E. J. 'L'auteur de l'église des Capucines de la Place Vendôme et ses deux projets de façade', *Bull. de la Soc. de l'hist. de l'art français* (1957), p. 259.

CLOUZOT, H. 'Saint-Maur', *Revue des Études Rabelaisiennes*, VII (1909), 259.

COLET, Abbé. *Annales du monastère de la Visitation de Dijon.* 1854.

Congrès Archéologiques: see SOCIÉTÉ FRANÇAISE D'ARCHÉOLOGIE.

CONTANT D'IVRY, P. *Les Œuvres d'architecture.* 1769.

COTTINEAU, Dom L. H. *Répertoire topo-bibliographique des Abbayes et Prieurés.* Mâcon, 2 vols. 1935–7.

COULTON, G. G. *Commentary on the Rule of St Augustine by Robertus Richardinus.* Edinburgh, 1935.

CROZET, R. *L'Abbaye de Noirlac et l'architecture Cistercienne en Berry.* 1952.

CROZET, R. 'Maillezais', *Congrès archéologique*, CXIV, La Rochelle, p. 80.

DAINVILLE, F. DE. 'Lieux de théâtre et salles des actions dans les collèges de Jésuites', *Revue d'histoire du théâtre*, II (1950), 185.

DAINVILLE, F. DE. 'Un Jésuite architecte inconnu, le P. Edmond Moreau', *XVIIe Siècle*, V (1956), 397.

DAMIRON, S. 'Dessins inédits d'architecture du XVIIIe siècle pour l'église Sainte-Geneviève', *Bull. de la Soc. de l'hist. de l'art français* (1961), p. 27.

DARGENVILLE, A. J. DEZALUER. *Vies de quelques peintres célèbres.* 1745.

DECORDEMOY, —. *Nouveau Traité de toute l'architecture.* 1714.

DE LASTEYRIE, C. *L'Abbaye de Saint Martial de Limoges,* 1901.

DELATTRE, P. (ed.) *Les Établissements des Jésuites en France, 1949–.* Published up to *Pinel,* Enghien and Wetteren, 1955.

DELATTRE, P. (ed.) 'Notice sur la vie et les œuvres de Frère Charles Turmel, Breton, Jésuite et architecte, 1597–1675', *Mem. de la Soc. d'hist. et d'arch. de Bretagne,* XXII (1942), 29.

DELFOUR, J. *Les Jésuites à Poitiers.* 1902.

DE L'ORME, PHILIBERT. *Le premier tôme de l'architecture.* 1567.

BIBLIOGRAPHY

DE MONTFAUCON, DOM BERNARD. *Monumens de la monarchie française.* 1729–33.

DENIFLE, Père H. *La Désolation des églises, monastères et hôpitaux en France pendant la guerre de cent ans.* 2 vols. Paris, 1897.

DERAND, F. *L'architecture des voûtes.* Paris, 1643.

DEREL, M. 'Constructions civiles du début de XVIIIe siècle à Saint-Martin-des-Champs à Paris', *Bull. de la Soc. de l'hist. de l'art français* (1956), p. 157.

DEREL, M. 'Le maître autel de Saint-Martin-des-Champs', *Bull. de la Soc. de l'hist. de l'art français* (1957), p. 159.

DES BROSSES, CHARLES. *Lettres d'Italie.* 1739.

DESHOULIÈRES, —. *Eglises de France, Cher.*

DE VASIÈRE, P. *Lettres d'Aristocrates.*

DONY D'ATTICHY, L. *Histoire générale de l'Ordre des Minimes.* 2 vols. 1624.

DUBOIS, P. *L'Abbaye de Valloires, guide du visiteur.* Abbeville, n.d. (c. 1950).

DUMOLIN, M. 'Le Val de Grâce', *Bull. de la Soc. de l'hist. de Paris* (1930), p. 92.

DURAND, G. *L'église de Saint-Riquier* (Petite Monographie). 1933.

DURANDEAUX, J. *Valloires.* 1953.

ERLAU, J. B. *L'ancien Carmel du Faubourg Saint-Jacques.* 1929.

EVANS, JOAN. *Art in Medieval France.* Oxford, 1948.

EYDOUX, H. P. 'L'église abbatiale de Morimond', *Bull. Mon.* CXIV (1956), 253.

EYGUN, F. 'Saint-Michel-en-l'Herm', *Cong. Arch.* CXIV, La Rochelle, p. 27.

FÉLIBIEN, M. *Histoire de la Ville de Paris.* 5 vols. 1725.

GALLET, M. 'L'œuvre de Pierre Desmaisons', *Bull. de la Soc. de l'hist. de l'art français* (1959), p. 91.

GERMAIN, MICHEL, *Monasticon Gallicanum.* Reprint, ed. Peigné-Delacourt, 1882.

GIGAS, E. *Lettres inédites.* Vol. II. *Lettres des Bénédictins de la Congrégation de Saint-Maur, 1652–1700.* Copenhagen, 1892.

GILLET, L. *Histoire artistique des Ordres Mendiants, étude sur l'art religieux en Europe du XIIIe siècle.* 1912.

GOUHIER, P. *L'Abbaye-aux-Hommes, Saint-Étienne de Caen.* Caen, 1960.

GUIBERT, L. *Destruction de l'Ordre et de l'Abbaye de Grandmont.* Paris and Limoges, 1877.

GUILLET DE SAINT GEORGES, G. *Mémoires inédits sur la vie et les ouvrages des membres de l'Académie.* 2 vols. 1854.

HAUTECŒUR, L. *Histoire de l'architecture classique en France.* 5 vols. 1943–.

HÉLYOT, P. *Dictionnaire des Ordres religieux*, ed. M. L. Badiche, in Migne, *Encyclopédie Théologique*, vols. XX–XXIII, 1847–59.

HÉLYOT, P. *L'Abbaye de Corbie.* Louvain, 1957.

HERRMANN, W. 'Desgodets and the Académie Royale d'Architecture', *Art Bulletin*, XL (March 1958), 23.

HERVIER, M. *Musées de Lyon. Le Palais des Arts, ancienne Abbaye royale des Dames de St.-Pierre.* Lyons, 1922.

HOUSSAYE, M. *M. de Bérulle et les Carmélites de France, 1575–1611.* 1872.

HUGO, C. L. *Sacri et Canonici Ordinis Praemonstratensis Annales.* 2 vols. Nancy, 1734.

HUXLEY, A. *Grey Eminence.* 1941.

IMBART DE LA TOUR, P. *Les Origines de la Réforme.* 4 vols. 1905–35.

JADART, H. *Dom Jean Mabillon, 1632–1707.* Rheims, 1879.

JADART, H. *Dom Thierry Ruinart, 1657–1709.* Paris and Rheims, 1886.

JOUIN, H. *Charles le Brun.* 1889.

JOUSSE, M. *Le Secret d'Architecture.* La Flèche, 1642.

KING, A. A. *Cîteaux and her Elder Daughters.* 1954.

LAMBERT, E. 'Un recueil d'abbayes Augustines préparé par les Génofévains', *Bull. de la Soc. de l'hist. de l'art français* (1945–6), p. 126.

LANSON, L. *Le Goût du Moyen Age en France au XVIIIe siècle.* Paris and Brussels, 1926.

LARAN, J. 'Une Vie inédite de François Perrier', *Mélanges offerts à M. Henry Lemonnier* (1913), p. 186.

LAUGIER, P. *Essai sur l'Architecture.* 2nd ed. 1755.

LAUGIER, P. *Observations sur l'architecture.* The Hague (Paris), 1765.

LA VARENDE, —. *L'Abbaye du Bec-Hellouin.* 1951.

LEBEUF, J. *Histoire de la ville et de tout le diocèse de Paris,* ed. H. Cocheris, 15 vols. 1745–60.

LECLER, A. 'Histoire de l'abbaye de Grandmont', *Bull. de la Soc. historique du Limousin,* tomes LIX–LX. Limoges, 1909–16.

LECOUTURIER, E. *Françoise-Madeleine de Chaugry et la tradition Salésienne au XVIIe siècle.* 2 vols. 1933.

LE FEBVRE, H. *Histoire chronologique de la province des Recollets de Paris.* 1677.

LE FEBVRE, I. A. *La Chartreuse de Notre-Dame-des-Prés, à Neuville, sous Montreuil-sur-Mer.* 1881.

LEKAI, L. J. *Les Moines Blancs.* 1957.

LEMONNIER, H. *L'art français au temps de Louis XIV.* 1911.

LENÔTRE, G. *Paris Révolutionnaire.* 1894.

LEPAUTRE, A. *Les Œuvres d'Architecture.* n.d.

LE SENNE, A. *La Chapelle du Lycée à Saint-Omer.* Saint-Omer, 1897.

LESPRAND, P. 'L'abbaye de Saint-Louis de Metz, chapitre noble de Dames', *Annuaire de la Soc. d'hist. et d'archéologie de la Lorraine,* XXXII (1923), 277.

MÂLE, E. *L'art religieux après le Concile de Trente.* 1932.

MARCHAND, L. A. *Souvenirs historiques sur l'ancienne Abbaye de Saint-Benoît-sur-Loire.* n.d.

MARIETTE, J. *L'architecture française.* Reprint of 1727 ed., ed L. Hautecœur. 3 vols. Paris and Brussels, 1927.

MARILLIER, L'Abbé. *Corbigny.* Paris and Nevers, 1887.

MARMONTEL, J. F. *Tableau de Paris.* Amsterdam, 1788.

MAROT, J. *Recueil des…Palais, Chasteaux, Eglises…dans Paris.* 1670.

MARRIER, Dom MARTIN. *Monasterii regalis Sancti Martini a Campis Historia.* 1636.

MARTÈNE, Dom. *Histoire de la Congrégation de Saint-Maur.* Ed. Charvin. 5 vols. Ligugé and Paris, 1928–31.

MENORVAL, E. DE. *Les Jésuites de la rue Saint-Antoine.* 1872.

MERCIER, S. *Nouveau Paris.* 1793.

MERLE, Dr. 'L'abbaye de Saint-Maixent', *Bull. de la Soc. hist. et scient. des Deux Sèvres,* 1957.

METHUEN, PAUL, Baron. *Normandy Diary.* 1952.

MIGNE, J. P. *Dictionnaire des Abbayes.* 1856. *See also* HÉLYOT, *Dictionnaire des Ordres religieux.*

MILLIN, A. L. *Antiquités Nationales.* 5 vols. 1790.

MOISY, P. 'Le recueil des plans jésuites de Quimper', *Bull. de la soc. de l'hist. de l'art français* (1950), p. 70.

MOISY, P. 'L'architecte François Derand, Jésuite lorrain', *Revue de l'hist. de l'église de France*, XXXVI (1950), 149. (Summary in *Bull. de la Soc. de l'hist. de l'art français* (1950), p. 7.)

MOISY, P. 'Portrait de Martellange', *Archivum historicum Societatis Jesu*, XXI (Rome, 1952), 289.

MOISY, P. 'Martellange, Derand, et le conflit du Baroque', *Bull. Mon.* CX (1952), 237.

MOISY, P. *Les églises Jésuites de l'ancienne assistance de France*. 2 vols. Rome, 1958.

MONGET, C. *La Chartreuse de Dijon*. Montreuil-sur-Mer. 3 vols. 1898.

MONTESSUS DE BALLORE, S. DE. 'La sculpture religieuse sur bois au XVIIe et au XVIIIe siècle: les modèles', *Bull. de la Soc. de l'hist. de l'art français* (1936), p. 235.

MOREY, M. P. *Notice sur la vie et les œuvres d'Emmanuel Heré de Corny*. Nancy, 1863.

MORTIER, R. P. *Flavigny, l'abbaye et Ursulines, la ville*. Lille, 1920.

OMAN, C. C. *English Church Plate*. 1957.

PELCOQ, J. *L'Abbaye de Mondaye*. Bordeaux, 1938.

PETZET, M. 'Un projet de Perrault pour l'église Sainte Geneviève à Paris', *Bull. Mon.* CXV (1957), 81.

PIGANIOL DE LA FORCE. *Description historique de la Ville de Paris et ses environs*. 10 vols. New ed. 1765.

PIHAN, —. *Histoire de Saint-Just-en-Chaussée*. 1885.

POINTEL, P. DE. *Recherches sur la vie et les œuvres de quelques peintres provinciaux de l'ancienne France*. 3 vols. 1847.

PRAT, J. M. *Essai historique sur la destruction des Ordres religieux en France au XVIIIe siècle*. 1845.

PROST, J. F. *Blondel et son œuvre*. Metz, 1860.

PROST, J. F. *Recherches historiques et critiques sur la Compagnie de Jésus en France du temps du Père Coton, 1564–1626*. 5 vols. Lyons, 1876.

RANCÉ, A. DE. *De la Sainteté et des Devoirs de la Vie Monastique*. 1683.

REMNANT, E. 'The Cloister of Jumièges', *J. Brit. Archaeological Assoc.* 3rd series. XX–XXI (1957–8), 107.

RENAUDET, A. *Préréforme et Humanisme à Paris, 1494–1517*. 1916.

RICHARDINUS. *See* COULTON, G. G.

ROSTAND, A. *L'œuvre architecturale des Bénédictins de la Congrégation de Saint-Maur en Normandie, 1616–1789*. Caen, 1940.

ROSTAND, A. 'Un grand constructeur et décorateur: Frère Guillaume de la Tremblaye, 1644–1715', *Revue Mabillon*, XLV (1945), 245.

ROSTAND, A. 'Les constructions mauristes à l'abbaye de Saint-Riquier', *Revue Mabillon* (July–Sept. 1958), p. 197.

ROUSSEAU, F. *Dom Grégoire Tarisse*. Lille and Paris, 1924.

ROY, M. *Artistes et monuments de la Renaissance en France*. 1934.

ROZET, —. *Mon Vieux Mâcon qui s'en va*. Mâcon, 1959.

RUINART, T. *Apologie de la Mission de Saint-Maur, apostre des Bénédictins en France*. 1702.

RUPPRICHT-ROBERT, V. *L'Église et le monastère du Val-de-Grâce, 1645–1665*. 1875.

RUSKIN, JOHN. *Diary*, ed. Joan Evans and J. Howard Whitehouse, 3 vols. 1956–9.

SAUVAL, H. *Histoire et recherches des Antiquités de la Ville de Paris*. 3 vols. 1724.

SERBAT, L. 'L'architecture gothique des Jésuites au XVIIe siècle', *Bull. Mon.* LXVI (1902), 315 and LXVII (1903), 84.

SIMON, Abbé. 'Dom J-B. Miserey, Moine de Saint-Maur, 1726–86', *Bull. de la Soc. des Antiqs. de Normandie*, XL (1933), 319.

SOCIÉTÉ DES ANTIQUAIRES DE PICARDIE. *La Picardie historique et monumentale*. Amiens, 1893.

SOCIÉTÉ FRANÇAISE D'ARCHÉOLOGIE. *Congrès Archéologiques*. Whole series.

THIBEAU, P. *La Crypte de Jouarre, La Chapelle-Montligeon*. 1950.

TOURNIER, R. *Les Églises Comtoises*. 1954.

TREVILLIERS, J. DE. *Sequania Monastica*. Vesoul, n.d. [*c.* 1930].

VALLERY-RADOT, J. *Le recueil de plans d'édifices de la compagnie de Jésus conservé à la Bibliothèque Nationale de Paris*. Rome, 1960.

VANUXEM, J. 'Les sculptures de l'église des Carmélites de la rue Saint-Jacques', *Bull. de la Soc. de l'hist. de l'art français* (1939).

VAUTHIER, M. G. 'Anne d'Autriche et l'Église du Val-de-Grâce', *Archives de l'art français*, nouvelle série VIII (1916), 146.

VILLARET, —. *Les Congrégations Mariales*.

VITRY, P. *Michel Colombe*.

WARD, W. H. *The Architecture of the Renaissance in France*. 2 vols. n.d. [1911].

INDEX

Figures in bold type refer to the plates

INDEX

Autun (Saône-et-Loire)
Augustinian Abbey of Saint-Symphorien, drawing of cloister, 74, **430**
Benedictine Abbey of Saint-Martin, panelling, 47, **227**
Cordeliers, monastic buildings, 115, **666, 669–70**
Jesuit College, chapel, 135, **783–4,** 139, **810**; grille, 135, 139 n.

Auxerre (Yonne)
Augustinian Abbey of Saint-Père-en-Vallée, 77, **465–6**
Benedictine Abbey of Saint-Germain: abbot's lodging, 53, **294**; cloister, 50, **274**; screens and other furnishings, 47
Benedictine Priory of Saint-Eusèbe, choir, 13 n.
Jesuit seminary, xv; chapel, 135–6
Ursuline convent, 89
Visitandines church, 99, **576**

Auxonne (Côte-d'Or), Ursuline convent, 91 n.

Avallon (Yonne)
Capuchin convent, now a theatre, 120
Jesuit college, 135 n.
Ursuline convent, 90
Visitandines, nuns' quarters, 98, **570**

Avignon (Vaucluse)
Cistercian nuns, Sainte-Cathérine, cloister, xiii
Dominican: Congrégation du Saint-Sacrement instituted at, 110; furnishings of church, 112
Jesuit college, 129
Ursulines, 88
Visitandines chapel, 96 n.

Bacquet, Père, buildings designed by, x n.
Balivière, M. de, commendatory abbot of Royaumont, abbot's lodging built for, 70, **419**
Bar, Catherine de (Mère Mechtilde), Nunnery founded by, 23
Bar-sur-Aube (Aube), Ursuline convent, 90
Barbeaux (Seine-et-Marne), Cistercian Abbey, high altar, 57, **303**
Barcelonnette (Basses-Alpes), Dominican church, 111 n.
Barlet, Victor, Louis and Lhuillier, architects of Saint-Vincent, Metz, 43, **197**
Barnabites, 141
Barnay, Dom Georges, abbot of Grandmont: arms of, 81 n.; reforms of, 81
Barré, Père Nicolas, Sœurs des Écoles Charitables du Saint Enfant-Jésus founded by, 95 n.
Barrière, Jean de la, abbot *in commendam* of Notre-Dame-des-Feuillants, 54–5
Bassac (Charente), Benedictine Abbey, stalls, 40
Bastide-de-Jourdans, La (Vaucluse), Benedictine, Notre-Dame-de-l'Hermitage, foundation of, 41

Bauer, Simon, stalls for Abbey of Le-Moûtier d'Ahun, by, 40, **194**
Baume-les-Dames (Doubs), Benedictine Nunnery: exterior of church, 53, **291**; interior of dome of church, 53, **290**
Baume-les-Messieurs (Doubs), secularized, 29 n.

Bayeux (Calvados)
Benedictine Abbey of Saint-Vigor: Dom Anselme Boisseau, Cellarer, acted as architect, 18; buildings at, planned by Dom Alexis Bréard, 33; Dom Denis Plouvier, architect, employed at, 18
Couvent de la Charité, 142, **821**
Franciscan house at, restored, 115 n.
Ursuline Convent, 91, **541**

Beaubec (Seine-Maritime), Cistercian Abbey, farm buildings and pigeon house, 57, **310**
Beaufort, Dom Eustache de, abbot of Sept-Fons, 56
Beaugency (Loiret), Augustinian Abbey: church, 75; monastic buildings, 75, **442**
Beaulieu (Corrèze), Benedictine church, support for pyx in, 62 n.
Beaulieu (Haute-Marne), entrance gate at Auberive formerly at, 67 n.
Beaulieu, or Belloc (Tarn-et-Garonne), Cistercian abbey, abbot's lodging, 57
Beaulieu-lès-Loches (Indre-et-Loire), Benedictine Abbey: Abbot's Lodging, 9, **11**; monastic buildings, 35, **133**

Beaune (Côte-d'Or)
Carmelites: chapel, 107, **624**; cloister, 107
Ursuline Convent, cloister, 91, **542**
Visitandines, Caves du Patriarche père et fils, xiv

Beaupré (Oise), Cistercian Abbey, organ case, 60
Beauregard-l'Evêque (Puy-de-Dôme), Minimes, 121
Beaurepaire (Nord), Augustinian Nunnery, 5 n., 75, **436**
Beauvais (Oise), *see* Saint-Quentin-lès-
Beauvoir (Saône-et-Loire), Cistercian Nunnery, 63
Bec-Hellouin, Le (Eure), Benedictine Abbey: Cardinal de Boissy abbot of, 7; married man as abbot of, 8; neglect of church, 7; monastery later a stud-farm, 147; restoration of, xi; Dom Guillaume de la Tremblaye architect at, 33; altar, 33 n.; cloister and cloister door, 20, **65, 66, 67**; corridor to cells, 50, **245**; guest house, 33, **119**; monastic buildings, 50, **244**; north court, 50, **254, 255**; refectory, 33, **123**; staircase to the cells, 50, **253**
Bégard (Côtes-du-Nord), Cistercian Abbey, monastic buildings, 68, **399–401**
Bellevaux (Nièvre), Premonstratensian, monastic buildings, xiv

INDEX

Chartres *(cont.)*
Cordeliers: monastic buildings, 115, **663**-4; door with Greek and Hebrew inscriptions, 115
St Paul, Sœurs de, founded at, 87 n.

Chastellux, Hélène de, Visitandines house at Avallon founded by, 98

Chateaubriand, François René Xavier, Vicomte de, cited, 104

Châteaudun (Eure-et-Loir), Benedictine Abbey of the Madeleine, 143; damage by fire and restoration, 9; monastic buildings, 36, **148–9**

Château-Gontier (Mayenne)
Benedictine Priory of Saint-Jean, baldaquin, 41 n.
Ursuline convent: church, 89–90, **526**; cloister, 89, **527–9**

Château-l'Hermitage, near Pontvallain (Sarthe), Augustinian Priory, drawing of monastic buildings, 74, **429**

Château-Remy, Augustinian Canons, monastic buildings, 75 n.

Chateauroux (Indre)
Augustinian Nunnery of Notre-Dame-de-Saint-Augustin, cloister and monastic buildings, 76, **447**
Capuchins, chapel and monastic buildings, 120, **697**

Châtillon-lès-Dombes (Ain), Sœurs de la Charité founded at, 86

Châtillon-sur-Seine (Côte-d'Or)
Augustinian Abbey of Saint-Pierre, church door and entrance, 76, **450**, **452**
Benedictine Nunnery, 23, **83**
Cistercian, Saint-Jean, stalls, 60 n.
Cordeliers, monastic buildings, 115, **667–8**

Châtillon-sur-Sèvre (Deux-Sèvres), Génofévain Abbey: church, interior, 79, **471**; altar with baldaquin, 79, **471**; wing of monastic buildings, 74, 75, **435**; abbot's lodging, 75

Châtre, La (Indre), Capuchin convent, 120

Chatrices-en-Argonne (Marne), abbey of Notre-Dame, 75

Chaulnes, Anne de, Abbess of Saint-Pierre, Lyons, 28

Chaumont (Haute-Marne), Jesuit College, chapel, 132, **745–6**

Chaumont-en-Vexin (Oise), Recollets, monastic buildings, 118, **696**

Chauny (Aisne), house of Clarisses, destroyed, x n.

Chauvelin de Richemont, Marie de, abbess of Abbaye de Beauvoir, 63

Chauvin, architect of priory of Mortagne-sur-Sèvre, 39, **186–7**

Chelles (Seine-et-Marne), Benedictine Nunnery: included in Maurist Congregation, 22; rebuilt, 49 n.

Cheminon (Marne), Cistercian abbey, reform of, 55 n.

Cherlieu (Haute-Saône), Cistercian Abbey, monastic buildings, 65, **366–7**

Chesneau, Père Pierre: Jesuit college at Clermont-Ferrand designed by, 132; Jesuit buildings at Montpellier attributed to, 137 n.

Chezal-Benoit (Cher): revised Benedictine rule of, 6; Congregation of St Maur joined by, 16

Chinon (Indre-et-Loire)
Augustinian Canons, 76 n.
Calvarian Nuns, surviving building, 23 n.

Ciboure (Basses-Pyrénées), Recollets, cloister, xiv

Cistercian Order, 54–70; abbots appointed *in commendam*, 54–5; architectural restrictions, 54; reformed Benedictine Order, 6; reforms, 54–6, 144, and subsequent division, 55, 145; division of dorters into cells, 63; houses in France, 2; inclusion of lay brethren, 65; royal commissioners at Chapters General, 69

Cîteaux (Côte-d'Or), Cistercian Abbey, 143; attempts at reform, 54–5; restoration of, xi; designs for, 67–8, **395–6**; cloister, 68, **397**; staircase, 68, **398**

Clagny, Château de, 33

Clairefontaine (Haute-Saône), Cistercian, cloister, xiii

Clairmarais (Pas-de-Calais), Cistercian Abbey, farm buildings, 57 n.

Clairvaux (Aube), Cistercian Abbey, 143; decline of, 145; reform of, 55 n.; visit of Queen of Sicily, 2; *boiseries*, 68; cloister, 63, 68, **409**; entrance door, 68, **402**; outer façade, 68, **403**; mausoleum for St Bernard, 147; staircase to abbot's lodging, 68, **410**

Clare, St, patroness of Franciscan nuns (Filles de Sainte Claire and Clarisses), 116

Clarisses Mitigées or Urbanistes, 116–17; 'Noble' Clarisses, 116

Claude, Frère, façade of Dominican church of Saint-Thomas-d'Aquin rebuilt by, 111

Clausse, Père Paul, Jesuit college at Chalons-sur-Marne by, 132

Clavas (Haute-Loire), Cistercian nuns, Saint-Philibert-de-Rioutor, monastic buildings, xiii

Clermont-Ferrand (Puy-de-Dôme)
Discalced Carmelites, church, 108, **640**
Jesuit College, 132, 138, **807**
Saint-Pierre-des-Minimes, church, 122, **715**

Cleves, Catherine of
Jesuit college at Eu founded by, 133

Clovis, King, statue of, 13

Cluny, Order, 6–53 *passim*, 146; reformed Benedictine Order, 6; Congregation of St Maur joined by, 16; houses in France, 2, closing of, 145

165

INDEX

Dames de l'Assomption, *see* Assomption *under* Paris

Dames Blanches, *see* Sœurs de la Présentation de Marie *under* Hospitallers

Danvin, Omer, pulpit of Notre-Dame de Saint-Omer carved by, 112 n.

Darney (Vosges), Recollets, monastic buildings, 118, **695**

Dathoze, Dom, buildings at Cluny by, 51

Decize (Nièvre)

Benedictine abbey: cloister, 10; portal, 12, **24**

Minimes: chapel, 121; cloister, 121, **707**; portal, **708**

Defrance, J. P., and Le Brument, monastic buildings at Saint-Ouen, Rouen, designed by, 50-1, **259-63**

Delafosse, engravings by, 48

Delpuech, F., lithograph of Capuchin Novitiate, Paris, by, **706**

Démis, Abbé, Sœurs de St Charles founded at Lyons by, 87 n.

Denis, Frère, ironwork at Saint-Denis by, 49, **241**

Deran, Père Adrian, chapel of Jesuit College, Vannes, by, 132, **747**

Derand, Père François: school buildings of Jesuit college at Orléans designed by, 129 n.; buildings of Jesuit college at Rouen by, 133, **749-52**; *see also* Martellange; with Charles Turmel, Jesuit College chapel, Rennes, by, 133, **754**

Desarnod, project for Noble Canonesses of L'Argentière, 80, **477**

Desgodets, Antoine, lectures on architecture, 42

Desmaisons, monastic buildings for Theatines erected in Paris by, 141

Deux-Jumeaux, Les, *see* Isigny

Dieppe (Seine-Inférieure)

Carmelite chapel, 107

Hospitalières de la Miséricorde de Jésus, 87

Jesuit church destroyed, x n.

Dijon, Guillaume de, abbot of Fécamp, tomb of, 22

Dijon (Côte-d'Or)

Augustinian Abbey of Saint-Étienne, façade of church, 78; Order of Hospitallers founded by canon of, 86

Benedictine Abbey of Saint-Bénigne: restoration of, 31; abbot's throne, 47, **225**; stalls, 12 n., 40 n.

Benedictine Abbey of Saint-Michel, façade, 11-12, **22**; portals, 12

Bernardines: plan and façade designed for, 60-1, **324-5**; second design (as built), 61, **326-7**; monastic buildings, 60, 63, **353**

Carmelite house, portal, 107

Cordeliers, cloister now Dominican, 115 n.

Hospitalières de Dijon et de Langres, 86

Jesuit College, 124; chapel, 129; monastic buildings, 129, **731**; oratory, 126

Ursulines, Congregation of, 88, 89

Ursuline Convent: buildings adapted to form Cité Administrative, x n.; plan, 91, **546**

Dinan (Côtes-du-Nord)

Dominican Sisters of St Catherine of Siena: church and conventual buildings rebuilt, 113, **657**; pulpit now at Saint Malo, 112 n.

Ursulines, house designed by Martellange, 88 n., 92

Doctrinaires, Pères, 141

Doctrine Chrétiennes, Les Pères de la, xii

Dôle (Jura)

Benedictine Abbey of Notre-Dame, reforms, 15

Bernardines, house of, 64

Carmelite house, 106 n.

Cordeliers: house rebuilt, 116, **672**; chapter-house(?), 116, **674**; cloister, 116, **673**; door, 114 n.

Jesuit College, elevation, 129

Dominicans, or Order of Friars Preachers: 110-13, 143; reforms, 110, 144; house in rue du Bac, Paris, asylum for Order, 146

Dorbay, François: Capuchins in Paris, buildings of, formerly ascribed to, 121 n.; Minimes church in Paris begun by, 121; Premonstratensian church, Paris, designed by, 83; Visitandine house in Paris designed by, 97

Douai (Nord)

Jesuit College, later Museum, destroyed, x n.

Recollets (English) chapel, 118, **692-3**

Doulevant-le-Château (Haute-Marne), Minimes, house burned, 122 n.

Draguignan (Var), Minimes chapel, xv

Duc, Gabriel Le, Augustinian church of Notre-Dame-des-Victoires, Paris, partly built by, 78

Duchesne, Dom Vincent, work at Besançon, Corneux, Faverney, Lons-le-Saunier, **98-9**, Orgelet, **354-5**, and Vaux-sur-Poligny by, 36-7; abbey of Saint Pierre, Chalons-sur-Saône by, 36, 39, **184-5**

Dufaur de Pibrac, Jerôme, abbot of Fleury, 31

Dufour, Père Antoine: building of Jesuit college at Dôle begun by, 129 n.; scholastic buildings at Besançon by, 133 n.

Dunkirk (Nord), Recollets church damaged, x n.

Duparc, Antoine, High altar for Charterhouse of Val-Benité by, 101, **584**

Duprat, Chancelier, abbot of Fleury: arms of, at Mozac, 12, **23**; Sanctuary of Fleury abbey enriched by, 8

Durocher, Abbot's lodging at Saint-Remi, Rheims, designed by, 53

167

INDEX

INDEX

Saint-Amand-de-Coly (Dordogne), destruction of monastic buildings, 71

Saint-Amand Montrond (Cher)
Carmelite Monastery, door, 105, **611**
Capuchin church, 119

Saint-Amant-de-Boixe (Charente), suppression of abbey, 41

Saint-Amour (Jura)
Annonciades, rebuilt, xiv
Visitandine convent, now Collège, xiv

Saint-André-le-Bas, *see* Saint-Chef

Saint Anthony of Vienne, Commanderies of, in France, 2

Saint-Antoine-des-Champs, *see* Cistercian Nunnery *under* Paris

Saint-Antoine-en-Viennois (Isère), Antonin Monastery: church, 140; monastic buildings and Curé's house, 140, **813–14**; occupied by Knights of Malta, 145 n.; stalls, 140–1

Sainte-Aure, Communauté de, 95

Saint-Bénigne, *see under* Dijon

Saint-Benoît-sur-Loire (Loiret), Benedictine Abbey of Fleury; description of, by Chenesseau, 14; reforms, 15; Congregation of St Maur joined by, 16; 'mausolée' of St Benedict, 22; Cardinal de Coligny abbot of, 8; Philippe de Lorraine abbot of, 31; Jerôme Dufaur de Pibrac abbot of, 31; Cardinal Richelieu abbot of, 14, 16; Claude Soublet abbot of, 8; Jean de la Trémoille, abbot of, 7; Dom Guillaume de la Tremblaye architect at, 33, 34; Abbot's lodging of Abbot Poncher, 9; gate with drawbridge, 21 n.; MSS. from library of, 8 n.; monastic buildings, 47; pulpit, 22 n.; sanctuary enriched by Abbot Duprat, 8; vicissitudes of, 1, 8

Saint-Bruno, *see under* Bordeaux *and* Lyons

Saint-Céré (Lot), Recollets: façade of chapel, 118, **686**; monastic quarters, 118

Saint-Charles, Sœurs de, 87 n.

Saint-Chef (Isère), Benedictine Abbey, Saint-André-le-Bas united to, 41

Sainte-Claire, Filles de, *see* Clare, St

Sainte-Colombe-lès-Sens (Yonne), Benedictine, refectory, xiii

Saint-Cosme-lès-Tours (Indre-et-Loire), Ronsard prior of, 8

Sainte-Croix, *see* Guingamp

Saint-Cyr (Seine-et-Oise)
Augustinian nuns: founded by Madame de Maintenon, 75, **437–441**
Ursuline convent, later Dames religieuses de Saint Louis, following Augustinian Rule, 72

Saint-Denis (Seine)
Annonciades, 117

Benedictine Abbey: Comte du Vexin appointed abbot *in commendam*, 31; Maurist reforms introduced into, 16; rebuilding by Robert de Cotte, 48; monastic buildings, **232, 235–41**
Carmelite church by Mique, 108–9, **641**, 143
Recollets, house of, 117

Saint-Eloi-lès-Noyon (Oise), Benedictine Abbey, Philibert de l'Orme abbot of, 8

Saint-Evroul d'Ouche (Orne), Benedictine Abbey: Dom Marc Rivard acting as architect at, 33; church rebuilt, 44; abbot's lodging and gate, xiii

Saint-Florentin (Yonne), Benedictine Priory: choir of church rebuilt, 12; doorways, 12; Easter Sepulchre, 12; high altar, equestrian figures, 12

Saint-Flour (Cantal), Jesuit chapel demolished, x n.

Saint-Fuscien-aux-Bois, *see under* Amiens

Sainte-Geneviève, Filles de, or Miramiones, 95; *see also* Augustinian Abbey *under* Paris

Saint-Georges-de-Boscherville (Seine-Maritime), Benedictine Abbey: Dom Marc Rivard acting as architect at, 33; chapter-house, 31, **107**; monastic buildings, 35, **134–5**; confessionals, 47

Saint-Georges-sur-Loire (Maine-et-Loire), Benedictine Abbey: façade of church, 46, **210**; monastic wing, 18, **39**

Saint-Germain-des-Prés, *see* Benedictine *under* Paris *and under* Pontlevoy

Saint-Germain-Laval (Loire), Recollets, cloister, 118, **691**

Saint-Gildas d'Auray (Morbihan), Benedictine Priory, church rebuilt, 21, **71**

Saint-Gildas-des-Bois (Loire-Atlantique), Benedictine church and monastic buildings, xiii

Saint-Gildas de Rhuis (Morbihan), Benedictine Abbey: 21; church, 38; cloister, 38, **170**

Saint-Hippolyte (Haut-Rhin), Ursuline Convent, 91, **544–5**

Saint-Jean-d'Angely (Charente-Maritime): Benedictine-Cluniac Abbey: church rebuilt, façade, 45, **203–5**; monastic buildings and entrance, 19, **50–1**

Saint-Jean-de-Côle (Dordogne), Génofévain Priory: church, 79; cloister, 73, **420**; abbot's lodging and monastic buildings, 73, **421**

Saint-Jean-de-Luz (Basses-Pyrénées), Recollets, cloister and fountain, 118

Saint-Jean-de-l'Osne (Côte-d'Or), Benedictine Abbey, church, 39, **180–1**

Saint-Jean-des-Prémontrés, *see under* Amiens

Saint-John of God, Brothers of, 86

Saint John of Jerusalem, Order of, 2, 141

Saint-Joseph, Congrégation des Sœurs de, foundation, 87 n., 142

INDEX